Beyond
the Nixon Shocks

NEW APPROACHES TO INTERNATIONAL HISTORY

Series Editor: Thomas Zeiler, Professor of American Diplomatic History, University of Colorado Boulder, USA

Series Editorial Board:
Anthony Adamthwaite, University of California at Berkeley (USA)
Kathleen Burk, University College London (UK)
Louis Clerc, University of Turku (Finland)
Petra Goedde, Temple University (USA)
Francine McKenzie, University of Western Ontario (Canada)
Lien-Hang Nguyen, University of Kentucky (USA)
Jason Parker, Texas A&M University (USA)
Glenda Sluga, University of Sydney (Australia)

New Approaches to International History covers international history during the modern period and across the globe. The series incorporates new developments in the field, such as the cultural turn and transnationalism, as well as classical high politics of state-centric policymaking and diplomatic relations. Written with upper-level undergraduate and postgraduate students in mind, texts in the series provide an accessible overview of international diplomatic and transnational issues, events, and actors.

Published:
Militarization and the American Century, David Fitzgerald
American-Iranian Dialogues, eds. Matthew K. Shannon
America's Road to Empire, Piero Gleijeses
The International LGBT Rights Movement, Laura Belmonte
Global War, Global Catastrophe, Maartje Abbenhuis and Ismee Tames
Globalizing the U.S. Presidency, eds. Cyrus Schayegh
Public Opinion and Twentieth-Century Diplomacy, Daniel Hucker
Europe's Cold War Relations, eds. Federico Romero, Kiran Klaus Patel, Ulrich Krotz
Canada and the World since 1867, Asa McKercher
Scandinavia and the Great Powers in the First World War, Michael Jonas

The First Age of Industrial Globalization, Maartje Abbenhuis and Gordon Morrell
Women and Gender in International History, Karen Garner
International Development, Corinna Unger
The Environment and International History, Scott Kaufman
Reconstructing the Postwar World, Francine McKenzie
Activism Across Borders since 1870, Daniel Laqua
Leftist Internationalisms, eds. Mathieu Fulla, Michele Di Donato
American Sport in International History, Daniel DuBois
Climate Change and International History, Ruth Morgan
The Fear of Chinese Power, Jeffrey Crean
An International History of US Immigration, Benjamin Montoya
From World War to Cold War, Andrew N. Buchanan

Forthcoming:
China and the United States since 1949, Elizabeth Ingleson

On July 15, 1971, in the NBC broadcasting studio in Burbank, California, President Richard M. Nixon announces his acceptance of an invitation by Premier Chou En-Lai to visit the People's Republic of China. Courtesy: Richard M. Nixon Presidential Library and Museum (National Archives and Records Administration).

Beyond the Nixon Shocks

Global Consequences since 1971

BY

THOMAS W. ZEILER

BLOOMSBURY ACADEMIC
LONDON · NEW YORK · OXFORD · NEW DELHI · SYDNEY

BLOOMSBURY ACADEMIC
Bloomsbury Publishing Plc

Bloomsbury Publishing Plc, 50 Bedford Square, London, WC1B 3DP, UK
Bloomsbury Publishing Inc, 1359 Broadway, New York, NY 10018, USA
Bloomsbury Publishing Ireland, 29 Earlsfort Terrace, Dublin 2, D02 AY28, Ireland

First published in Great Britain 2026

Copyright © Thomas W. Zeiler, 2026

Thomas W. Zeiler has asserted his right under the Copyright, Designs and Patents Act, 1988, to be identified as Author of this work.

Series design by Catherine Wood

Cover image: Courtesy Richard M. Nixon Presidential Library and Museum (National Archives and Records Administration)

All rights reserved. No part of this publication may be: i) reproduced or transmitted in any form, electronic or mechanical, including photocopying, recording or by means of any information storage or retrieval system without prior permission in writing from the publishers; or ii) used or reproduced in any way for the training, development or operation of artificial intelligence (AI) technologies, including generative AI technologies. The rights holders expressly reserve this publication from the text and data mining exception as per Article 4(3) of the Digital Single Market Directive (EU) 2019/790.

Bloomsbury Publishing Plc does not have any control over, or responsibility for, any third-party websites referred to or in this book. All internet addresses given in this book were correct at the time of going to press. The author and publisher regret any inconvenience caused if addresses have changed or sites have ceased to exist, but can accept no responsibility for any such changes.

A catalogue record for this book is available from the British Library.

A catalog record for this book is available from the Library of Congress.

ISBN: HB: 978-1-3503-5748-8
PB: 978-1-3503-5747-1
ePDF: 978-1-3503-5750-1
eBook: 978-1-3503-5749-5

Series: New Approaches to International History

Typeset by Deanta Global Publishing Services, Chennai, India
Printed and bound in Great Britain

For product safety related questions contact productsafety@bloomsbury.com.

To find out more about our authors and books visit www.bloomsbury.com and sign up for our newsletters.

To Rocio, always there

Contents

List of Illustrations x
List of Abbreviations xiii

Introduction: The Nixon Shocks 1

1 The American Century Fades 5

2 *Pentagon Papers* Shock 17

3 Aftershock: Abuse of Power 29

4 China Shock 63

5 Aftershock: From Engagement to Conflict 79

6 Economic Shock 111

7 Aftershock: Globalization 133

8 Trade War 155

9 Aftershock: Crises 179

Conclusion: Consequences of the Nixon Shocks 203

Bibliography 209
Index 219

Illustrations

Figure 2.1. Senator Mike Gravel and Daniel Ellsberg stand in front of "our favorite machine"—the copier used to reproduce the *Pentagon Papers* in June 1971. Courtesy of Daniel Ellsberg Papers, Robert S. Cox Special Collections and University Archives Research Center, UMass Amherst Libraries 19

Figure 2.2. Effective August 9, 1974, Nixon left the White House. He and Pat Nixon say goodbye to Vice President Gerald Ford and Betty Ford on the White House lawn before boarding the presidential helicopter and retirement in California. Courtesy: Richard M. Nixon Presidential Library and Museum (National Archives and Records Administration) 26

Figure 3.1. Reagan meets with his National Security Planning Group regarding arms sales to Iran on November 25, 1986. Clockwise from the President's left are Secretary of State George Schultz and CIA Director William Casey. Secretary of Defense Caspar Weinberger is seated to Reagan's right. Courtesy: Ronald Reagan Presidential Library 38

Figure 3.2. Nixon and Clinton give pre-impeachment advice to Trump. Courtesy of Kevin KAL Kallaugher, *The Economist*, kaltoons.com 57

Figure 4.1. Two long-time enemies shake hands in Mao Zedong's residence on February 21, 1972. Courtesy: Richard M. Nixon Presidential Library and Museum (National Archives and Records Administration) 71

Figure 4.2. At the opera, Nixon speaks with Jiang Qing (Madame Mao), while Secretary of State William Rogers and Premier Zhou Enlai (on Nixon's right) and Pat Nixon and Kissinger (to Jiang Qing's left) await the performance. Courtesy of Richard M. Nixon Presidential Library and Museum (National Archives and Records Administration) 73

Figure 5.1. President Bush and his wife, Barbara, visit Tiananmen Square in Beijing on February 25, 1989, four months before the massacre. Courtesy of the George H. W. Bush Presidential Library and Museum 84

ILLUSTRATIONS

Graph 5.1. Thomas Hout, "A New Approach to Rebalancing the U.S.-China Trade Deficit," *HBR* (December 20, 2021), https://hbr.org/2021/12/a-new-approach-to-rebalancing-the-u-s-china-trade-deficit. 94

Figure 5.2. Regardless of American efforts to restrain its trade, China was an exporting behemoth from the late 1990s onward. Courtesy: Bet_Noire and iStock. 104

Graph 5.2. Laura Silver, "Pressing China on Human Rights—Even if It Hurts Economic Relations—Has Americans Bipartisan Support," *Pew Research Center* (April 6, 2021), https://www.pewresearch.org/short-reads/2021/04/06/pressing-china-on-human-rights-even-if-it-hurts-economic-relations-has-americans-bipartisan-support/. 108

Figure 6.1. At Camp David, "Coach" Nixon conferred with his "quarterback," the nationalist Treasury secretary, John Connally. Courtesy Richard M. Nixon Presidential Library and Museum (National Archives and Records Administration) 121

Figure 6.2. Nixon poses after his televised economic address on August 15, 1971. Courtesy Richard M. Nixon Presidential Library and Museum (National Archives and Records Administration) 126

Graph 7.1. Jonas Tallberg, Karin Backstrand, Jan Aart Scholte, and Thomas Sommerer, "Global Governance: Fit for Purpose? SNS Democracy Council Report 2023," *SNS* (May 2023), https://www.sns.se/en/articles/sns-democracy-council-2023-global-governance-fit-for-purpose/. 145

Figure 7.1. WTO headquarters in Geneva, Switzerland. Courtesy of the World Trade Organization 151

Figure 8.1. Nixon welcomes Prime Minister Eisaku Sato to Washington, DC for US-Japan summit talks. Courtesy Richard M. Nixon Presidential Library and Museum (National Archives and Records Administration) 166

Figure 8.2. Sato (left, with translator) listens as Nixon speaks at the Western White House in California on January 7, 1972. Looking on, left to right, are Secretary of State William Rogers, John Connally, US Ambassador to Japan Armin Meyer, and a contented Commerce Secretary Maurice Stans. Courtesy: Richard M. Nixon Presidential Library and Museum (National Archives and Records Administration) 172

Graph 8.1. Takashi Miwa, "What Can We Learn from the History of Trade Wars," *Nomura* (August 2018), https://astonishingceiyrs.blogspot.com/2022/10/history-of-trade-wars.html. 172

ILLUSTRATIONS

Figure 9.1. During the first oil crisis and after the Yom Kippur War in November 1973, Nixon meets with Israeli Prime Minister Golda Meir, as Kissinger looks on. Courtesy: Richard M. Nixon Presidential Library and Museum (National Archives and Records Administration) 184

Figure 9.2. President George W. Bush speaks at a meeting of G7 leaders on October 11, 2008, as the Great Recession brings chaos to markets. Courtesy of the George W. Bush Presidential Library 194

Graph 9.1. US Census—Foreign Trade Statistic Citation: "Balance of Trade," *Higher Rock Education and Learning*, Inc., https://www.higherrockeducation.org/glossary-of-terms/balance-of-trade. 194

Abbreviations

AFL-CIO	American Federation of Labor-Congress of Industrial Organizations	**NAFTA**	North American Free Trade Agreement
APEC	Asian-Pacific Economic Cooperation forum	**NATO**	North Atlantic Treaty Organization
ASEAN	Association of Southeast Asian Nations	**NBA**	National Basketball Association
CIA	Central Intelligence Agency	**NSC**	National Security Council
EU	European Union	**OPEC**	Organization of Petroleum Exporting Countries
FBI	Federal Bureau of Investigation	**PNTR**	Permanent Normal Trade Relations
FISA	Foreign Intelligence Surveillance Act	**PRC**	People's Republic of China
GATT	General Agreement on Tariffs and Trade	**SALT**	Strategic Arms Limitations Talks
IMF	International Monetary Fund	**TPP**	Trans-Pacific Partnership
MFN	Most-Favored-Nation trade treatment	**UN**	United Nations
MITI	Ministry of International Trade and Industry (Japan)	**WMDs**	Weapons of Mass Destruction
		WTO	World Trade Organization

Introduction
The Nixon Shocks

The domination of the United States abroad and its enviable way of life at home appeared in the rear-view mirror for many Americans by the summer of 1971. A struggling economy and social unrest deepened the notion that the post-Second World War so-called "American Century" had run its course after just a quarter of that time. Not everything had always been rosy since the war, to be sure, but the widely shared perception of commanding success was important while hard statistics of affluence did not lie. But by 1971, the United States was in trouble both in material terms and in its national psyche. Confusion, anxiety, and resentment replaced optimism. The happy days of the American Century faded into memory.

In stepped President Richard M. Nixon over the three months of summer in 1971. He boldly launched dramatic policy shifts designed to rekindle American power and prosperity and to guarantee his reelection. Regarding the latter, in June, to counter dissent, he attempted to suppress the press that led to his eventual demise and seemed to usher in an era of presidential abuse of power thereafter. In July, he inaugurated a diplomatic opening to the People's Republic of China that forever altered the global balance of power. Then, in August, Nixon suddenly ended the gold standard and devalued the dollar in a policy that profoundly changed the world economy. At the tail end of the summer, in September, he threatened a trade war with Japan that signaled an era of economic, political, and social crises to follow. This is the story of each of those initiatives and their consequences over several decades.

It is no exaggeration that, in the short and long term, these four initiatives transformed the United States and the world. The China and gold/dollar plans were labeled the "Nixon Shocks" by Japan but just as stunning were Nixon's abuse of power and bellicose threats in trade. Nixon's summer of shocks reshaped the nation and the world. Not every inch of the following post-1971 history related to these shocks; indeed, there are plenty of other policies and events that had consequences for later history. But the shocks did influence politics, the economy, and society in many ways that resonated over the decades up until today. So, Watergate begot later "gates" and scandals; the debate over engagement or conflict with China could not have happened without Nixon's visit to Beijing in 1972; his economic Shock actually heralded the onset of flexible exchange rates that we have today; and his trade war with Japan foreshadowed subsequent concerns with that country and China, as well as the nationalism of more recent years. Nixon, of course, could not predict the effect of his actions over the next decades, but these shocks can help us understand the history of 1970 and how they oftentimes shaped our current times.

Beyond the Nixon Shocks explores over a half century of American and international history since 1971 within the context of what was once a heyday of optimism during the roughly thirty glorious postwar years of growth, stability, and general peace in the Western world. Those three decades in which the American Century reigned are the subject of Chapter 1. There was turmoil in that period, but it did not upend the consensus that the country was on the right track, at least until the late 1960s when Nixon took office. His shocks of 1971 brewed in this mix of decline, anxiety, and determination to transform America and the world.

After setting up the demise of the American Century, the book pairs chapters in a sequence. That is, one chapter discusses a "shock" and is followed by a chapter of the consequences of that shock over the next decades.

Like all politicians, President Nixon's reelection (in 1972) was his top priority. A successful campaign strategy depended, in part, on withdrawing from the Vietnam War. Thus followed his first shocking initiative of the summer of 1971. In June, the *New York Times* published excerpts from the *Pentagon Papers*, a top-secret investigation that damned previous presidents for deceiving the public about the Vietnam War. Nixon feared that the report would undermine US foreign policy and hurt his reelection chances. The subject of Chapter 2, his failed attempt to suppress the *Pentagon Papers* led to his undoing in the Watergate affair that resonated thereafter regarding the abuse of power in US politics (Chapter 3).

The two actual "Nixon Shocks" followed the *Pentagon Papers* saga. In the first, Nixon announced in July his visit to an arch-enemy, the People's Republic of China. This most dramatic reversal of US foreign policy in a generation (Chapter 4) served as the precursor to the subsequent roller-coaster of embrace, engagement, and animosity between the two superpowers, which Chapter 5 explores.

Chapter 6 addresses the second Nixon Shock of August 1971 when the President addressed the nation about America's declining fortunes in the international and domestic economies. He had a double charge: to re-balance the international financial system that so taxed US resources by straining the dollar and to fight inflation at home. His decidedly nationalistic economic aggression actually wrecked the postwar exchange system, though doing so planted seeds of globalization for decades thereafter (Chapter 7).

Nixon coupled this economic Shock with a textile trade war with Japan. This came to a head in September 1971 when he unprecedentedly considered invoking the Trading with the Enemy Act against a friendly nation for the first time ever, in peacetime no less (Chapter 8). In essence, this was the third Nixon Shock, though it is not labeled as such. This was only the first of many economic crises to follow and spoke to the downsides of globalization in the ensuing years that soured many on the neoliberal idea of market capitalism (Chapter 9).

These chapters show the influence of the summer of shocks, providing context to our contemporary times. Back then, democracy, politics, economic well-being, and the complexities of foreign policy in a dangerous world were of paramount concern. They remained so and even became more intense. The trajectory from 1971 affected society in both negative and positive ways over a half century later.

It should be noted that this book does not cover every issue in American history at the time nor is the domestic arena given primacy except as foreign policy issues touch on it. This is, essentially, a study of America in the world and the world's impact on America. It devotes much space to economics, though politics, diplomacy, society, and culture are important as well. Furthermore, each of the chapters deals with subjects that have already been analyzed by scholars and experts; *Beyond the Nixon Shocks* serves as a synthesis of scholarship and history, which is the objective of this *New Approaches to International History* series. In short, the hope is that students will understand the Nixon's Shocks' influence in the history of twentieth-century America as well as in the present.

***

I wish to acknowledge Professor Sarah Sokhey and her STUDIO program for undergraduate research at the University of Colorado Boulder, which brought me assistants Ashley Eddy, Daniel Nickum, Noah Quarton, and Alia Davis—Alia also orchestrated a great bibliographical presentation for our group. Then-graduate students Erin DaCosta, Ben Montoya, Sarah Gavison, and Nick Swails were essential in rounding up sources.

I am also indebted to staff at several libraries, including Ryan Pettigrew and Michael Pinckney at the Richard M. Nixon Library, Mckenzie Morse at the George H. W. Bush Library, Jeremy Smith in the UMass archives, and photograph archivists at the George W. Bush Library and WTO Library.

I would be remiss not to single out Maddie Smith, the editor of this NAIH series at Bloomsbury Press, whom I count not only as a reliable source of guidance and editorial excellence but also as a long-time friend. I have had the pleasure of serving as the chief editor for this series that has been made possible by Maddie, who both got married and renovated her house in the years I wrote this manuscript! I am forever thankful to her.

There is always a last but not least, but in this case, she should be first and foremost. My spouse, partner, and best friend, Rocio, has been the essential part of my life. Our kids—in their own right wonderful people who I thank for keeping me happy and honest—(and a grandkid) would agree. As I write this and look back, I acknowledge my great fortune, and especially the best luck in the world that the bus system in Paris deposited us both together some forty-four years ago. That was ten years after the Nixon Shocks and the beginning of a near-half century of happiness for me!

1
The American Century Fades

Publisher Henry Luce proclaimed "the first great American Century" in *Life* magazine in February 1941. Also the founder of *Time*, *Fortune*, and *Sports Illustrated* magazines, this media baron influenced US foreign policy with pioneering photojournalism. An internationalist Luce now urged his Republican Party to assume the mantle of leadership in global affairs.

In his words, "America as the dynamic center of ever-widening spheres of enterprise, America as the training center of the skillful servants of mankind, America as the Good Samaritan, really believing again that it is more blessed to give than to receive, and America as the powerhouse of the ideals of Freedom and Justice" possessed "a vision of the 20th Century to which we can and will devote ourselves in joy and gladness and vigor and enthusiasm." The founders had long imagined that Americans must put that theory into practice.[1]

Such was the basis of the American Century. In 1941, its optimism and determination shaped US power, politics, and society. By 1971, that "vigor and enthusiasm" had faded.

***

When Luce wrote his editorial, the United States was not yet in the war that launched the American Century. Even before its entry, however, America was a colossus providing aid to France, Britain, and the Soviet Union in their fight against German and Italian fascism and resisting Imperial Japan as it swept across Asia and the Pacific. Once fully mobilized with thirty-one million registered in the draft and some fifteen million inducted into service (including five million women volunteers), the United States exerted its power across multiple continents by air, land, sea, media, and invention.

---

[1] Henry R. Luce, "The American Century," *Life*, February 17, 1941, reprinted in *Diplomatic History* 23, no. 2 (Spring 1999): 171. See also George C. Herring, *The American Century and Beyond: U.S. Foreign Relations, 1893* (New York: Oxford University Press, 2017), ix.

By late 1943, America had almost singlehandedly turned back Japan's advance while invading Europe through Italy in preparation for opening a second front against Nazi Germany in France. A massive workforce churned out war goods used by allied forces that landed at Normandy in June 1944 and rolled toward Berlin, meeting Soviet forces coming from the other direction and defeating Adolf Hitler's Third Reich by May 1945. Three months later, the Untied States assailed Japan, dropping two atomic bombs secretly created at enormous expense. This world war without mercy ended with Japan's surrender in September 1945.

Americans took stock of atrocities (the Holocaust), casualties (over sixty million people dead), and domestic tensions arising from racism, though this so-called "Good War" had united them in ways that downplayed social and class divisions through a sense of solidarity. They had high expectations for a future guided by American ideals on a prosperous home front and in peace abroad. The fear of a renewed depression persisted, but the mood was upbeat because of healthy productivity at home and a new international order abroad, governed by a United Nations and economic institutions dominated by the United States. Americans understood that their country stood alone at the top of the global military and economic hierarchy as the hope for postwar peace. Journalist Walter Lippmann concluded that "What Rome was to the ancient world, what Great Britain has been to the modern world, America is to be to the world of tomorrow."[2]

With millions of veterans returning home, Washington seemed to make good on many of the wartime promises, at least for a large majority, though the country still faced major challenges. Civil rights moved slowly as Black and Brown citizens did not share in the largesse of the economy, though the trend toward desegregation in sports and the military crossed into schools and public places to undermine the system of Jim Crow racism by the 1960s. The Cold War, moreover, provoked fear and intolerance at home under the scourge of a second "Red Scare" that ruined lives and exacerbated intolerance. Americans were worried about the communist threat from abroad, which was intensified by repeated crises centered on Soviet aggression in Europe, the "fall" of China to communism, a stalemated war in Korea, and the beginnings of the US commitment to South Vietnam by the mid-1950s.

Americans focused mostly on the domestic economy, however. Industry converted its wartime production to consumer goods that typified the postwar economic boom. The ensuing years of stability, profits, and good

---

[2] James T. Patterson, *Grand Expectations: The United States, 1945-1974* (New York: Oxford University Press, 1997), 8.

jobs were unparalleled in American, if not world, history. Such growth, and the contentment that came with it, derived as well from union strength. Organized labor accounted for over a third of workers who exercised their power to raise wages and improve conditions for members. Economic trends all pointed upward in this American Century. Confident consumers cashed in their savings for houses, cars, and appliances, all advertised as the route to happiness. Postwar foreign assistance programs like the Marshall Plan to Europe stimulated output even more by putting billions of dollars in the hands of nations that then bought US exports produced in American factories and farms.

The famous "Kitchen Debate" between Soviet leader Nikita Khrushchev and Vice President Richard Nixon in 1959 epitomized the consumer happiness underlying the American Century. At a national exhibition in Moscow displaying US products, Nixon conceded that Soviet rockets were powerful but that modern technology and affordable machines gave housewives back home an easier life than the one experienced by Soviet women. Capitalist democracy worked, that is, in contrast to communism's forced and outmoded treatment of people.

No administration, regardless of political affiliation, deviated much from the commitment to prosperity for all that Nixon implied in the Kitchen Debate. This was the message of moderate Republicanism under the popular President Dwight Eisenhower in the 1950s and of moderate Democrats under John Kennedy and Lyndon Johnson in the next decade. For the latter, the robust economy gave them license to extend the New Deal government activism of Franklin Roosevelt to correct society's remaining ills, such as poverty and racism. Nixon had expressed the vision, and reality, of the American Century.

A fundamental driver of the economy was spending on defense as well as on consumer goods, both of which were intertwined. Eisenhower wanted to cut defense budgets, but the result was the opposite during the Cold War. A nuclear arms race ensued that became part of a culture of atomic fear, yet the suburbs distracted provided a distraction from Armageddon. The superpower conflict spurred a transformation in the nation's geography; people moved south and west to the Sunbelt, aided by an extensive interstate highway system that made suburban living possible for millions. Women and minorities also benefited, though not equally with white men. Nonetheless, the Cold War national security state was so prevalent that Kennedy issued challenges to "a new generation" to adventure abroad in the Peace Corps and win the superpower race to put a human on the moon.

Tempered by nuclear fears, Americans were generally optimistic about the future. By the mid-1960s, Johnson could declare his War on Poverty under an everlasting Great Society that reached into media, education, healthcare, and housing, bringing benefits not only to those on welfare but also to the soaring working and middle classes. All the while, the country had ample means to conduct an expanding war against communism in Vietnam.

The postwar boom and Cold War consensus molded perceptions that the American Century would endure—well—for a century or even more. Circumstances of power and wealth imprinted on Americans that a perpetually high standard of living was not only a dream but a fact of life. They expected their politicians to deliver the policies so that business could deliver the goods. Huge automobiles like the Cadillac with its thousands of pounds of chrome and tailfins not only made General Motors the biggest corporation in the world but also convinced Americans that size, growth, and well-paying and secure jobs were limitless.

Culture exemplified such a horizonless future. While major industries as tires, steel, glass, and petroleum supported the automobile with robust employment, other sectors such as fast food (McDonald's) and drive-in movies were offshoots of the car culture. Television reflected the idyll of suburbia (made possible by the car), with trifling portrayals of everyday life in *I Love Lucy* and *Leave It to Beaver*. Middle-class youth even had the luxury of rebellion. Pop culture in the form of rock 'n roll, television programming, and civil rights and antiwar movements in universities stimulated revolutionary ideas against the very notion of abundance even though kids had grown up with such prosperity. No matter the surge of generational conflict, the American Century was, in the words of the eminent economist John Kenneth Galbraith, the product of "the affluent society."[3]

***

And then by the late 1960s, holes appeared in this age of plenty. Indeed, there had always been losers among the winners. Small farmers, for one, were victims of technological innovation and corporate Big Agriculture's efficiency. Similarly, while labor unions peaked in the late 1950s, automation reduced the number of workers in extractive and manufacturing industries. Overall, the US workforce shifted from blue-collar manufacturing to white-collar service occupations. Low-wage labor like custodians and food servers continued to eke out a living. With the boom in suburbs and the Sunbelt, and white flight

---

[3] John Kenneth Galbraith, *The Affluent Society* (New York: Houghton and Mifflin Co., 1958). See also William L. O'Neill, *American High: The Years of Confidence, 1945–1960* (New York: Free Press, 1986); Kenneth T. Jackson, *Crabgrass Frontier: The Suburbanization of the United States* (New York: Oxford University Press, 1987); Raymond A. Mohl, *Searching for the Sunbelt; Historical Perspectives on a Region* (Knoxville, TN: University of Tennessee, 1990); Lynn Spigel, *Make Room for TV: Television and the Family Ideal in Postwar America* (Chicago, IL: The University of Chicago Press, 1982); David Farber, *The Age of Great Dreams: America in the 1960s* (New York: Hill and Wang, 1994).

intensifying due to urban violence and racism in the 1960s, city infrastructure and urban cohesion also began to decay.

Johnson did not create a truly Great Society; no matter the safety nets for the poor and elderly, destitution remained. Middle-class bureaucrats (overseeing federal programs), real estate developers (pursuing slum clearance for gentrification), and physicians (guaranteed fees under Medicaid and Medicare) reaped benefits from the War on Poverty. Yet persistent racism and systemic poverty remained for some twenty million Americans. In addition, escape to a comfortable life for racial minorities was much slower than for whites. Liberals clamored for a redistribution of wealth while grassroots conservatives saw anti-poverty projects as handouts. Long muffled by the largesse of the American Century, divisions in society and politics gaped larger by the end of the decade as the economy strained to meet expectations as well as fund spending at home and abroad.

Perception was key. The decline in urban areas and a militant civil rights movement that responded to the decay provoked an eruption of violent rioting across the country from California to New Jersey, reaching a peak in 1967. White middle-America watched the turmoil on television along with protests against an ever-hopeless Vietnam War. The Democrats seemed unable to control the streets. Deeper and wider rifts roiled the nation in a backlash against civil rights and Black (and Brown and Red and Gay) Power, a more strident feminist movement that unsettled conservatives and religious observers, a feeling that baby boomers faced a less promising future than their parents, and falling confidence in unions. In the background was the sentiment that since the Kennedy assassination in 1963, a nation of supposedly misbegotten baby boom youth guided by a Supreme Court in favor of more social freedoms and rights had veered from its moral compass. The American Century seemed to be unraveling, and with it, Roosevelt's postwar liberal state.

***

The year 1968 summed up the stresses in the American Century. In January, North Vietnam launched an attack on America's ally South Vietnam called the Tet Offensive that reached all the way into the US embassy in Saigon. The event made the war seem senseless and thus spurred over 200 antiwar protests in the first half of the year, including campus riots in Mexico, France, and Germany. At the end of March, President Johnson stunningly withdrew from the presidential race. A few days later, the civil rights icon, Martin Luther King, Jr., was murdered, and then tragedy struck again when Democratic Party candidate and brother of the former president, Robert Kennedy, was slain in June.

In the second half of 1968, the trauma spiraled ever downward. The Democratic convention in Chicago in August devolved into an antiwar and counterculture melee outside of the hall and on the nominating floor itself, where party leaders and insurgents clashed. Aghast, the nation watched the chaos on television. In foreign affairs, there was no progress in Vietnam, while a Soviet suppression of one of its rebellious satellite nations, Czechoslovakia, nullified America's promise of liberation. That October, the Olympics in Mexico City witnessed US athletes giving the Black power salute on the medal podiums, actions that certainly dismayed mainstream liberals and angered patriotic conservatives.

Meanwhile, the segregationist George Wallace ran for president, mounting for the first time in nearly a half century a viable third-party candidacy. He attracted white working-class voters dismayed by civil rights and social programs that did not serve them and anxious about the violence in the streets. Many of these Democrats turned to Wallace, who won five states in the general election in November 1968. Others banked on the Republican nominee, Richard Nixon.

To top off the misery, the world also experienced the most serious economic crisis since the Great Depression in 1968. Speculation against a bellwether of economic and political stability—gold—reached a fever pitch that petrified leaders and the markets. For the first time since the war, moreover, the domestic economy showed signs of stress. Prices rose due to spending on Vietnam and poverty programs. The economy polarized Americans.

Nixon cleverly instigated a culture war to woo those in economic distress. He tried to appeal to Wallace voters and conservatives with a "southern strategy" of slowing down government civil rights activism and punishing protesters with a law-and-order Republican Party platform. They were part of his supposed "Silent Majority" who prized a tough foreign policy, including prosecuting the Vietnam War, and who believed in obeying authority, hard work, and family values. They blamed government overspending on things that did not benefit them and despised the turmoil in the streets. These so-called "forgotten Americans" could comprise a "new American majority," Nixon claimed.[4]

---

[4] Robert M. Collins, "The Economic Crisis of 1968 and the Waning of the 'American Century,'" *The American Historical Review* 101, no. 2 (April 1996): 396–422; Matthew D. Lassiter, *The Silent Majority: Suburban Politics in the Sunbelt South* (Princeton, NJ: Princeton University Press, 2006), 5. See also Paterson, *Grand Expectations*, 738–9; Dan T. Carter, *The Politics of Rage: George Wallace, the Origins of the New Conservatism, and the Transformation of American Politics* (Baton Rouge, LA: LSU Press, 2000), 324324,–370; Allen J. Matusow, *The Unraveling of America: A History of Liberalism in the 1960s* (New York: Harper & Row Publishers, 1984), 398–442; Mary C. Brennan, *Turning Right in the Sixties: The Conservative Capture of the GOP* (Chapel Hill, NC: University of North Carolina Press, 1995), 122–9.

He read the electorate correctly. The Silent Majority came his way. Along with the right and center of the Republican establishment, blue-collar, average Americans delivered him a narrow electoral victory in November 1968.

***

President Richard Nixon had long prepared for the White House. Before becoming Eisenhower's vice president, he served three terms as a congressman from Southern California just after the Second World War. Nixon was a political brawler, garnishing that reputation as a vehement anticommunist during the second Red Scare and then as a clever manipulator of the media and public when he was accused of financial wrongdoing as the vice presidential candidate in 1952. He stayed on the ticket after portraying himself as a down-home, honest common man in a gutsy but maudlin appearance on the then-novel medium of television. This ardent Cold Warrior spent the 1950s as Eisenhower's foreign policy emissary, tapping into the mainstream worldview in favor of robust US global involvement to stop the spread of communism. This included covert intervention in the Global South and public support for anticommunist regimes like the Republic of Vietnam, birthed in 1954 and dependent thereafter on American aid.

Schooled as a hardline anticommunist internationalist, Nixon also styled himself as a realist who understood that by 1969 the United States could no longer hold onto the outright hegemonic power of the American Century. Along with realist Henry Kissinger, the President devised a foreign policy that conceded the relative decline in US power. Neither practiced realism consistently; they responded to domestic pressures and ideological challenges as well as to the hard facts of international power. Nonetheless, a willingness to address America's competitive role in a changed world became the basis for their approach to foreign policy.

To achieve the aims of bolstering US power while lessening the dangers of the Cold War, Nixon had an eye on compromise by accepting nuclear parity with the Soviet Union right off the bat at his first press conference. Yet he and Kissinger also cleverly planned to play off the Soviet Union against its ideological rival, the People's Republic of China. These were two communist powers with such mutual disgust that they had shot at each other on their border and had even considered mutual nuclear attacks. The new President saw an opportunity to thaw the two-decade-long freeze in relations with Beijing while continuing to engage Moscow. Both initiatives would advance US interests by also ending the nightmare of the Vietnam War, a conflict that had brought down his predecessor, Lyndon Johnson. Nixon vowed not to be another political victim of the war and also to reformulate foreign policy to account for the new realities of post-hegemony on the part of the United States.

This was the thinking behind the broad policy of détente. Nixon and Kissinger needed to muffle dissent over the Vietnam War to quell domestic antiwar disturbances. To do so, the administration planned to replace US troops with Asian ones. Meanwhile, regional powers would be enlisted in the peace effort; China, for instance, might pressure North Vietnam to negotiate an end to the war. Nixon and Kissinger also planned to reduce American commitments that had become too expensive, such as upholding the Bretton Woods monetary system that so taxed the dollar. Realism did not mean Nixon surrendered US dominance. Instead, he recognized that the American Century had merged with a new era of parity in which foes might work for peace while friends could help share America's burden of leadership.

The administration made clear its intention to restore US power in a transformed world power structure and domestic arena. As historian George Herring has written, "the postwar years were over; a new and uncertain era was taking form." Not only were the Chinese and Soviets challenging US authority but Western European allies and Japan chafed at US control. Growth, moreover, had slowed.

In 1969, Nixon's first year in office, observers also saw a nation divided in ways not seen since the Civil War over 100 years before. Nixon's inaugural parade witnessed violent protests, symbolic of the political, social, and economic upheavals that wracked the country. Crime rates continued to skyrocket, including 600 bombing incidents in 1969 alone, and then doubled the next year. With "the left screaming revolution and the right demanding law and order, the center seemed to be crumbling," concludes Herring; America was in trouble.[5]

***

Vietnam preoccupied the new administration. By 1969, about 34,000 US military personnel had been killed in Vietnam with tens of thousands more injured. The war had long traumatized the nation ever since Johnson had sent the first US troops in 1965, while also escalating an air war that dropped triple the bomb tonnage on a country the size of California than had been used in all theaters in the Second World War. As a result of the casualties and the style of war, baby boomers rebelled in the streets by staging huge demonstrations. Congress increasingly joined in the dissent. Johnson passed the baton of Vietnam to Nixon, who had promised during the 1968 campaign to wind down the war and bring the troops home.

Like past ones, his administration faced a tricky calculation. If the United States abandoned South Vietnam, its resolve would be questioned by

---

[5]Herring, *The American Century*, 462, 463. See also Mario De Pero, *The Eccentric Realist: Henry Kissinger and the Shaping of American Foreign Policy* (Ithaca, NY: Cornell University Press, 2009), 6–11; Jussi M. Hanhimaki, *The Rise and Fall of Détente: American Foreign Policy and the Transformation of the Cold War* (Washington, DC: Potomac Books, 2013), 37–52.

enemies and friends alike. This lack of credibility might conjure up an image of strategic weakness that could undermine the Nixon-Kissinger grand design for peace and security. This plan was based on opening the diplomatic door to China, negotiating with the Soviets on disarmament, and enlisting allies to reform the capitalist world economy. Extrication from the Vietnam War, then, was linked to an array of priorities related to détente. Equally, Nixon believed that domestic strife over the war would continue to tear apart the country, denting support for internationalism at home and sparking isolationism. He was determined to end the war "honorably," meaning America's ally in Saigon would remain standing with US military aid but not troops.

Yet, this balancing act resulted only in recrimination at home and defiance abroad during Nixon's first four-year term. The administration tried pressuring Hanoi through Soviet and Chinese diplomatic channels and by restricting communist aid to North Vietnam and escalating bombing. None of these actions got Hanoi's compliance for peace at the bargaining table.

Vietnamization also did not calm down the domestic front. Massive demonstrations took place in 1969; in October alone, some two million people across the nation marched against the war, many for the first time. Twenty-thousand businessmen on Wall Street demonstrated while in midtown Manhattan over 100,000 protesters heard luminaries from Lauren Bacall and Woody Allen to New York's mayor denounce the war. Congress discussed Vietnam for the longest time up to that point (four hours) while 50,000 people stood at the Washington Monument to hear Coretta Scott King, the dead civil rights leader's wife, explain the war's destructive force on the country. In London, a Rhodes Scholar, Bill Clinton from Arkansas, organized a protest of 1,000 people in front of the US embassy.

Nixon tried to ignore the demonstrations by focusing on military plans. South Vietnam's military remained weak, and corruption plagued the Saigon government. Thus, he took a bold chance in the spring of 1970 by sending US and South Vietnamese troops into Cambodia. North Vietnam had violated Cambodian neutrality, using the vulnerable nation as a supply route and staging area for troops infiltrating South Vietnam. The communists presumed Cambodia was off-limits to US bombing because such aggression would destabilize the government there, widen the Vietnam War into another theater, and provoke protesters at home. That is exactly what happened, however, which is why Nixon hoped to keep his Cambodia campaign secret.

The incursion proved disastrous, at least for Cambodians and for Nixon politically. Beginning in late April 1970, bombing eventually destabilized the neutral government, causing a civil war won by the vicious Pol Pot, who perpetrated a horrific genocide on his own people in the years to come. For Nixon, the domestic reaction hurt him the most and ultimately ruined his presidency.

Furious antiwar demonstrations erupted when word got out about the widening war. Some 350 colleges and universities went on strike, and over 500 of them closed. Roughly two million students or a quarter of all American campuses marched in outrage against Nixon's Cambodia war. Tragically, four students at Kent State University were killed on May 4 by National Guardsmen brought in to keep order. Ten days later, two students lay dead, and twelve more were injured when police fired on protesters at Jackson State College in Mississippi. The response in Congress matched that of the furious antiwar movement. In a symbolic gesture, the Senate terminated its blanket permission for prosecuting the war under the Tonkin Gulf Resolution of 1964. More to the point, Congress tried to end funding for operations in Cambodia. An amendment eventually fell short in the House, but Nixon got the message.

***

President Nixon countered with such vitriol and emotion that he seeded his own demise. He had already ordered wiretaps on Kissinger's aides on the National Security Council (NSC) to determine who had leaked word of the ongoing secret bombings of Cambodia to the press. He later complained that in the first five months alone of his presidency, at least twenty-one major stories had leaked from NSC files. The wiretaps would find the perpetrator while he continued secretly bombing Cambodia. The wiretaps expanded to seventeen individuals by 1971.

While previous presidents had eavesdropped, Nixon's actions more methodically violated freedom and privacy. For instance, he authorized the infamous Huston Plan, one of the gravest constitutional infringements in history. Revealed in the Watergate hearings, the Huston Plan called on the Federal Bureau of Investigation (FBI), the Central Intelligence Agency (CIA), and other intelligence services to spy on "radicals" by opening their mail, using electronic surveillance, and even committing burglary. There was even a suggestion to detain agitators in special camps in Western states. Agencies resisted the Plan, but Nixon's intentions were clear when it came to dealing with domestic dissent: stifle it through legal or criminal means.

His aides wrote up a list of enemies to whom he directed his wrath. They would harass these foes of the President by instigating IRS probes into their tax returns, among other distasteful and illegal operations. All the while, Nixon labored to project a positive image of morality and fairness, but his personal underside of hatred and paranoia became prominent.

As it was for Lyndon Johnson, so for Nixon: the Vietnam War became a curse. As the North Vietnamese refused to negotiate, the South Vietnamese failed abysmally in an incursion into Laos in early 1971. In one of the worst riots in the nation's capital, militant protesters blocked bridges and roads, and mobs broke windows, leading to violent police retaliation and the arrest of over 12,000 people. By mid-1971, public support for the war had fallen to an all-time low, with just 29 percent believing that the United States was right to send troops to Vietnam. A whopping 58 percent thought the war was immoral. Still, surveys revealed that half of the respondents backed the invasion of Cambodia and more than that blamed students for the violence at Kent State. In sum, polls showed ambivalence but also basic approval for Nixon's policies, especially from "hard hats"—flag-waving blue-collar workers who counter-attacked against protesters.[6]

***

In this maelstrom, Henry Luce's call to greatness in an "American Century" had all but been lost. Actually, the term got thrown into the dustbin of history, treated as delusional idealism during the acrimonious 1970s. By the new millennium the term garnered criticism as an arrogant expression of supposed American exceptionalism or as an impulse toward territorial or cultural empire.[7]

In any case, the existence of an American Century came under severe questioning by June 1971. To Richard Nixon's consternation a secret report on the Vietnam War was released that month. The reaction prompted the biggest constitutional crisis since the Civil War, with consequences apparent today.

---

[6]Stanley I. Kutler, *The Wars of Watergate: The Last Crisis of Richard Nixon* (New York: Alfred A. Knopf, 1990), 103–8; Herring, *The American Century*, 466–71; Paterson, *Grand Expectations*, 751, 755–6. See also Charles DeBenedetti and Charles Chatfield, *An American Ordeal: The Antiwar Movement of the Vietnam Era* (Syracuse, NY: Syracuse University Press, 1990); Richard M. Nixon, *RN: The Memoirs of Richard Nixon* (New York: Simon & Schuster, Inc., 1990), 387–9; Rick Perlstein, *Nixonland: The Rise of a President and the Fracturing of America* (New York: Scribner, 2008), 424–5.
[7]Andrew J. Bacevich, *The Short American Century: A Postmortem* (Cambridge, MA: Harvard University Press, 2012).

2

Pentagon Papers Shock

The political intrigue could not have been better scripted. Two acquaintances—economist Daniel Ellsberg and *New York Times* correspondent Neil Sheehan—brought down a president of the United States. The seminal issue of the day, the Vietnam War, undermined an imperial presidency when Nixon tried to suppress freedom of expression by critics in the press. His efforts at coercion and claims of executive privilege ultimately blew up in his face in the Watergate affair. Thus, a foreign policy problem—Vietnam—remade the domestic political landscape, and the battle over executive privilege remained a fixture for decades. Ellsberg and Sheehan initiated the confrontation by publishing the *Pentagon Papers*. In doing so, they forever changed the tenor of American politics and the workings of democracy itself.

***

Daniel Ellsberg, worked at the think-tank, the RAND Corporation, that employed America's foremost minds on issues ranging from nuclear arms to healthcare. In 1967, he joined thirty-three other analysts to produce a 47-volume, 7,000-word series of documents entitled, *The History of U.S. Decision-making in Vietnam, 1945–1968*, which had been commissioned by Secretary of Defense Robert McNamara. Known as the *Pentagon Papers*, the report showed that US leaders had long known that the Vietnam War was a losing cause. President Lyndon Johnson in particular had lied to the public and Congress to cover up that fact. Ellsberg believed he had a duty to expose the lies that justified the Vietnam War as a matter of war and peace and, at the heart of the matter, right and wrong.

Troubled by his role in the foreign policy establishment, Ellsberg secretly photocopied the *Pentagon Papers*. In 1970, after the powerful chair of the Senate Foreign Relations Committee, J. William Fulbright, and the antiwar Senator George McGovern delayed releasing the report, Ellsberg circulated the documents to his friend Neil Sheehan. Ellsberg asked Sheehan to take notes, but the journalist copied the entire report in Boston-area outlets while Ellsberg was on vacation. Sheehan then flew copies to his homes in Washington, DC and New York City, handing over the *Pentagon Papers* to the *New York Times*. The newspaper posted the first of nine excerpts on June 13, 1971, before the Nixon administration got a court injunction to halt publication. The Supreme Court would review the validity of this blocking order.

Meanwhile, Ellsberg returned from the West Indies. While eluding FBI agents who had begun a manhunt for him, he handed over the *Pentagon Papers* to Ben Bagdikian, a former Rand associate who was national editor of the *Washington Post*. Ellsberg regretted that he had not revealed the documents to newspapers back in Fall 1969. Now he hoped that "informed Americans will direct their public servants to stop lying and to stop the killing and dying by Americans in Indochina."[1]

Ellsberg then turned himself into the US Attorney's office in Boston, eventually facing up to 115 years in prison under the Espionage Act. But a day later, on June 29, 1971, Senator Mike Gravel entered over half of the *Pentagon Papers* (which he had received from Bagdikian) into the Senate's official record. The cat was out of the bag.

A day after Gravel acted, the Supreme Court ruled against Nixon's injunction, allowing the *New York Times* and the *Washington Post* to publish the *Pentagon Papers*. The publication was a sensation, galvanizing the antiwar movement as well as public cynicism about the veracity of American leaders. Nixon had a political problem on his hands created by the Vietnam War, but his response turned the *Pentagon Papers* into a legal issue as well.

***

The *Pentagon Papers* did not impugn Richard Nixon because the report's timeline ended before he became president. They were actually embarrassing to the Democrats who had presided over the escalation of the Vietnam War. Yet the bruising Cambodian fiasco and the continued incompetence of South Vietnam's military sunk him into a deep gloom about a war that he hoped to end before his 1972 reelection campaign. Depression came second, however, to his utter rage toward the press and foreign policy establishment whom he accused of irresponsibility and treachery. That he went to court to cease the printing of the report and indict the leaker, Daniel Ellsberg, under the Espionage Act showed his fury.

As Nixon later explained, "I saw the government's ability to function effectively in international affairs being undermined by leaks which I felt were a violation of law as well as of the code of honorable behavior." He "had

---

[1] Daniel Ellsberg, *Secrets: A Memoir of Vietnam and the Pentagon Papers* (New York: Viking Penguin, 2002), 287, 292, 408.

FIGURE 2.1. *Senator Mike Gravel and Daniel Ellsberg stand in front of "our favorite machine"—the copier used to reproduce the* Pentagon Papers *in June 1971. Courtesy of Daniel Ellsberg Papers, Robert S. Cox Special Collections and University Archives Research Center, UMass Amherst Libraries.*

no patience with the argument that the people who leaked information did so because they opposed the war on moral grounds." Said Nixon, Ellsberg was a "rat," while National Security Advisor Henry Kissinger considered him the most dangerous person in the country. The administration resorted to a fortress mentality to defend against leaks and treasonous acts.

Nixon acknowledged the political dangers of moving against the two newspapers. In his eyes, though, the release of the *Pentagon Papers* represented a violation of the principle that government experts, not the press, should determine the impact of a top-secret document. Not acting against publication "would be a signal to every disgruntled bureaucrat in the government that he could leak anything he pleased while the government simply stood by."[2] That the *Pentagon Papers* case gave the press leeway over policymakers showed a lack of discipline at best and a betrayal of national interests at worst. There was a personal motive as well; Nixon had hated the press for decades and sought revenge for perceived slights.

When the Supreme Court upheld the freedom of the press, Nixon was ever more infuriated. The leak occurred just a month before he announced his plan to travel to China, and secret Paris Peace talks with the North Vietnamese were also underway. Now his credibility, as a tough negotiator toward Hanoi, was at stake. On June 28, while Ellsberg stood outside a Los Angeles courthouse where a grand jury had indicted him on one count of theft of government property and one count of unauthorized possession of documents related to national defense, Nixon expressed his utter contempt. "I considered what Ellsberg had done to be despicable and contemptible—he had revealed government foreign policy secrets during wartime."[3]

The President and his advisors grew more paranoid, fearing Ellsberg would publicize some 173,000 classified documents in his possession since his days at RAND. Reports by Kissinger and others posited that Ellsberg was smart but emotionally unstable. Perhaps his psychiatrist, Lewis Fielding, would know more or at least discredit Ellsberg as unhinged. Perhaps the "Plumbers," an illicit White House policing group tasked with uncovering the sources of leaks, could poison Ellsberg's food with a dose of LSD before he spoke at a fundraiser. Surely he would then be labeled a madman. In any case, as the President's chief of staff, H. R. Haldeman, noted at the time, Nixon compared Ellsberg to Alger Hiss, a State Department official accused of harboring communist sympathies who the red-baiting Nixon had prosecuted in the 1940s. According to the President, like Hiss (and Julius Rosenberg, who had been executed in 1953 for passing secrets to the Soviet Union), Ellsberg was a liar and a spy who must be nailed for stealing the *Pentagon Papers*.

***

Richard Nixon now entered the dark realm of personal politics, especially as he entered an election year and Vietnam still loomed as a top political issue. He believed that as president he possessed the authority to safeguard the nation. That is, his executive privilege permitted him to crack down on dissent and perceived illegal activities that might undermine foreign policy. Moreover, he

---

[2] Nixon, *RN*, 390, 509. George C. Herring, *America's Longest War: The United States and Vietnam, 1950–1975*, 4th ed. (New York: McGraw-Hill, 2002), 300.
[3] Dominic Sandbrook, "Salesmanship and Substance: The Influence of Domestic Policy and Watergate," in *Nixon in the World: American Foreign Relations, 1969–1977*, eds. Fredrik Logevall and Andrew Preston (Oxford: Oxford University Press, 2008), 87.

could not be held accountable for damage caused to people or organizations; that is, there was no abuse of power. Perhaps, perhaps not. Yet such thinking led to his downfall as he traveled down this unconstitutional road.

Even if he seemed paranoid, the *Pentagon Papers* ordeal revealed Nixon's hatred of the press (whom he saw as a worthy adversary), his pursuit of enemies, and his embrace of secrecy. History was repeating itself. This was a conspiracy against Richard Nixon, a continuation of media and Democratic efforts to destroy him over the past quarter century.

Indeed, Kissinger had told him earlier that his tough-guy image was at risk if he did not act strongly because any idiot bureaucrat could publish secrets while Nixon weakly stood by. The press, the President told his cabinet, is "only interested in news or in screwing me."[4] His future vice president, Gerald Ford, later reflected that Nixon's pride led to his personal contempt for weakness in people. For instance, he bitterly labeled legislators who wanted to retreat from Vietnam as "soft." Ellsberg was a different sort; he had acted as a bold, worthy but loathsome adversary.[5]

Did Ellsberg and colleagues at the liberal Brookings Institution in Washington have other documents, maybe one on plans for a bombing halt in Vietnam? Word came that the Soviet embassy had acquired a copy of the *Pentagon Papers* even before they were sent to the *New York Times*. J. Edgar Hoover at the FBI seemed to be dragging his feet on an investigation. The President wanted those documents and the Ellsberg types turncoats stopped dead in their tracks. "If the FBI was not going to pursue the case, then we would have to do it ourselves."[6] In short, Nixon knowingly prepared to break the law.

***

In mid-July, 1971 White House aides went into action on Nixon's orders. His chief counsel and assistant on domestic affairs, John D. Ehrichman, organized the anti-leak project. He tapped Egil Krogh as its head and placed under him a former Kissinger aide and lawyer, David Young. Joining them were E. Howard Hunt, a former CIA agent, and G. Gordon Liddy previously of the FBI, both rightwing ideologues bereft of moral qualms about using illegal methods against perceived enemies. Young jokingly put up a sign identifying himself as a "Plumber" assigned to plug leaks. The group investigated the FBI, NSC, CIA, and even the White House itself. It also focused on Ellsberg

---

[4]Sandbrook, "Salesmanship," 87. See also Kutler, *The Wars*, 114–6.
[5]Gerald R Ford, *A Time to Heal: The Autobiography of Gerald R. Ford* (New York: Harper & Row Publishers, 1979), 35.
[6]Nixon, *RN*, 513, also 390, 511. See also H. R. Haldeman, 303, 331; David Rudenstine, *The Day the Presses Stopped: A History of the Pentagon Papers Case* (Berkeley, CA: University of California Press, 1996), 66; Perlstein, *Nixonland*, 584; Robert D. Schulzinger, *A Time for War: The United States and Vietnam, 1941–1975* (New York: Oxford University Press, 1997), 291.

by breaking into his psychiatrist's office over Labor Day weekend to find information on his intentions, motivations, and any co-conspirators who deviously plotted alongside of him.

President Nixon may or may not have been informed but he thought that even these covert investigations were not aggressive enough. He also knew the Plumbers had carried out an "unprecedented, unwarranted, or unthinkable" violation of privacy and criminal action as he later confessed. When he grilled Ehrlichman about other plans for the Plumbers Nixon learned that they might bomb the liberal Brookings Institution though they had largely failed to produce much fodder against his enemies. That he seemed impotent to use government toward his own ends sent the President into fits. Maybe the Internal Revenue Service should be wielded to harass Democrats and their supporters, he pondered, like "Jews" and other "cocksuckers." At that time, however, Nixon held that the Plumbers reflected "my sense of urgency about discrediting what Ellsberg had done and finding out what he might do next."[7]

While some of the Plumbers dropped out of the secret group, Liddy, Hunt, and other recruits (Cuban exiles, for instance) continued Nixon's illicit work against his critics. They engaged, for instance, in wiretaps and burglaries into the next year. Their actions proved to be momentously ill-advised.

***

Nixon focused on the domestic scene when it came to his reelection in November 1972 even though he trumpeted his foreign policy accomplishments. He gave Henry Kissinger wide latitude in negotiations with the Chinese, Soviets, and North Vietnamese (as well as European allies) while he focused on crime and bread-and-butter issues, namely inflation. By mid-1971 the antiwar movement's influence had peaked despite outcries over Cambodia and the *Pentagon Papers*. His popular Vietnamization plan explained why; it steadily reduced US troops from the 543,000 when he had taken office to just over 24,000 by the end of 1972. Combat deaths nearly ceased by then as well. As a result, in the 1970 midterm elections foreign affairs barely made a ripple. To Nixon's disappointment Democrats picked up nine seats in the House of Representatives and eleven governorships.

The results frustrated Nixon because he had delivered the goods abroad. Even though he had not ended the Vietnam War (that announcement came in October 1972 to the dismay of the Democrats) he led in public opinion

---

[7]Nixon, *RN*, 514. See also Carolyn Eisenberg, "Remembering Nixon's War," in *A Companion to the Vietnam War*, eds. Marilyn B. Young and Robert Buzzanco (Malden, MA: Blackwell Publishing, 2008), 270; Perlstein, *Nixonland*, 594, also 584; Keith W. Olson, *Watergate: The Presidential Scandal That Shook America* (Lawrence, KS: University Press of Kansas, 2016), 18; Kutler, *The Wars*, 112–4.

polls regarding foreign policy. When the Democrats virtually handed him the election by nominating a progressive peacenik, Senator George McGovern, Nixon reveled in the comparison with himself as the international statesmen. "The real issue is patriotism, morality, religion, not the material issues of prices and taxes," he told his aides. Staking out a whopping 32 percent lead over McGovern, newspaper editors lauded his accomplishments in foreign affairs. Yet foreign policy also came back to bite him due to the *Pentagon Papers* fiasco. Nixon complained that his persecution by liberals, the press, and other enemies was unfairly linked to his prosecution of the Vietnam War.[8]

Nixon understood the immorality of lying, cheating, and cover-ups but he rationalized that such behavior was essential to defending the United States in the Cold War. After all, his predecessors had done the same (Kennedy had lied over the failed Bay of Pigs operation in Cuba in 1961 and Johnson had done so regarding Vietnam). In his eyes, Nixon's only mistakes were misjudging the path to achieve the desired ends. The true evil were unpatriotic critics who abetted international communism, which must be contested even by unpalatable or illegal means.

In the end, though, his abuse of power tested the very foundations of the democratic process. Writes legal scholar David Rudenstine, Nixon did not grasp his inability to control two institutions—the press and the courts. They were not fully accountable to politicians and, as in the case of the *Pentagon Paper*, they could weaken the executive branch. Moreover, just because the President claimed that press disclosures would seriously damage future military, diplomatic, and intelligence operations did not prove that such harm was a certainty. Without specific proof the government "cannot expect the courts to defer to national security officials," adds Rudenstine, even if judges lacked the training and knowledge of those experts. As District judge Murray Gurfein noted in turning back the administration's injunction against the *New York Times* to publish the *Pentagon Papers*, "the Security of the Nation is not at the ramparts alone. Security also lies in the value of free institutions."[9]

The 1972 election seemed a foregone conclusion. Nixon would romp thanks to a backlash of conservatives, populists, and moderate Democrats alienated by the left wing of their own party. Nixon embellished his image as a foreign policy guru and the economy seemed primed for the election year. When upstart George Wallace won some primaries but was forced to leave the race when he was paralyzed by an attempted assassination, Nixon's prospects grew even stronger. Democrat McGovern's campaign seemed ill-

---

[8]Sandbrook, *The Influence of Domestic Policy*, 97. See also Patterson, *Grand Expectations*, 762–5; Olson, *Watergate*, 175, 179.
[9]Rudenstine, *The Day*, 6, 356.

fated from the start. The press discovered that his vice presidential nominee had sought mental health treatment for depression, which led McGovern to dump him. Regardless, he appeared indecisive and too extreme on the issues. Nixon cruised to victory with nearly 61 percent of the popular vote, winning every state but Massachusetts. Democrats held Congress though Nixon won from across the social spectrum, including such traditional Democrats as southerners, Catholics, urban residents, and blue-collar workers.

Nixon's only real problem before his reelection lay with his latent paranoia and insecurity and his burning resentment toward political enemies. These negative personality traits caused him to double down to ensure victory during the campaign. And that is where the bumbling Plumbers entered the picture, just months before his huge victory in November.

***

Early in the morning of June 17, 1972 G. Gordon Liddy sent five of Plumbers into Democratic Party headquarters in the Watergate apartment and office complex in Washington, DC. It was not their first attempted incursion into the Watergate. This time around they wanted to repair a malfunctioning bugging device on the phone of Democratic National Committee Chairman Lawrence O'Brien. Security personnel discovered and arrested them. A search turned up their contact information that traced back to the White House, to an E. H. Hunt, an original Plumber who now worked for the Committee to Re-Elect the President.

Over the next two years, the Watergate scandal as it was called (thereafter, other government misdeeds were tagged with a "gate" to suggest a presidential violation), unraveled Nixon's second term. Investigative journalists found not only White House connections to the break-in but they exposed Nixon's myriad abuses, such as illegal campaign donations, sabotage of political enemies, and unlawful attempts to silence critics (as the *Pentagon Papers* episode suggested). Nixon's personality plus the revelations about the Watergate affair from a grand jury, Senate inquiries and hearings, and the press revealed an untoward abuse of executive power. By April 1973, numerous Nixon advisors had resigned, including his entire White House staff and the Attorney General. Many of them decided to save their own skins and talk.

These deserters were bad enough but then word came that Nixon had tape recorded all conversations in the White House. Investigators immediately sought these recordings to discover Nixon's complicity in the Watergate affair through his secret talks with aides and Plumbers about the break-in. The President refused to turn over the tapes, citing executive privilege and a constitutional separation of powers. The special prosecutor assigned to scrutinize the break-in, Archibald Cox, as well as Senator Sam Ervin and his congressional investigative committee, took Nixon to court. In October 1973, the President himself ordered Cox to stop his pursuit of the tapes and when the special prosecutor refused, Nixon ordered the Attorney General to fire Cox. The Attorney General refused to do so, resigning alongside his second in command at the Justice Department. Eventually, the Solicitor General, Robert Bork, did Nixon's bidding and terminated Cox. This so-called "Saturday Night Massacre" damaged Nixon's standing among Americans who could readily identify another abuse of power.

By February 1974, the House began impeachment proceedings and two months later, Nixon released written transcripts of the tapes. While the House Judiciary Committee considered several articles of impeachment, one—Article IV—dealt with Nixon's lies to Congress about US operations in Vietnam. As one historian has argued Nixon (and his chief foreign policy advisor, Henry Kissinger) lied about Vietnam because of electoral considerations; the President, they alleged, must stay the course to look patriotic to Americans. The issue of Vietnam (and the *Pentagon Papers*) was later dropped from the impeachment proceedings but Article IV showed the linkage of foreign policy to the domestic arena.[10]

For his part Nixon had excised damning evidence from the tapes yet what remained was bad enough. The recordings revealed that he ordered aides to shut down the Watergate investigation and cover up his involvement. As a result of the transcripts he lost all credibility, his claim of executive privilege crashing against the tide of overwhelming censure by Congress, voters, the press, and his own Republican allies. As the House readied to vote on impeachment in July 1974 the Supreme Court ordered him to turn over the remaining tapes. One of those recordings revealed Nixon demanding that his aide, H. R. Haldeman, send CIA operatives to impede the FBI's investigation of the Watergate caper. All of his congressional allies now jumped ship, convinced of his guilt. Nixon had few, if any, supporters left. As a result, he resigned from the presidency on August 9, having destroyed himself by his own grievances and his unconstitutional behavior stemming from the *Pentagon Papers*.

***

Indeed, the Vietnam War had already prompted restraints on presidential authority. Under the War Powers Act of 1973, for the first time in history, Congress required notification from the president within two days of the deployment of military forces that were then required to be withdrawn after sixty days (now ninety days) barring congressional endorsement. As Nixon and Kissinger understood (Congress overrode Nixon's veto), the War Powers Act clearly weakened the authority of the executive branch in foreign policy. They blamed Congress' meddling and its Watergate investigation for losing

---

[10]See Carolyn Woods Eisenberg, *Fire and Rain: Nixon, Kissinger, and the Wars in Southeast Asia* (New York: Oxford University Press, 2023), 7, 14.

FIGURE 2.2. *Effective August 9, 1974, Nixon left the White House. He and Pat Nixon say goodbye to Vice President Gerald Ford and Betty Ford on the White House lawn before boarding the presidential helicopter and retirement in California. Courtesy: Richard M. Nixon Presidential Library and Museum (National Archives and Records Administration).*

the Vietnam War. In Nixon's view, Hanoi shunned peace and invaded South Vietnam, knowing that the War Powers Act prevented a reassertion of American military power in Southeast Asia. Considering the war was already lost, this was a dubious opinion. Still, the War Powers Act signaled that presidential authority, including executive privilege, would be contested thereafter.[11]

In addition, Nixon's firing of Archibald Cox led to an independent counsel law that protected special prosecutors. That 1978 legislation became the foundation for future investigations of criminality by Presidents Ronald Reagan and Bill Clinton. Thus, there was a direct line from Vietnam and the *Pentagon Papers* to late-twentieth-century politics. The issue of abuse of power through claims of executive privilege reappeared over the next decades.

---

[11]Olson, *Watergate*, 22–59, 123–67; Herring, *The American Century*, 504; Sandbrook, "Salesmanship," 99.

3

Aftershock
Abuse of Power

Watergate became the historic gold standard of exploitation of executive power but it was not the last case. When he tried to suppress the *Pentagon Papers*, Nixon let his worst impulses overwhelm his presidency. Thus, Watergate was a lesson in character as well as criminality. Some of his successors did abuse their power, though only one, Donald Trump, possessed even worse character flaws than Nixon.

***

Ronald Reagan enjoyed an immensely popular presidency in the 1980s due, in part, to his skill at deflecting criticism and scandal. Indeed, Colorado Congresswoman Patricia Schroeder called him the "Teflon President," referring to a chemical coating on pans that prevented foreign substances from sticking. Nothing bad seemed to stick to Reagan. But he could not avoid the fallout from the next "gate" to threaten a presidency: Irangate or the Iran-Contra affair.

During the President's second term, the Reagan administration's illegal activities on behalf of Nicaraguan anticommunists became public. Although his popularity and age ruled out resignation, Reagan's reputation suffered. Like Nixon, he tried to assert executive prerogatives in foreign policy though Congress resisted. Nevertheless, the Cold War granted to the executive branch authority over international affairs. Concludes historian James Patterson, the Iran-Contra scandal showed that "the constitutional balance of American government . . . remained heavily tilted toward 1600 Pennsylvania Avenue on military and foreign policy concerns" and would remain so.[1] That trend ultimately saved Reagan.

---

[1] Patterson, *Grand Expectations*, 781.

Before the Iran-Contra affair nearly made him a lame-duck president, however, Ronald Reagan enjoyed perfect timing, credentials, and outlook for a nation mired in economic misery and global problems. Amid post-Watergate cynicism about leaders stepped Reagan, a conservative who welcomed the demise of the liberal New Deal state but whose political pragmatism attracted a wide variety of voters. These included evangelicals seeking morality in society, a working class disenchanted by the end of the American Century, free-market "neoliberals" sick of economic regulations, and a majority of the South where white people wanted civil rights slowed. Traditional conservatives (like his vice president, George H. W. Bush), who sought limited government and low taxes at home, joined him, and so did disenchanted Democrats. "Neoconservatives," pushing militant anticommunism overseas, hoped to win the Cold War through a robust national security state and powerful military, providing dynamism (and controversy) alongside the domestic neoliberals.

A former actor and movie industry union organizer, Reagan had turned conservative as the Cold War wore on and when influenced by his second wife, Nancy. By 1964, he embraced the extreme conservatism of Republican presidential candidate Barry Goldwater. Two years later, Reagan won the first of two terms as governor of California where he asserted conservatism but compromised on the environment, abortion, and taxes. From there, he used this big state as a springboard to national prominence, though he failed to win the Republican presidential nominations in 1968 and 1976. Reagan was the right leader at the right time in 1980, however, as Americans were down on the economy and their standing abroad, particularly after the Soviets mocked President Jimmy Carter's preoccupation with American hostages held in Iran by invading Afghanistan in 1979.

Earnest with a sunny disposition conveyed by superbly simplistic, vivid, and optimistic messages that pledged freedom at home from government oversight and taxes and freedom abroad against communism, Reagan—the "Great Communicator"—pledged to "make America great again." The oldest candidate nominated for president up to that time, Reagan trounced the hapless Carter. Four years later, with the economy humming and a huge defense buildup underway to bankrupt the Soviet Union, Reagan claimed it was "morning in America"—a new era of restored prosperity and respect overseas.

Reagan lacked foreign policy experience and the knowledge or interest about the world necessary for leadership but he had such deeply held views about the American mission abroad that he imbued his presidency with a messianic vision to spread US values around the world, safeguard the global community from nuclear conflagration, and defeat communism. In large part, after the Cold War almost turned into war in late 1983 due to mistakes and his assertiveness against communism, his vision succeeded as he restored

America's self-esteem debilitated by the Vietnam War, uncertainty over détente, and Carter's crises. Eventually, Reagan negotiated on nuclear arms control with the new Soviet leader, Mikhail Gorbachev, though he urged him to allow Europeans, especially Germans, their freedom from tyranny. The United States, he held, was simply exceptional as a symbol of morality, democracy, and prosperity.

Reagan set out to undermine communist evil by any means possible, particularly in the Global South, where he was unsparing. His fight against Middle Eastern terrorism to prevent Soviet inroads in the region largely failed but it did harden the Cold War even more. He aided any insurgent "freedom fighters" against communism in Asia, Africa, the Middle East, and Latin America and the Caribbean. Reagan lamented the passing of the American Century though he promised its return and thought that the country could go it alone to fight communism, especially in vulnerable regions.

That was about the extent of his instructions to his foreign policy team; Reagan's mind was not cluttered with the arcana of decision-making like his predecessors. He could be pragmatic but he was largely an anticommunist ideologue when it came to global affairs. The administration ranged from hard-core anticommunist internationalists like Secretary of State George Shultz, who leaned toward cooperating with allies and advocated cautious diplomacy to William Casey, the director of the Central Intelligence Agency (CIA), a staunchly anticommunist backer of subversion and dirty tricks who preferred action to Wilsonian ideology. Reagan tamed some of his own bellicose rhetoric and fell somewhere in between, a unilateralist willing to cooperate. But he rarely probed for options in foreign policy.

He governed by intuition, notes White House journalist and Reagan biographer, Lou Cannon, and that left the specifics to others. His inattention to the issues and laissez-faire attitude with advisors allowed too much freedom to opportunism in the administration. These included covert operations that Casey masterminded oftentimes without Shultz's knowledge. His advisors also feuded with the State Department despising the National Security Council and Caspar Weinberger's Department of Defense, and vice versa. Nancy Reagan tried to insulate her husband from the hardliners in the NSC but doing so simply isolated him from decisions. In sum, chaos often reigned in an administration run by a President who let his advisors roam free and fight each other.[2] That approach resulted nearly in his downfall.

---

[2] Gary W. Reichard, *Deadlock and Disillusionment: American Politics Since 1968* (Malden, MA: Wiley-Blackwell, 2016), 188; Lou Cannon, *President Reagan: The Role of a Lifetime* (New York: Simon & Schuster, 1991), 172–8; Herring, *The American Century*, 562–72; Michael Schaller, *Reckoning with Reagan: America and Its President in the 1980s* (New York: Oxford University Press, 1992), 122.

What Reagan did do clearly was set the agenda. He determined to defend the Free World against its terrorist agents: Iran, Libya, North Korea, Cuba, and Nicaragua. In November 1985 he called these five a "new international version of Murder, Incorporated" united in their "fanatical hatred of the United States, our people, our way of life, our international stature." He would not allow these "outlaw states" to intimidate, terrorize, or attack the United States.[3] Disposing of Libyan-sponsored terrorism the administration turned its focus on Nicaragua.

***

The "Contras" (the opposition to the leftist Sandinista government in Nicaragua) became fodder for the Reagan Doctrine or the policy of covert action to support "freedom fighters" among people of the Global South who defended themselves against communism. Reagan's obsession with communism linked to the notion that Central America was the major battleground of the Cold War. He and Casey were dead set on liberating the region from a supposed "red tide" by backing a rightwing government in El Salvador, ridding the tiny Caribbean nation of Grenada from Marxist rule, and supporting freedom fighters in Nicaragua against the Sandinistas.[4]

Although the administration failed to overthrow the Sandinista government (it would be voted out in an election in 1990), in his eyes, Reagan saved the nation by largely destroying it in the name of rolling back communism (meaning not only the Nicaraguan government but its supposed Cuban and Soviet sponsors). Decades later even his critics would pine for such clarity to combat aggressors. For instance, historian Tom Nichols argued for continued support to Ukraine in 2024. "Reagan's detractors will point to his policies in Central America and elsewhere as examples of what can happen when righteous fixation on noble ends leads to the justification of bloody and repulsive means. But Reagan . . . was right to view opposition to the Kremlin as both strategically necessary and morally just, as it is again today."[5]

In 1981, when Reagan took office, the United States faced grim challenges south of the border. Having backed ruthless pro-American dictators for decades Washington then encountered revolutionaries against such rule. Fidel Castro had overthrown Cuban ally Fulgencia Batista in 1958 and a few years

---

[3]Richard Reeves, *President Reagan: The Triumph of Imagination* (New York: Simon & Schuster, 2005), 264.
[4]Document 2: Ronald Reagan, "Presidential Finding on Covert Operations in Nicaragua, September 19, 1983," in *The Iran-Contra Scandal: The Declassifed History*, eds. Peter Kornbluh and Malcolm Byrne (New York: The New Press, 1993), 12.
[5]Tom Nichols, "Ukraine Needs American Weapons, Not More GOP Drama," *The Atlantic*, January 31, 2024, https://www.theatlantic.com/newsletters/archive/2024/01/ukraine-needs-american-weapons-not-more-gop-drama/677314/. See also Herring, *The American Century*, 585.

later, Dominican Republic strongman Rafael Trujillo was assassinated. A post-Watergate Congress highlighted the myriad abuses of human rights by these governments, including the overthrow by the CIA of democratically elected leaders in Guatemala in 1954 and Chile in 1973.

The Reagan administration countered that President Jimmy Carter's campaign for human rights further loosened Latin America from Washington's orbit. Nicaraguan Sandinistas had toppled long-time dictator Anastasio Somoza, a loyal, anticommunist friend of the United States, and now represented a Cuban-style "Soviet beachhead" in the Western hemisphere. Americans generally opposed sending troops to Central America, a phobia that the President derided as a "Vietnam Syndrome" of unwillingness to engage militarily abroad. Reagan's first secretary of state, Alexander Haig, pushed the region to the top of the foreign policy agenda as an aggressive response to Castro's Cuba. Haig reportedly shouted in the White House, "Give me the word and I'll make that island a fucking parking lot."[6]

In Nicaragua Reagan's troubles with dysfunctional decision-making began with $20 million in funding for a covert operation to train 500 Contras in Honduras. But the CIA's William Casey had larger ambitions: overthrow the Sandinista leader, Daniel Ortega, and plant a pro-American government in Managua. The United States sponsored a covert war from 1981 to 1984 that grew less secret; Reagan soon referred to the Contras as America's brothers-in-arms against the supposed "Moscow-Havana axis" of communism.

It was a dirty war. The Contras grew to an army of 10,000 soldiers who never threatened Ortega's rule but rebels greatly damaged the country. They committed human rights abuses against long-oppressed peasants while wrecking hospitals, homes, schools, and entire villages. The CIA took over operational command in late 1982, guiding the Contras to demolish fuel storage facilities. The next year the United States held military exercises with 4,000 troops in neighboring Honduras to intimidate Ortega's Sandinistas. The secret war that Reagan crowed about soon provoked a backlash at home as some Americans feared a repeat of the Vietnam tragedy. This was not a popular uprising against communism.

Most Americans were not persuaded that the Contra cause in Nicaragua was worth the slide toward involvement or the expenditures. Congress intervened late in 1982 under the Boland Amendment, named for its Democratic sponsor, to forbid the use of US funds to overthrow Ortega. The administration cleverly insisted that it was merely trying to stop Nicaraguan aid to leftist guerillas in El Salvador, thereby dodging the restrictions, but this

---

[6]Schaller, *Reckoning*, 123.

was simply an underhanded way to undermine the legislative branch. In 1984, congressional debate erupted into furor when the press uncovered the mining of Nicaraguan ports by the CIA, which was a clear violation of international law and an act of war. Casey had nothing but contempt for "those assholes on [Capitol] Hill" who got involved with his covert war.[7]

Reagan, too, despised the legislative branch when it tried to undermine the power of the presidency in foreign affairs, calling Congress a "meddlesome committee of 535" who unjustly demanded oversight of his office. Yet even some Republicans, including the arch-conservative Senator Barry Goldwater, were infuriated by the illicit war. In October 1984, Congress cut off all funding for the Contras. Reagan responded by instructing advisors to save them: "do whatever you have to do to help these people keep body and soul together."[8]

He found the very person to accomplish this objective in Oliver North, a US Marine lieutenant colonel who worked out of the White House for the National Security Council with a team of zealous anticommunists. North was energetic, charming, and cared little about the law. His squad of "cowboys" also had nothing but contempt for government institutions—a perfect mindset for abusing constitutional power. His mission focused on the wishes of Ronald Reagan, who North worshipped. The President thought North something of a free agent who often failed to inform him of the money flowing to the Contras but these NSC cowboys took their orders from Casey. He told them to stay out of sight of Congress and the rest of the executive branch, especially the State Department that tediously sought to honor the law. As historian George Herring summed up, Casey and North so "privatized U.S. foreign policy" that they sent the administration down a rabbit hole of presidential abuse of power.[9]

The Iran-Contra affair grew from the roots of this unholy and illegal apparatus of secret money and intentions. Reagan authorized requests for funding from other nations that totaled $50 million as well as from wealthy rightwing Americans like the beer baron, Joseph Coors. It was not enough to sustain the Contras. As a result, in early 1986 North orchestrated his "neat idea" to transfer the massive funds gleaned from the unlawful sales of arms to Iran (see below) to the Contras through Swiss bank accounts. This was done over the objections of Secretary of State George Shultz and the Pentagon's Caspar Weinberger. Shultz became increasingly assertive about coming clean on these underhanded transactions.

---

[7]Herring, *The American Century*, 59; Kyle Longley, *In the Eagle's Shadow: The United States and Latin America* (Wheeling, IL: Harlan Davidson, Inc., 2002), 291, 298.
[8]Malcolm Byrne, *Iran-Contra: Reagan's Scandal and the Unchecked Abuse of Presidential Power* (Lawrence, KS: University Press of Kansas, 2014), xxi. See also Schaller, *Reckoning*, 149–53.
[9]Herring, *The American Century*, 592. See also Byrne, *Iran-Contra*, 45–8; Douggles Brinkley, ed., *The Reagan Diaries* (New York: HarperCollins Publishers, 2007), 453.

North established Project Democracy, a private corporation set up to fund Reagan's freedom fighters. In reality the project focused on Nicaragua. It had its own ships, planes, and landing strips in Central America—all secret—and set up dummy corporations and bank accounts—all secret—with codes provided by North. Some of the operatives of what was called the "Enterprise" profited substantially from the funding arrangements in which millions of dollars disappeared into illicit accounts. The shenanigans could not be contained just to North's office. He tried to cover up the administration's involvement in the swirl of multi-million dollar donations and payments under Project Democracy but others bungled his efforts. When a story broke in November 1986 that Reagan had sold arms to America's hated enemy, Iran, to free hostages in the Middle East, the Contras story exploded.[10]

***

Central America occupied one side of the Iran-Contra affair. The other sprung from terrorism in the Middle East and the impasse with Islamic Iran since the late 1970s. The administration supported Iraq's Saddam Hussein in a draining war beginning in 1980 against the hated Ayatollah Khomeini of Iran but Iran also presented Washington with an opportunity. Reagan obsessed about extricating seven American hostages held in Lebanon, a nation embroiled in a civil war. Tehran had indicated that it could get the release of the hostages from a pro-Iranian faction in a trade for American arms needed in Iran's flagging war against Iraq. Reagan zeroed in on a deal. He confessed that he would even do something illegal (such as trading arms for hostages with Iran, an avowed enemy) to bring the hostages home.

American policy had long denied weapons to nations linked to terrorism and Reagan had publicly pledged not to bargain with terrorists. Furthermore, arms transfers to Iran were legally embargoed and Congress had to be informed of any deviation from that prohibition. But CIA Director Casey believed that arms might moderate Tehran toward the United States, preserving a balance of power in the Middle East against the Soviets who aided Iraq in the war against Iran. Arms might even encourage Iranian politicians to confront the Ayatollah's half decade of rule. NSC Advisor Robert McFarlane held out to Reagan a grand vision of an overture to Tehran being the equivalent of Nixon's to China ten years before.

Whatever the reasoning a plan went forward that no responsible policymaker—Shultz, Weinberger, Casey, or White House staff—monitored until too late. In typical fashion, Reagan was detached. As aides often noted

---

[10]Byrne, *Iran-Contra*, 144–167; Cannon, *President Reagan*, 68; William M. LeoGrande, *Our Own Backyard: The United States in Central America, 1977–1992* (Chapel Hill, NC: University of North Carolina Press, 1998), 587.

he was easily distracted and could not remember what he had done or said. These weaknesses played into the hands of NSC fanatics led by McFarlane, his deputy and successor, John Poindexter, and Oliver North. They planned their secret scheme, Project Democracy, right under Reagan's nose in a White House basement office.

Project Democracy secretly sold 2,004 TOW anti-tank missiles and fifty HAWK anti-aircraft missiles to Iran in 1985–6, covered by Israel and a shady Iranian arms dealer as the intermediaries. With Reagan's approval, Poindexter and North also traveled to Teheran with false passports, presenting a cake and a Bible signed by the President as good faith gestures. North even gave a member of Iran's feared Revolutionary Guard a private late-night tour of the White House. In exchange they got assurances that Iran would assist in the release of the hostages in Lebanon. Unsurprisingly, North and company lost out on their end of the bargain and they violated the law in the process. The supposed inept "rug merchants" in Teheran took them for a ride on the hostage release though Iran became an ATM machine, buying the missiles through Israel with cash that ended up in the hands of the Contras.[11]

Irangate resulted in scandal for the Reagan administration. When the scandal became public, Reagan's credibility took a huge hit. The results of the illicit dealing yielded just three, not seven, hostages who were then simply replaced when terrorists seized three new captives. Reagan tried to explain away the deal by arguing that he hoped to deny the Soviets an edge in the Persian Gulf but few took the bait.

Then he stonewalled, knowingly giving misleading statements in a nationally televised address on November 13, 1986. The "charges are utterly false" that his administration had shipped arms to Iran for hostages, as the Iran-Contra controversy stewed. "Our government has a firm policy not to capitulate to terrorist demands. That no-concessions policy remains in force, in spite of the wildly speculative and false stories about arms for hostages and alleged payoffs."[12] As journalist Lou Cannon summed up, Reagan's speech to the nation "was neither accurate nor believable."[13] The President lied to cover up his misdeeds and people knew it.

---

[11] Cannon, *President Reagan*, 708; Document 88: Oliver North, "Release of American Hostages in Beirut," April 4, 1986 in Kornbluh and Byrnes, eds., *The Iran-Contra Scandal*, 319–23; Bacevich, *The Short American Century*, 179.

[12] Address to the Nation on the Iran Arms and Contra Aid Controversy, November 13, 1986, *The American Presidency Project*, https://www.presidency.ucsb.edu/documents/address-the-nation-the-iran-arms-and-contra-aid-controversy. See also Reichard, *Deadlock*, 118–9; Byrnes, *Iran-Contra*, 206–29, 236–54, 265–7; Document 64: John Poindexter, Memorandum for the President, "Covert Action Finding Regarding Iran," January 17, 1986 in Kornbluh and Byrne, eds., *The Iran-Contra Scandal*, 232–5.

[13] Cannon, *President Reagan*, 683.

The scandal pierced his Teflon reputation. Reagan suffered ridicule and, most seriously, incurred charges of criminal activity as well. His approval ratings that had leapt to 73 percent after his summit meeting with Soviet Premier Mikhail Gorbachev in Iceland weeks before now fell under 25 percent. Reagan made things worse by misstatements on the types and number of arms and that Israel had not been involved at all. He could not recall what he knew about the affair or when he knew it. He had not just broken the arms embargo law—he had committed crimes.

A hostile Democratic Congress relished the opportunity to hunt this wildly admired Republican who had so outmaneuvered them but posse was late in coming. Democrats had grounds to prosecute when it was discovered that the funds from the arms sales to the Iranians were diverted to the Contras in Nicaragua, which violated congressional sanctions on aiding these insurgents. Congress began hearings into the affair.[14] The Iran-Contra scandal erupted. Like Nixon in Watergate Reagan was accused of abusing executive power.

***

The scandal likely exceeded Watergate in its breach of the law. Iran-Contra echoed Watergate in terms of the number of investigations, press and congressional involvement, resignations and firings of White House personnel, and executive branch cover-ups and, ultimately, in findings of guilt. Even when news of the arms sale went public, the Justice Department delayed its investigation to allow the NSC time to cover up the scheme.

Reagan learned that Israel had sold the missiles at a great profit, with the excess billions of dollars deposited into Swiss bank accounts before being sent to the Contras. Oliver North and his secretary, Fawn Hall, shredded thousands of documents that showed their wrongdoing in bypassing legal strictures on aiding the Contras, though they could not get rid of everything. (Hall tried to do so by cramming papers into her boots and exiting the building.) Enough documents remained behind to incriminate North, Hall, and five others. NSC Advisor Poindexter, who briefed the full national security team on the illegal transfers of funds, deleted over 5,000 emails, although they, too, were later recovered. His predecessor, the incompetent McFarlane, had already doctored a history of the Iran arms affair to appear as if Reagan had no knowledge of Project Democracy. The administration claimed, just like Nixon had regarding the Watergate break-in, that the President was unaware of his aides' transgressions.

Indeed, Reagan pleaded ignorance of the entire affair and then forgetfulness as an aging leader, but this was clearly an abuse of power. His diary (he

---

[14]Byrnes, *Iran-Contra*, 288–94; Reichard, *Deadlock*, 127; LeoGrande, *Our Own Backyard*), 438.

FIGURE 3.1. *Reagan meets with his National Security Planning Group regarding arms sales to Iran on November 25, 1986. Clockwise from the President's left are Secretary of State George Schultz and CIA Director William Casey. Secretary of Defense Caspar Weinberger is seated to Reagan's right. Courtesy: Ronald Reagan Presidential Library.*

scrupulously logged his thoughts and actions) showed surprise at certain points after he discussed matters with advisors. Yet he did know about the transfer of arms to Iran; the problem for investigators was, as with Nixon and Watergate, when did Reagan know about Iran-Contra and what did he know? One diary entry on December 5, 1985, revealed a briefing by the NSC in which he scribbled about the complexity of the "undercover effort to free our 5 hostages held by terrorists in Lebanon" and that "I won't even write in the diary what we're up to."[15]

There was no evidence that Reagan knew about the diversion of funds to the Contras. Nevertheless, he did not inquire into who had authorized the Iran-to-Contras transfers. And he praised North, exclaiming "Ollie, you're a national hero" whose neat idea "is going to make a great movie one day." According to the special prosecutor later assigned to the case, aides had built a wall around Reagan in an effort to seal him off from complicity in the scandal.[16] The fence was not quite high enough, however.

---

[15] Reichard, *Deadlock*, 128.
[16] Leogrande, *Our Own Backyard*, 483. See also Lawrence E. Walsh, *Firewall: The Iran-Contra Conspiracy and Cover-up* (New York: W. W. Norton & Company, 1997), 15.

After Democrats gained congressional seats in the midterm elections in November 1986, legislators leveled two charges against the administration. First, Reagan had pledged never to bargain with terrorists, but he had done so, thereby violating the government's stated neutrality policy in the Iran-Iraq War. Second, the administration had breached Congress' ban on military aid for the Contras. Both houses of Congress launched hearings into the Iran-Contra affair in the summer 1987, calling 500 witnesses over six weeks to Capitol Hill. Investigations revealed that Reagan knew about the dealings and even approved much of Oliver North's plans. Later, the President boasted that Iran-Contra had been his idea all along.

He might have said this in part due to the performance of the resolute and handsome North, who appeared at the hearings for six days. Wearing battle ribbons on his uniform, this patriot pledged to fight communism as a stalwart Reagan loyalist. North preeningly confessed he was prepared "to take a spear to the chest" to protect his superiors.[17] He also admitted to having no qualms about the illegality of his actions. Americans either tuned out of the hearings or held that communism was a far greater evil than lying. Many engaged in "Olliemania" by celebrating North, who received thousands of calls and telegrams in support. Even some Capitol Hill police took photos with him during breaks in his testimony while young men flocked to barbers for military-style Ollie haircuts.

In the end the Democratic majority charged Reagan with violating the Boland Amendment ban on funding the Contras, while Republicans pretended that the entire affair looked like a partisan issue. They walked a dangerously undemocratic road. The Republican minority report took issue with the Democrats for placing obstacles in the way of Reagan's anticommunist foreign policy, alleging that they were unconstitutional infringements on the executive branch's prerogatives in international affairs. Even more, Republicans held that the president's authority over foreign policy superseded that of Congress over appropriations; hence, when Congress cut funding to the Contras, it violated the Constitution. In a handy reversal of the executive privilege argument, the administration, wrote Reagan's defenders, was legitimately frustrated by the "abuses of power and irresolution by the legislative branch" and should ignore Congress.[18] What stupefying logic, charged lawyers, that actually endorsed the unconstitutional abuse of power.

Nonetheless, following the appointment of a three-person review committee under Republican Senator John Tower, who Reagan banked on being friendly to him, and after the firing of North and receiving Poindexter's resignation, the

---

[17]Schaller, *Reckoning*, 167.
[18]LeoGrande, *Our Own Backyard*, 501, also 497.

President was forced to appoint a special prosecutor, Independent Counsel Lawrence Walsh, in December 1986. Tower interviewed Reagan, stunningly watching the President read off a note to answer the question of whether he had approved of the missile sales. Was the President senile?[19]

By the time Walsh came on the scene Reagan's approval ratings had plummeted to around 40 percent. Walsh's probe into Iran-Contra yielded convictions of Poindexter and North for a conspiracy to defraud the United States though their felonies were later reversed. North even went on to become a darling of the Republican rightwing, nearly winning a Senate seat in Virginia in 1994. Published that year, Walsh's report concluded that Reagan and then Vice President Bush knew about the Iran-to-Contras diversion of funds. By either his knowledge or encouragement of the affair, Reagan, by 1994 diagnosed with Alzheimer's, had committed the most serious breach of executive branch wrongdoing since Watergate.

***

Reagan boasted to a skeptical public that he had won a critical battle in the Cold War despite an abuse of power that he denied. In general, though, many Americans excused his actions because they suspected his age undermined his mental reasoning. Indeed, when he last spoke publicly about Iran-Contra he earnestly took full responsibility but held that he did not trade arms for hostages. "My heart and my best intentions still tell me that's true, but the facts and the evidence tell me it is not." He came off as a lovable, doddering old warrior. As historian Gary Reichard concludes, "seeming to fall asleep at the wheel was far less damaging to Reagan than possible culpability for unconstitutional operations and lying under oath."[20] Indeed, even the special prosecutor concluded that Reagan's actions "fell well short of criminality which could be successfully prosecuted" because "it could not be proved beyond a reasonable doubt that President Reagan knew of the underlying facts of Iran/Contra that were criminal or that he made criminal misrepresentations regarding them."[21] The President was asleep at the wheel but supposedly not a law-breaker.

Scholars Malcolm Byrnes and Peter Kornbluh argued even before Walsh's ruling that Iran-Contra did not happen in a vacuum. It was bigger than Reagan, with roots that grew across the world—in Washington, Tel Aviv, Tehran, and Managua—into a jungle of complex circumstances that overlapped with covert

---

[19]Max Boot, *Reagan: His Life and Legend* (New York: Liveright Publishing Corporation, 2024), 669.
[20]Reichard, *Deadlock*, 129, also 130. See also Byrnes, *Iran-Contra*, 297; Cannon, *President Reagan*, 717.
[21]Byrnes, *Iran-Contra*, 321.

operations directed by officials at the highest levels of the US government.[22] Before the congressional hearings got underway in February 1987, the friendly Tower Commission had already placed blame on Casey and the CIA rather than the White House. That charge could never be proven because Casey lay in a coma from a massive stroke that soon took his life. The Commission exonerated Reagan though it took him to task for his lack of oversight in the national security policy process. The Reagan charm remained popular as did his accomplishments like a booming economy and disarmament with Moscow.

Reagan could be accused of being irresponsible because his contempt for government led to flawed governance which allowed his minions to run rampant. Like his idol Franklin Roosevelt he believed in making Americans feel better about themselves. He succeeded. He defined his times like Roosevelt had defined the 1930s or Eisenhower the American Century. Reagan was undeniably honest; he was not personally corrupt, as historian Max Boot argues. Yet he thought little about the trust invested in him because he disdained government. And even as he held government as an institution to be fraudulent he never thought his appointees might be corrupt. He paid a price for such thinking, in this scandal and in others that flew out of his control, many of them emanating from the Justice Department. In sum, because of his leadership style and view of government, the Iran-Contra affair threatened his political survival. He ended up as a diminished figure by the end of his term.[23]

In subsequent years, Reagan was feted as the Republican's visionary until Donald Trump seized control of the GOP. The 1980s had faded from view. The Soviet Union soon crumbled and the President got credit for ending the Cold War. Democratic capitalism triumphed and the United States stood alone to remake the world in its globalized image. Nixon, too, had seen his reputation improve when he became an elder statesman until his death in 1994. Perhaps Americans could forgive abuses of power; like history, voters moved on.

***

History could be kind, especially when aided by clever packaging by the Reagan team and Republican allies that attempted to mute the serious legal violations of the Iran-Contra affair. Arraignments of the principals involved provoked the ire of Republican loyalists. When North, Poindexter, and Weinberger were hauled before the courts Senate Minority Leader Bob Dole—a future Majority Leader and presidential candidate—demanded that Walsh end his inquiry. He accused Walsh of "browbeat[ing] two people into guilty pleas, threatening to

---

[22]Malcolm Byrnes and Peter Kornbluh, *The Iran-Contra Affair: The Making of a Scandal, 1983–1988* (Alexandria, VA: The National Security Archive, 1990), 27.
[23]Cannon, *President Reagan*, 793–5, 830–2; Boot, *Reagan*, 679.

ruin them financially if they didn't roll over . . . and with the indictment of Mr. Weinberger, his credibility is now zero as well."[24]

Republican presidential candidate George H. W. Bush managed to fight off reporters during the campaigns of 1988 and then again in 1992. They wondered when he knew about the Iranian arms deal. Reagan wrote in his diary that Bush had not been involved and Bush himself brushed off the accusations as unfair and the entire scandal as silly. Nixon had lacked a luxury that Reagan and Bush enjoyed: partisan politics abetted a cover-up for them. Worse, both presidents' avoidance of criminal prosecution gave a greenlight to future presidents to violate the Constitution. They actually banked on getting away with illegal deeds.[25]

***

The abuse of power did not end with Reagan. The affair involved much more than just Cold War posturing. As scholar William LeoGrande sums up, from start to finish Reagan officials "lied about what they were doing—publicly, privately, repeatedly, and egregiously."[26] And George H. W. Bush continued to stonewall by shoving aside the convictions brought by Walsh.

Bush completed Reagan's cover-up by pardoning Secretary of Defense Weinberger, one of six players set free (McFarlane, Assistant Secretary of State Elliott Abrams, and three mid-level CIA officials were the others). He dismissed their convictions as the "criminalization of policy differences," that is, he intervened because in his view Iran-Contra was a political dispute, not a constitutional one.[27] What Weinberger might have revealed about Bush will never be known but likely he would have testified to the vice president's engagement in the affair.

Walsh saw right through Bush's reasoning. The President had undermined the basic principle that no American was above the law. In a statement after the pardon of Weinberger Walsh wrote that Bush demonstrated that "powerful people with powerful allies can commit serious crimes in high office—deliberately abusing the public trust—without consequences."[28] That surely resonated some thirty years later when Donald Trump claimed immunity

---

[24] Walsh, *Firewall*, 419.
[25] Reichard, *Deadlock*, 131, who cites Will Bunch, *Tear Down this Myth: How the Reagan Legacy Has Distorted Our Politics and Haunts Our Future* (New York: Free Press, 2010). See also Brinkley, *Reagan Diaries*, 643.
[26] LeoGrande, *Our Own Backyard*, 587.
[27] Byrnes, *Iran-Contra*, 331, also 324–6.
[28] Document 101: Lawrence Walsh, Response to Presidential Pardons, December 24, 1992 in Kornbluh and Byrnes, eds., *The Iran-Contra Scandal*, 377. See also Jeffrey A. Engel, *When the World Seemed New: George H.W. Bush and the End of the Cold War* (Boston, MA: Houghton Mifflin Harcourt, 2017), 84.

from prosecution for his efforts to overthrow the 2020 election results and the Supreme Court granted it.

The frustrated special prosecutor also overplayed his hand by pursuing conspiracy charges that required evidence on a bunch of complicated actions but he did prove that Iran-Contra was different from Watergate because the cover-up started by one president carried over to the next one. This was the very essence of the rule of law. That principle applied all the way back to English kings of the thirteenth century and was "commonly viewed as the antithesis of autocracy, restraining government officials, including the president, from unauthorized conduct toward individuals," wrote Walsh. The rule of law ensured a balance of power among the three branches of government and compelled unelected bureaucrats to comply with congressionally enacted laws. Reagan and Bush showed contempt for it. Iran-Contra was a criminal conspiracy of the highest order that undermined the Constitution of the United States.[29]

***

Nixon's crimes undermined faith and credibility in politics and politicians while Reagan's hurt more abroad. For instance, arms control negotiators saw their START talks grind to a halt due to Reagan's preoccupation with the scandal. Gorbachev, for one, realized Reagan was hamstrung by Iran-Contra.

The notion that the Cold War justified the Contras tragically affected Latin America. In the case of Nicaragua subsequent negotiations led by Costa Rica resulted in a peace proposal, one that Reagan tried to sabotage for the rest of his term. The plan brought a cease-fire in the Contra war in March 1988 and two years later led to elections that the leftwing Sandinista president, Daniel Ortega, lost. Reagan focused on human rights to score propaganda points against the Soviet Union but he did not have the same empathy toward Latin America.

Such disdain led to suffering. In the wake of the Contra war some 30,000 Nicaraguans lay dead, added to 80,000 killed in El Salvador. Proportionally, this amounted to more lives lost when compared to US deaths in the Civil War, both world wars, Korea, and Vietnam combined. Despite the fact that Latin America as a whole gained seven civilian democracies during the 1980s—a claim touted by the Reagan team—Nicaragua remained one of the world's poorest nations. Furthermore, rampant inflation, huge debt, and extremist-fed violence plagued the entire region. Central America, moreover, witnessed brutal drug wars and an outflow of migrants.[30] Reagan's scandal made life worse in the region.

***

---

[29]Walsh, *Firewall*, 456–7, xiii, 517, also 519–21, 531. See also Byrnes, *Iran-Contra*, 329, 333.
[30]Herring, *The American Century*, 592–94; Byrnes, *Iran-Contra*, 336; Andrew J. Kirkendall, *Hemispheric Alliances: Liberal Democrats and Cold War Latin America* (Chapel Hill, NC: University of North Carolina Press, 2022), 228–30.

The Monica Lewinsky scandal that led to President Bill Clinton's impeachment in 1998 also represented an abuse of power with foreign policy implications. The nation's first baby-boomer president Clinton won the White House in 1992 by beating out incumbent George H. W. Bush and a third-party insurgent, Texas billionaire Ross Perot. An investigation into his wife Hillary's firing of the White House travel staff brought charges of "Travelgate" was the opening salvo of a chain of accusations against Clinton for corruption.

With Clinton on the defensive Republicans sailed into the midterm elections of 1994 and triumphed in both the Senate and the House, the latter under the leadership of Democratic antagonist, Speaker Newt Gingrich. Yet the President outmaneuvered the Republicans by placing limits on welfare to attract independents and by benefiting from a booming economy that got him get reelected in 1996. Clinton then instigated a scandal that nearly toppled his presidency.

An earlier probe into the Clintons' investments in a failed real estate corporation in Arkansas called Whitewater and accusations that the President used the Federal Bureau of Investigation (FBI) for political purposes led to the appointment of Special Prosecutor Kenneth Starr. The Whitewater project implicated financial advisor, Vincent Foster, recently an assistant White House counsel who had worked at Hillary's Little Rock law firm and whose suicide seemed tied to Clinton's malfeasance perhaps to cover up a conspiracy of some sort. Hillary persuaded her husband not to turn over any of their private papers for review by the press. His opponents erupted with such a rising chorus of accusations of abuse of power that Clinton gave in by appointing the special prosecutor.[31]

Starr could not pin the Whitewater charges on Clinton. Reports of the President's extramarital affairs, consorting with a nightclub dancer, and sexual harassment stemming back to when he was governor of Arkansas (and likely earlier) did stick, however. Bill Clinton had a reputation as a scoundrel, and an arrogant one at that.

The most serious charge arose from his presumed sexual relations with a 21-year-old White House intern named Monica Lewinsky. The *Washington Post* broke the allegations on its front page in January 1998. Starr turned his spotlight on the affair, which Clinton tried to hide by denying the relationship to a grand jury. The President, most implausibly, even contested the very definition of a sexual relation, claiming that oral sex was not sex. He later confessed to this misleadingly inane statement.

---

[31]John F. Harris, *The Survivor: Bill Clinton in the White House* (New York: Random House, 2005), 103–9.

Clinton eventually confessed to something and Starr recommended impeachment proceedings. In the first impeachment case since President Andrew Johnson's three years after the Civil War the House, along partisan lines, approved two charges of perjury and obstruction of justice in December 1998. The case then went before the Senate, which found insufficient constitutional grounds to impeach Clinton for high crimes and misdemeanors. A majority polled held that Clinton's sexual improprieties did not warrant impeachment or were not a public matter as long as they did not affect his performance in office. Yet this time around the Republicans, on the defensive in Watergate and Iran-Contra, occupied the moral high ground.[32]

***

Clinton was off the hook but he was wounded, if not crippled, for the remainder of his presidency. The scandal's effects lingered. Any big domestic reforms to Medicare and Social Security, for instance, were out of the question, as neither his party nor the Republicans would negotiate on his behalf. Poor Vice President Al Gore, moreover, carried the immoral taint of serving in the Clinton administration into his 2000 election campaign. The Republican candidate, George W. Bush, emphasized character and honesty in this closest of elections in American history in which surely Clinton's distasteful behavior cost Gore votes.

In foreign policy the Lewinsky affair had consequences as well. Enmeshed in his legal trials Clinton could only deal in a limited way with terrorists in Sudan and Afghanistan, the latter connected to 9/11 sponsor, Osama bin Laden. The President launched cruise missile attacks in these countries but he could not lead campaigns or even send US troops because he lacked credibility. Add in an ineffective bombing of Saddam Hussein in Iraq, the beginning of the air campaign in Kosovo to protect Muslim victims of war criminal and Serbian President Slobodan Milosevic, and a halt to normalizing trade relations with China and the ledger showed that Clinton was hamstrung by his sexual indiscretion.

On the constitutional front Republican foes argued that no president was above the law. This one had lied under oath regardless of whether this was a private matter. He had also undermined the notion that the chief executive should be beyond reproach by upholding high moral standards (though Republicans hypocritically changed their tune two decades later regarding Donald Trump's indictments for rape and payments to a porn star). Clinton had not only used the power of his office to besmirch Monica Lewinsky's

---

[32]Peter Baker, *The Breach: Inside the Impeachment and Trial of William Jefferson Clinton* (New York: Scribner, 2000), 160–87; Harris, *The Survivor*, 350–61; Reichard, *Deadlock*, 212–20; Bill Clinton, *My Life* (New York: Alfred A. Knopf, 2002), 774.

reputation but he had obstructed justice for personal gain. His defenders, however, considered such thinking prudish. When the independent counsel authorization expired in 1998 some said good riddance because the Whitewater investigation yielded little evidence of wrongdoing. Still, like Nixon and Reagan, Clinton exited office under a cloud of executive abuse of power.

Once again Watergate cast a long shadow. Clinton had disgraced the presidency, further deepening cynicism toward politicians. "Twenty-five years of self-destructive, internecine stupidity had finally borne its fruit," wrote journalist Joe Klein. "The public was disgusted—in a vague, bored way—with almost everyone associated with public life."[33] Public disenchantment was a grave outcome for a democracy.

The Lewinsky scandal seemed the kickoff to subsequent party warfare. Clinton put liberals in a bind for defending him and the right simply hated him for his liberal successes. Like Reagan, Clinton survived his scandal. He actually turned the tables, blaming the "power lust of my accusers" as a much greater threat to democratic government than his actions. That was galling though like Nixon (and unlike Reagan) he had hurt himself more than others.[34]

***

Arab terrorists hijacked an American Airlines flight with ninety-two passengers on board on its daily flight to Los Angeles just fifteen minutes out of Boston's Logan Airport on September 11, 2001. They overpowered the pilot and crew then veered the plane south to New York City, crashing it into the North Tower of lower Manhattan's World Trade Center. The plane hit between floors ninety-three and ninety-nine, causing an immense explosion and fires that killed over 1,000 people on the floors above and below. Reading to elementary schoolers in Florida President George W. Bush was informed just before 10:00 a.m. of this horror. It was the deadliest plane crash in aviation history and the worst in the history of terrorism.

The second worst occurred seventeen minutes later. A United Airlines plane on the same scheduled route from Boston crashed into the South Tower of the World Trade Center. All sixty-five passengers and crewmembers and the five terrorists who had commandeered the plane perished, as did 600 people in the upper reaches of the South Tower and many below it as well. The extensive structural damage collapsed both the North and South Towers into rubble within a few hours, trapping hundreds of civilians and rescue workers below.

---

[33] Joe Klein, *The Natural: The Misunderstood Presidency of Bill Clinton* (New York: Doubleday, 2002), 182, also 196–201.
[34] Clinton, *My Life*, 847. See also David P. Schippers, *Sellout: The Inside Story of President Clinton's Impeachment* (Washington, DC: Regnery Publishing, Inc., 2000), 178–9.

In Washington, DC there was more carnage. Terrorists crashed an American Airlines flight headed from Dulles Airport to Los Angeles into the Pentagon in Washington, DC killing all sixty-four people on board and 125 in the building though it missed Secretary of Defense Donald Rumsfeld who was inside at a breakfast meeting at the time. A fourth plane flying from Newark to San Francisco also headed for the nation's capital with the likely intention of striking the Capitol. Heroic passengers seized control from the terrorists and crashed this United flight in a field in Pennsylvania, killing the forty-four passengers on board. Osama bin Laden, the leader of the Al Qaeda terrorist network, claimed responsibility for murdering 2,977 people on a tragic day that changed history.

Destruction of the World Trade Center, a symbol of America's global economic dominance (and for the terrorists, imperialism) and the attack on the Pentagon, representing America's military reach, shifted attention from globalization to national security. The United States had blithely watched the fall of communism during the 1990s, enjoying unrivaled, near unilateral power around the world. Shattering the notion of the American Century redux 9/11 thrust the inexperienced Bush into a foreign policy role he was ill-prepared for and prompted major transformations in national security policy.

* * *

The son of the former president, George W. wished to focus on the economy once in the White House; the terrorist attacks derailed those desires. Bush had been a middling student at Yale, the only president with an MBA (from Harvard), and co-owner of the Texas Rangers major league baseball team. He became president after serving as governor of Texas. Bush took advice from an internationalist, Secretary of State Colin Powell. But in the wake of 9/11 his Vice President, former Pentagon chief Dick Cheney, and Secretary of Defense Donald Rumsfeld, held sway over him. They were hardliners skilled in bureaucracy and resentful of the withdrawal of American power after the Vietnam War. As neoconservatives they pursued America military supremacy and global power, shoving aside Powell's diplomatic approach.

Caught by surprise on 9/11 the neocons sought to reassure anxious Americans and reshape the national security structure (creating the Department of Homeland Security and reforming intelligence agencies). They also wanted revenge on the perpetrators. Included in their security overhaul was bypassing the 1978 Foreign Intelligence Surveillance Act (FISA), which prohibited spying on citizens without approval from the FISA court, with the USA PATRIOT Act. Passed by Congress, the Act allowed the government to eavesdrop into private email and telephone communications without a court's assent for the purpose of gathering foreign intelligence. Phone companies and internet providers had to disclose communications if requested by law enforcement agencies. Bush agreed with these fundamental infringements of civil rights, determined to extinguish the terrorist evil in the world.

Congress also approved a resolution within a week of the terrorist attacks to place America on a war footing. Three weeks later, in October 2001, invasion operations of Afghanistan began, supported by two dozen nations. They aimed to chase from power the Taliban Islamic fundamentalists who had allowed Al Qaeda to train on Afghan territory. The capital of Kabul fell in mid-November after allied forces swept through the country. The Taliban eventually recovered, inducing America's longest war until the United States withdrew from Afghanistan twenty years later.

The abuse of power, though, arose not in Afghanistan but due to the Bush officials' perception of a major obstacle to their neoconservative global agenda: the existence of Saddam Hussein in Iraq. After reformulating grand strategy along the lines of a tough aggressive model of pursing freedom, democracy, and free-enterprise through preemptive (rather than reactive) military strikes and economic dominance, conservatives cheered such activist and globalist "Wilsonianism in boots."[35] A key symbol of anti-Americanism Saddam proved the perfect foil for the bloodthirsty and self-righteous neocons.

***

In Bush's words Saddam was "a sworn enemy of America" who had warred against the United States, praised the 9/11 attacks, and tried to assassinate his father. The Iraqi dictator not only threatened neighbors but had invaded two of them, Iran and Kuwait. Saddam violated international demands while defying UN resolutions. His brutal rule included torture, raping political opponents in front of their families, disfiguring dissidents with acid, and dumping tens of thousands of Iraqis in mass graves. And Saddam not only "pursue[d] weapons of mass destruction. He had used them" against Kurds, noted Bush. The President "could only imagine the destruction possible if an enemy dictator passed his [weapons of mass destruction] to terrorists. With threats flowing into the Oval Office daily—many of them about chemical, biological, or nuclear weapons—that seemed like a frighteningly real possibility."[36]

Saddam had long been a thorn in America's side yet even worse than his tyranny, invasions, and mockery of American policies and presidents (including Bush's father) was the belief that he harbored weapons of mass destruction (WMDs). These could destabilize the Middle East and prevent the exercise of US power against terrorism. It did not matter whether he did or did not have the weapons; the Cheney-led neocon "Vulcans" wanted Saddam's head. WMDs, though, were mere rumors. Nonetheless, the administration intended to fabricate, if necessary, a war to overthrow the dictator. This was

---

[35]Herring, *The American Century*, 648, also 640–55. See also Reichard, *Deadlock*, 236, 238–9.
[36]George W. Bush, *Decision Points* (New York: Crown Publishers, 2010), 228–9.

all pure hubris. A worried Colin Powell tried to stem the tide toward conflict but the decision for war was foreordained by the Vulcans.

The abuse of power came in the selling job for an invasion and overthrow of Saddam. As a British diplomat told his bosses in London, "intelligence and facts were being fixed around the policy." That is, while all indications pointed to no WMDs that truth was inconvenient for Cheney and Rumsfeld. They did not want to hear from the "reality-based community," they confessed, "we create our own reality." Working with information from shady exiles they then leaked it to the press, cherry-picking information that fit their preconceptions and giving their audience what they wanted to hear. The intelligence was rigged and Vulcan assumptions were just that: theory. Not only were there no nuclear weapons but neither were there drones being readied with poisonous chemicals to drop on the United States nor stockpiles of enriched uranium to produce nuclear weapons.

Veracity was not the point, however. Instead, overthrowing Saddam—regime change, as it was called—was part of the larger war on terror that Bush had announced and on which he based his foreign policy. The logic of a preventive war on terrorism was unbounded by rationality or truth.[37]

Accompanied by a drumbeat of propaganda and half-truths spewed from Washington, war came. Vice President Cheney proclaimed that there was "no doubt" that Saddam had WMDs while National Security Advisor Condoleezza Rice warned that if he did not possess nuclear weapons at the moment, they were certainly on the way. Bush spoke of Saddam as a sponsor of terrorism who sought WMDs. Why wait until he had them? His new doctrine introduced in 2002—preemptive war—meant not waiting around "for the final proof, the smoking gun that could come in the form of a mushroom cloud."[38]

Most Americans fell in line, for the moment at least. Realists thought a war in Iraq a distraction from more important issues while young liberal activists in MoveOn.org used the new internet to mobilize a virtual antiwar protest in early 2003 in Washington, DC. A smattering of congressional members dissented. But Americans recalled the horrors of 9/11 and trusted in their government to protect them. Bush and Cheney "bullshitted" legislators in both parties with pressure and information. Some Democrats, like John Kerry and Hillary Clinton, questioned how to go to war and not whether it should be fought. There was no debate, little discussion, and merely an insistence that allies should be asked to join a coalition as they did in the Persian Gulf War a decade before.

---

[37]Herring, *The American Century*, 650, 651; Reichard, *Deadlock*, 237.
[38]Reichard, *Deadlock*, 266–7.

The neocons even balked at this idea, wanting to go it alone, but Bush preferred international support. He asked Secretary of State Powell to make the case before the United Nations after proposing a resolution to enforce sanctions against Iraq with military operations. The allies refused an automatic authorization for war though the Security Council approved a compromise, warning Iraq of "serious consequences" if it failed to comply with earlier demands including destroying its supposed WMDs under inspection by UN officials. In ensuing debate France backed off a commitment to support the United States as a last resort, Britain's Tony Blair stood with Bush despite an outcry in London, and Germany refused to participate. An outraged Congress renamed French fries "freedom fries" in the House cafeteria, targeting "sissy" France and "Old Europe" pacifism.

European obstructionism—to allow weapons inspectors to do their work in Iraq before going to war—delayed UN action into late January 2003. Having set March 10 as the launch date for war Bush sent the respected Powell to the United Nations. Powell resisted a bellicose statement written by Cheney but acted the loyal soldier as he exhibited shoddy photographs of WMDs and even a vial of anthrax. Inspectors later discredited all of his evidence. Pressure intensified on members of the Security Council to vote in favor of war and isolate France, which planned to veto a resolution. Bush warned that nations must "show their cards, let the world know where they stand when it comes to Saddam." His words ultimately failed to move the UN; arm-twisting yielded votes only from Britain, Spain, and Bulgaria. In mid-March Bush gave up on the United Nations as he and Prime Minister Blair went to war without the support of their allies.

Operation Iraqi Freedom began on March 20, 2003. It displayed the awesome power of Anglo-American military might that resulted in capturing key cities, then the government and Saddam Hussein, who was executed a few years later. Iraq turned to democracy, though it was shaky. Accusations of US soldiers mistreating captives soon got front page news. Part of this was because these troops faced increasingly lethal opposition from insurgents. As Iraq deteriorated Bush and Cheney admitted to the problems while they insisted that the nation have faith in the mission. Even when his Republicans lost the Congress in 2006 Bush doubled down with a surge of soldiers that peaked the next year at 168,000 troops. Nevertheless, he could not avoid the conclusion that this war was a fiasco.[39]

The neocons, including Bush, were responsible. The Iraq War cost well over 100,000 civilian lives as well as 4,431 Americans and nearly 32,000 US

---

[39]Thomas E. Ricks, *Fiasco: The American Military Adventure in Iraq* (New York: Penguin Books, 2006), 46–101.

casualties. The economic cost was staggering; estimates ranged from $3 to $7 trillion dollars, including veterans benefits and other debts to be paid well into the twenty-first century. Bush himself was a casualty, exiting office as an unpopular "war president" who had blood on his hands by tolerating brutal interrogations of prisoners and watching as Americans came home in body bags—all in the name of a dubious strategy in the long war on terror.[40] Democrats defied earlier predictions of a permanent Republican majority because of the war and an antiwar Democrat, Barak Obama, triumphed in the 2008 presidential election.

***

Lying and bullying paid off in that the neocons got their war but they lied all the same. This was a "story of spin, scandal, and the selling of the Iraq War," wrote two authors. The road to war was surely an abuse of power.[41] As the insurgency gained momentum critics questioned the rationale behind the conflict. Roughly 1,400 inspectors scoured Iraq and found no WMDs. Yet Bush had already proclaimed victory. He rationalized the Iraq War as a triumph for democracy that ended a tyrant's rule and represented a catalyst for a predicted global democratic revolution under American tutelage.[42]

Historians parsed the record, judiciously weighing evidence of why Bush went to war. Some reasons focus on provocation from Saddam Hussein or hubris in pushing Bush's broad-ranging and idealistic global "Freedom Agenda" or the arrogance of power or bureaucratic dysfunction or electoral politics or the fear emanating from 9/11 that give his team a blank check to fight terrorism. Things went wrong and Bush got things wrong. But these are excuses, no matter how much they are derived from the assiduous research of historians into archives and interviews with participants.[43]

The bare essentials of this case rested on the facts that the administration lied, covered up, obfuscated, and bullied friends. More willing to act then honestly examine the evidence (and lack of it), an incurious President Bush was at fault. Because of his preconceived notions, his disposition to advisors, and his lack of preparation in foreign policy George W. Bush bought the claims that Saddam had been behind the 9/11 attacks. He thought it totally conceivable

---

[40]Reichard, *Deadlock*, 276.
[41]See Michael Isikoff and David Corn, *Hubris: The Inside Story of Spin, Scandal, and the Selling of the Iraq War* (New York: Crown Publishers, 2006).
[42]Herring, *The American Century*, 649–65.
[43]Melvyn P. Leffler, *Confronting Saddam Hussein: George W. Bush and the Invasion of Iraq* (New York: Oxford University Press, 2023); Melvyn P. Leffler, "An Illuminating Hand-Off," in *Hand-Off: The Foreign Policy George W. Bush Passed to Barack Obama*, eds. Stephen J. Hadley, Peter D. Feaver, William C. Imboden, and Meghan L. O'Sullivan (Washington, DC: Brookings Institution Press, 2023), 635–57.

that this evildoer was up to no good. All the psychoanalysis and careful vetting by historians cannot deny the facts; Bush and his team masterminded a war by a con job of propaganda. Colin Powell knew it, the National Security Council, including Rice and her deputy (and future NSC Advisor) Stephen Hadley, knew it, and so did America's allies. Some, like Rice and Hadley, may get credit for seeking firmer evidence of WMDs yet they bowed to the message that Saddam had to go.[44]

This was not a scandal, though it should have been. Still, the Iraq War did have the same effect of the Nixon-Reagan-Clinton abuse of power. The lobbying for war made Americans ever more cynical of politicians, the political process, and even the value of democracy. The eventual outcome proved divisive, polarizing, and destructive to civility.

That is, Americans had had enough of the establishment. They grew so skeptical and disenchanted by the conflicts in Iraq and Afghanistan that they rebelled. With two wars going badly and an economic downturn that rivaled the Great Depression in 2008–9, voters opened the door to the White House to a shameless demagogue. Taking advantage of resentment and circumstances Donald Trump swept into power. Bush was immediately responsible because Americans reacted against the disasters in Afghanistan and Iraq. And over the longer term Trump was the fitting culmination of a half century of abuse of power that began with Richard Nixon.

***

Donald Trump faced a staggering ninety-one criminal charges in four cases after his first term in office ended, in 2021, becoming the first president to be indicted. Prosecutors incriminated him on felony counts to overturn the 2020 election, election interference in the state of Georgia, paying hush money to a porn star and cooking the financial books of the Trump Organization to influence the election of 2016 (for which he was found guilty on thirty-four felony counts), and hoarding classified documents at his residence in Florida. The first two were the most serious abuses of power because they led to his instigation of an insurrection against Congress on January 6, 2021 to halt the constitutionally mandated validation of electors. His violations included fraudulent claims about voters, assembling a fake slate of electors, and calls to Georgia officials urging them to find additional votes to put him ahead in the ballot count.

All of these efforts failed; he could not prevent President-elect Joe Biden's inauguration (which Trump, breaking with tradition, did not attend). There was a transition of power but it was not cooperative and peaceful. On the other

---

[44]Robert Draper, *To Start a War: How the Bush Administration Took America into Iraq* (New York: Penguin Books, 2012), 268–371, 401.

hand, regardless of his criminal behavior he was also reelected in 2024 and prosecutors had to drop the charges against him, knowing he would obstruct them anyway. Perhaps Americans were more forgiving, suffered from amnesia, or simply did not care about his multiple abuses of power.

Charged with insurrection and conspiracy that violated his oath of office to uphold the Constitution, Trump claimed executive privilege. In June 2024 his conservative appointees on the Supreme Court seemed to agree, granting him partial immunity in the classified documents case after which another of his judicial appointees overseeing that trial dismissed the case. He seemed to enjoy immunity from prosecution for any of his actions taken as president.

Trump's multiple abuses of power did not necessarily affect foreign affairs except in the classified documents case though they all showed the extent of his constitutional, civil, and criminal violations. Other crimes–covert relations with Russia and meddling in the affairs of Ukraine, for which he was impeached—did relate to the international arena. History shows that Trump was not alone in his behavior though he was the most frequent perpetrator and the worst of the lot from Nixon onward. After all, no other president was a convicted felon.

The processes of the Watergate affair re-emerged with allegations of Moscow's interference in the 2016 US presidential elections and Trump associates' secret connections to Russian agents and officials. The charges triggered the appointment of Robert Mueller, a former FBI director under three presidents, as a special counsel to oversee an investigation into Trump's actions. A swath of bipartisan leaders in government and the private sector held the Republican lawyer Mueller, a decorated US Marine who had served in the Vietnam War, in the highest esteem as a person of impeccable credentials and honesty.

Appointed on May 17, 2017, just eight days after Trump had fired FBI director James Comey for refusing to drop an investigation into former national security advisor, Michael Flynn, Mueller launched his probe. Flynn had lasted just twenty-two days before resigning after revelations that he had had conversations with the Russian ambassador to the United States, Sergey Kislyak, about defaming Democratic candidate Hillary Clinton. Flynn lied that he had never talked to Kislyak and then made a plea deal with Mueller to cooperate with his investigation. He did so but Trump later pardoned him of all crimes.

Mueller's charge targeted links between the Russian government and Trump's campaign. US intelligence agencies had reported that not only had Russian leadership favored Trump over Clinton but that President Vladimir Putin had personally ordered his agents to undermine Clinton. Doing so, Putin hoped, might also have the greater effect of casting doubt on the American democratic process. Mueller added a criminal investigation into potential conspiracy and obstruction of justice by Trump and members of his campaign staff and administration. Trump's closest confidants like his lawyer, Michael Cohen, would plead guilty to campaign violations by the candidate and go to jail for being complicit. His campaign chairman, Paul Manafort, pleaded guilty and cooperated with Mueller's team. The Russia probe spanned into Trump's presidency.[45]

Mueller also knew full well about Trump's moral depravity, a man steeped in sexual indiscretions and possible criminal behavior with women and in his business dealings. As the years went on he would know much more about Trump's salacious behavior as well as confirm his childish personality. The newcomer to the White House provided grist for the rumor and the legal mills.

The Mueller investigation lasted nearly two years during which time a grand jury summoned numerous witnesses, including Trump's son Donald Jr., to answer questions. Mueller also held private interviews with some principals, including advisor Steve Bannon who struck a deal not to appear before the grand jury. As well, the Republican-controlled Senate Intelligence Committee and the Democratic House Intelligence Committee referred several individuals to Mueller for criminal inquiries after they made false statements to Congress. Those subpoenaed revealed a complicated story of influence-peddling, Russian hacking into the Clinton campaign, tampering with evidence, and lying to Congress. A long-time advisor to Trump, Roger Stone was arrested in January 2019 on most of these charges and for leaking hacked Democratic National Committee emails to Wikileaks, a site renowned for publicizing damaging classified information. Because Stone had also discussed this information with the Trump campaign he was subsequently convicted though Trump commuted his sentence.

Mueller indicted a total of thirty-four people and three companies, of which eight pleaded guilty or were convicted of felonies. These included Trump associates and campaign officials. Thirteen Russians were accused of election interference. Because many under indictment had gotten close to candidate Trump a logical question surfaced: did he commit crimes, know of crimes committed on his behalf, and obstruct the investigation to cover up the trail of Russians?

In his 448-page report issued to Attorney General Bill Barr on March 24, 2019, Mueller did not absolve Trump of illegal actions. At a press conference a few months later he explained that "if we had confidence that the president clearly did not commit a crime, we would have said that." Mueller held up

---

[45]Office of the Director of National Defense, "Background to Assessing Russian Activities and Intentions In Recent U.S. Elections," January 6, 2017, chrome-extension://efaidnbmnnnibpcajpcg lclefindmkaj/https://www.dni.gov/files/documents/ICA_2017_01.pdf (accessed February 9, 2024).

because a sitting president could not be charged with a federal crime while in office. That his, the special prosecutor left open whether Trump was guilty or not but he certainly did not exonerate him. There was no doubt that Trump had panicked over the investigation, accusing then attorney general Jeff Sessions of not protecting him (as if the Justice Department was his personal legal defense agency) and seeking to have Mueller fired.[46]

Appointed to get Trump off the hook Attorney General Barr explained away the Mueller report. In a letter to Congress Barr conceded Russian interference in the election though he claimed that campaign officials had not been involved in these efforts. Regarding obstruction of justice the Attorney General argued that Mueller had drawn no conclusion on that charge. Thus, the Justice Department saw no reason to prosecute Trump. The White House claimed Barr had vindicated Trump, who called the whole Russian affair a hoax.[47]

Trump had obstructed justice. Barr's loyalty aside, Mueller would not say definitively because an indictment might further disrupt a near-ungovernable presidency. Furthermore, a sitting president could not stand trial. And an indictment would be unfair given there was no due process for Trump to defend himself. If Congress suspected his guilt then it could begin impeachment proceedings. What saved him were subordinates who refused his most extreme instructions.[48] Trump was actually lucky not to have Nixon's loyal Plumbers working for him.

The Mueller investigation showed that Trump's brush with the law stacked up to Nixon's criminality as well as Reagan's in Iran-Contra. While Watergate's prosecutors indicted sixty-one people, Mueller's thirty-four suspects was still a substantial number. Furthermore, twenty-six of those indicted were Russian so the Mueller inquiry internationalized the abuse of power. The probe into Trump was short but intense with indictments issued faster than in earlier special counsel investigations, although not primarily against government

---

[46]David Smith, "Robert Mueller Breaks Silence to Insist he Did Not Exonerate Trump," *The Guardian*, May 29, 2019, https://www.theguardian.com/us-news/2019/may/29/mueller-says-trump-was-not-exonerated-by-his-investigation. See also Chris Megerian, "Mueller Finds No Conspiracy, But Report Shows Trump Welcomed Russian Help," *Los Angeles Times*, April 18, 2019, https://www.latimes.com/politics/la-na-pol-mueller-report-trump-russia-collusion-20190418-story.html; Dareh Gregorian and Julia Ainsley, "Mueller Report Found Trump Directed White House Lawyers to "Do Crazy s—"," *NBC News*, https://www.nbcnews.com/politics/donald-trump/mueller-s-report-trump-sections-blacked-out-released-public-n990191 (accessed February 9, 2024).

[47]Michael S. Schmidt and Charlie Savage, "Barr Goes Beyond Mueller in Clearing Trump on Obstruction, Drawing Scrutiny, *New York Times*, March 24, 2019, https://www.nytimes.com/2019/03/24/us/politics/mueller-trump-obstruction-of-justice.html (accessed February 9, 2024).

[48]Adam Edelman, "Trump Failed at Obstruction Because His Aides Refused to Carry Out Orders, Mueller Finds," *NBC News*, May 20, 2019, https://www.nbcnews.com/politics/donald-trump/mueller-trump-failed-obstruct-because-his-aides-refused-carry-out-n996071 (accessed February 9, 2024).

officials as in Watergate. In addition, the Russia interference case came close to bringing down a president, as in the case of Iran-Contra. Trump escaped like Reagan and Clinton—damaged and ridiculed, but not destroyed.[49] In Trump's case prosecutors discovered many other opportunities to get him. The Russia investigation faded, replaced by impeachment just months after Mueller released his report.

***

The first impeachment (the second arose from a single charge of incitement of an insurrection on January 6, 2021) began with an inquiry from September to November 2019 and ended with acquittal by the Republican Senate in February 2020 (Republicans also cleared him in the second impeachment trial). The two articles of impeachment (Nixon would have confronted three articles and Clinton faced two) adopted by a Democratic House of Representatives were abuse of power and obstruction of Congress. That the impeachments were highly partisan affairs ultimately allowed Trump to survive.

Impeachment followed a House finding that Trump had asked Ukraine to interfere in the 2020 election by investigating his opponent, Joe Biden, for malfeasance. To prod along Ukrainian President Volodymyr Zelensky, Trump threatened to withhold military aid that Ukraine needed to fight Russian aggression in its eastern provinces. Trump also promoted a wild conspiracy theory that Ukraine, rather than Russia, lurked behind the 2016 election interference. In particular, the House inquired into a phone call on July 25, 2019, between Trump and Zelensky as a National Security Council member listened in, along with a dozen or so other US officials including Secretary of State Mike Pompeo. The NSC official, Alexander Vindman, blew the whistle on Trump, who, two days after his acquittal by the Senate, fired him.

Three House committees deposed seventeen witnesses, some of whom testified behind closed doors. Then the House voted on the two articles of impeachment. One witness, Ambassador to the European Union Alexander Sondland, whom Trump also later dismissed, described meetings with his lawyer and former New York City Mayor (and hero of 9/11) Rudy Giuliani, who told Sondland he took orders from the Oval Office. Giuliani verified the demand for a quid pro quo to Zelensky—military aid for a public inquiry into Biden—over the phone.

Trump's main conspiracy theory about his Democratic opponent alleged that while vice president in 2015 Biden had helped his son, Hunter, procure a lucrative position on the board of a Ukrainian natural gas company. That Hunter

---

[49] Amelia Thomson-DeVeaux and Julia Wolfe, "Is the Russia Investigation *Really* Another Watergate?", *FiveThirtyEight*, March 22, 2019, https://projects.fivethirtyeight.com/russia-investigation/ (accessed February 9, 2024).

FIGURE 3.2. *Nixon and Clinton give pre-impeachment advice to Trump. Courtesy of Kevin KAL Kallaugher,* The Economist, *kaltoons.com.*

had business dealings with foreign entities while his father held such a high office exposed Joe to accusations of a conflict of interest. (Weeks before leaving office President Biden raised eyebrows by pardoning his son of all crimes). In addition, the administration charged that a Democratic National Committee email server had been hacked by Ukrainians in the 2016 election.

Trump blocked a 400 million dollar aid package to coerce Zelensky's cooperation. After the July phone call, a White House budget official quietly told the Pentagon to withhold assistance. Trump demanded that Zelensky go public about the investigations into the Bidens and Ukrainian cyberspies. Vindman broke a story that sounded an awful lot like the episode that Mueller explored in which Trump solicited foreign help for his reelection. Acting White House Chief of Staff Mick Mulvaney blurted out that such pressure tactics for a quid pro quo were used all the time before realizing he had spilled the beans about this illegal deal.

Several credible witnesses, including former Trump administration officials, trooped to Capitol Hill to confirm the story of coercion by the White House. When pressed, Trump called the entire affair a witch hunt and said that Democrats had gotten the phone call totally wrong. He had only called Zelensky to congratulate the former television star on his election. Curiously, though, the Ukrainian president had taken office three months before! In truth, Trump had criminally extorted a foreign government to benefit his reelection.

The Republicans complained about an unfair political tarring propagated by bureaucrats who disagreed with Trump's policies. The Democrats had the evidence, however. Republicans actually politicized the matter by voting against impeachment in both houses of Congress. Many, including Senator Majority Leader Mitch McConnell, would come to regret their decision when Trump encouraged the January 6 insurrection and then captured his third nomination as their presidential candidate in 2024. His reign of terror may have ended by permanent removal from office; impeachment would have made him constitutionally ineligible from ever running again. But party loyalty outweighed the facts and morality. Only Senator Mitt Romney voted for impeachment, on one count.[50]

Trump's unconstitutional foreign entanglement almost cost him his job while it hurt the country, if not the world. His criminality further polarized the country at a time of impending crisis; the COVID-19 global pandemic was just weeks away from the impeachment trial. This scourge, that killed twenty million people over the next few years, demanded national unity to tame it. Trump's very existence in the White House hindered the response to the pandemic. And now even more trouble was brewing.

*　*　*

In June 2023, a grand jury indicted Donald Trump and two aides at his Mar-a-Lago residence on forty felony counts for mishandling classified documents. This represented the first federal indictment of a former US president. Most of the charges brought by Special Counsel Jack Smith were based on the Espionage Act for top-secret documents Trump had taken with him from the White House to Florida and to his Bedminster golf club in New Jersey. The rest included making false statements and engaging in a conspiracy to obstruct justice. After arraignment, the three pleaded not guilty to the charges. A trial date was set for Spring 2024, though complications delayed it through Fall.

All official presidential documents must be transferred to the National Archives and Records Administration at the end of a president's term; in this case fifteen boxes of papers turned up missing early in 2022. The FBI had evidence that Trump personally oversaw the removal of the documents to his estates. Under subpoena he certified that he intended to return the

---

[50] "Trump Impeachment: The Short, Medium and Long Story," *BBC*, February 5, 2020, https://www.bbc.com/news/world-us-canada-49800181; Alexander Vindman, "What I Heard in the White House Basement," *The Atlantic* August 1, 2021, https://www.theatlantic.com/politics/archive/2021/08/trump-ukraine-call-impeachment-vindman/619617/; Peter Baker, Maggie Haberman, Danny Hakim, and Michael S. Schmidt, "Trump Fires Impeachment Witnesss Gordon Sondland and Alexander Vindman in Post-Acquittal Purge," *New York Times*, February 7, 2020, https://archive.ph/20200208061052/https://www.nytimes.com/2020/02/07/us/politics/alexander-vindman-gordon-sondland-fired.html (accessed February 9, 2024).

materials. In reality he hid them from his lawyers and the FBI, who confirmed that because he had moved them he subverted justice. The FBI recovered over 13,000 documents at Mar-a-Lago in August 2022. More than 300 of them were classified with national defense secrets and thus covered under the Espionage Act. Trump claimed he had every right to the documents under the Presidential Records Act but lawyers confirmed that the Espionage Act superseded that legislation.

The affair turned even more unseemly due to Trump's violent rhetoric. He called for retribution after his indictment, which he labeled an "act of war." While Republicans in Congress largely remained silent, a House member, Adam Kinzinger, announced that Trump "will be held accountable." Even his former attorney general, Bill Barr, ridiculed the idea that Trump was a victim since due diligence was followed to investigate him. Lawyers agreed that a conviction would almost certainly mean time in prison.[51]

Two issues complicated the case. First were the accusations against Biden for similarly moving documents to his personal residence after stepping down as vice president in 2017. In February 2024, however, a special counsel opposed criminal charges because the President had cooperated with investigators. It turned out that Biden had accidentally retained the files and then willingly gave them up. On the contrary, the National Archives had repeatedly asked Trump to return the documents but he had not done so. Jack Smith charged him with conspiring to block investigators from recovering the classified files.

Second, the looming 2024 presidential election gave Trump a platform to grieve about unfair treatment. He cited a double standard—a supposed "two-tiered system"—in which Biden went free while Trump was persecuted for the same thing. The election played a major part in muddling his trial in the case.[52] Indeed, weeks after Trump was reelected in November 2024 Smith asked for dismissal of the documents case because it was unconstitutional to

---

[51] Scott Wong, "Trump Allies Say Biden is 'Weaponizing' DOJ Against His Chief 2024 Rival Following Indictment," *NBC News*, June 8, 2023, https://www.nbcnews.com/politics/donald-trump/trump-indictment-republicans-say-biden-weaponizing-doj-rcna87962; Michael S. Schmidt, Alan Feuer, Maggie Haberman, and Adam Goldman, "Trump Supporters' Violent Rhetoric in His Defense Disturbs Experts," *New York Times*, June 11, 2023, https://www.nytimes.com/2023/06/10/us/politics/trump-supporter-violent-rhetoric.html; Jake Swearingen, Cheryl Teh, and Taylor Berman, "Nobody Is Above the Law: How the World Reacts to Trump Being Indicted for the Second Time," *Business Insider*, June 9, 2023, https://www.businessinsider.com/trumpworld-reacts-to-the-mar-a-lago-indictment-2023-6; Gareth Evans, "Trump is 'Toast' If Indictment Correct, William Barr Says," *BBC News*, June 12, 2023, https://www.bbc.com/news/world-us-canada-65875898 (accessed February 9, 2024).

[52] Peter Charalambous, "Why Biden and Trump's Classified Documents Cases Aren't the Same: Experts," *ABC News*, February 8, 2024, https://abcnews.go.com/US/biden-trump-classified-documents-trumps-alleged-obstruction-led/story?id=107663 (accessed February 9, 2024).

prosecute a sitting president. The special counsel also terminated the January 6 case against Trump to subvert the 2020 election. Smith did note that the judges who issued the dismissals were merely following the law though it was also likely Trump would pressure his Justice Department to withdraw the charges anyway. The government stood by the merits of both cases because Smith had abundant evidence that Trump had committed crimes. Trump was lucky to be reelected, which got him off the hook under the Constitution, though once he left the White House he could possibly be relitigated.

***

When it came to abuse of power in legal, decision-making, and ethical senses Trump was the worst of all US presidents in history. Regarding constitutional offenses even his argument of presidential immunity from federal criminal prosecution for all acts taken when in office was, as the courts held, wrong although the Supreme Court obscured the matter by granting him partial immunity. If Trump was correct then a president could do anything while in office, a betrayal of the constitutional separation of powers in which the legislative and judicial branches (and elections) can rein in a bad presidential egg. But Donald Trump thought himself above the law.

Trump was a repeat offender in this regard, clearly the outlier of presidential abusers of the Constitution. Nixon was sneaky, Reagan lax, Clinton sleazy, and Bush narrow-minded. They were all liars. To be sure they protected themselves and violated public trust. But all of them ultimately followed the rule of law. All of them spoke of how they cherished democracy and the United States. They also took advice, backed down, and expressed misgivings, however tepidly. Finally, although they certainly had their personal foibles they behaved like mature adults, never engaging in immature, unpresidential name-calling. Trump might push an "America First" agenda but he cared not for America nor democracy nor the rule of law. Donald Trump cared about Donald Trump—cry baby, con artistry, and narcissist rolled into one after a lifetime of fraudulent, corrupt, and unethical dealings.

In short, Trump was not qualified to be president, lacking the experience, knowledge, and temperament to serve in the nation's highest office. Just the number of felony counts against him—ninety-one—should indicate that his abuse of power made him the champion culprit of illegal acts among occupants of the White House. Trump might have been the culmination of a history of executive abuse by embodying how bad things could get. It might be instructive to ask: what would other presidents—including Nixon, Reagan, Clinton, and Bush—think of Trump as their successor? Likely, they would be embarrassed for their country.

Still, Trump derived from a line of presidential behavior of contempt that stemmed from the *Pentagon Papers* decades before. Richard Nixon remained an apparition in US politics. American democratic processes were put to the test by the power wielded by the executive branch and the notion that presidents had leeway beyond the checks-and-balances of the Constitution to conduct foreign policy (or, in Clinton's case, sexual affairs). The courts—and the court of public opinion—decided otherwise. Nixon set a precedent of illegal actions when he targeted Daniel Ellsberg. His offenses repeated, in various forms, from 1971 onward.

Offending presidents had abused power before Nixon but he opened the way to threats to democracy that still trouble the country and the world. Under Trump they spiraled downward in gravity and scope. Chillingly, misdeeds may now seem commonplace—everybody does it argue presidential defenders. Abuse of power may seem like normal procedure according to a public that disparages civic duty and the conduct of its leaders, including the most powerful: the president of the United States. The country, after all, elected then reelected Donald Trump. Citizens travel down this road of cynicism, especially toward the Constitution, at their peril.

4

China Shock

On the evening of Thursday, July 15, 1971, Richard Nixon changed the world. In a three-minute television address to the nation from studios in Burbank, California, the President announced his acceptance of an invitation from the Premier Zhou Enlai to visit the People's Republic of China (PRC) the following year. Nixon sought to thaw relations between the two nations after a freeze in official communications since Mao Zedong's revolution in 1949. Listeners were stunned. They saw this historic effort at rapprochement as a major alteration in the balance of power in Asia and a gigantic reversal in US foreign policy. This was the first of two Nixon "shokkus," as the stunned Japanese called them, that have reverberated to this day.

Nixon designed this first Shock to build a lasting peace in the world, though that was not really why he accepted Zhou's invitation. Rather, he sought to open the door to the PRC as a means of activating his policy of détente—the easing of Cold War tensions with the other superpower, the Soviet Union. Détente hinged on attaining US interests: accords with Moscow to limit nuclear weapons and slow the arms race, extricating from the Vietnam War on which Nixon's 1972 reelection chances hinged, boosting the sliding economy at home and abroad, and acknowledging a new era of parity in world power.

With 750 million people in 1971, a number that doubled over the next half century, China could attract trade and investment to benefit US prosperity. Such engagement with capitalism might coax Beijing away from its destabilizing revolutionary ideology. Nixon's leap of faith recognized an impending "Pacific Century" of Asian power. The China Shock, in short, had grand strategic consequences in the decades to come.

***

The international strategic blueprint of Nixon and his National Security Advisor, Henry Kissinger—their "Grand Design"—undergirded the announcement on China. This plan involved détente with the Soviet Union, focusing on nuclear disarmament as well as warming toward the People's Republic. Western and

Eastern Europe were also integral parts of the Grand Design; both regions played intermediary roles between the superpowers. Détente emerged during the Kennedy years after the Cuban Missile Crisis and tensions over the Berlin Wall. A decade later Nixon placed détente at the top of his agenda because the Soviets had gained near equality in nuclear strength with the United States, thus changing the global balance of power.

Realism and real-world circumstances replaced ideology in Nixon-Kissinger calculations. Moscow seemed to have jettisoned its plan for global revolution; it sought instead to maintain its position of power relative to America. Furthermore, the United States no longer enjoyed its outright military or economic hegemony of the American Century. Nixon bet that the Soviets were willing to negotiate mutual coexistence within the Cold War context. His solid credentials as a hardline anticommunist allowed him political cover at home to gesture to enemies.

That approach could also play to America's advantage. Exploiting the triangle of power between Washington, Moscow, and Beijing might bring pressure to bear on problems while maintaining the United States as an essential player on the world stage. The two communist nations had long despised each other, a conflict fueled by ideological fissures dating back to diverging interpretations of Leninism and Stalinist rule. Kissinger and Nixon believed they could further drive a wedge between the two communist rivals by fostering arms control, economic growth, confidence among European allies stuck between US and Soviet missiles, and withdrawal from the Vietnam War. Soviet-Chinese hostility, in other words, served American purposes if Washington drew closer to both.

To a large extent, Moscow mirrored Washington's thinking. The Russians did not abandon their ideological struggle against democratic capitalism. Unlike the Nixon team, they opposed linking disparate issues—arms, trade, Jewish emigration, and China—into discussions with the United States. They were willing to talk, however. When Nixon announced in his 1969 inaugural address a new "era of negotiation," they picked up the signal of accommodation and engaged in arms control talks. These complicated negotiations yielded the hallmark Strategic Arms Limitation Talks (SALT I) agreements that, for the first time, placed limits on offensive and defensive nuclear systems. SALT II talks followed.[1] Détente was underway.

***

Through détente's linkage of issues, Nixon also wanted the PRC to influence communist North Vietnam to end that war and then open the Chinese

---

[1] Herring, *The American Century*, 472–6.

economy and integrate into the world community. Talks with Beijing were also good politics as they would steal thunder from liberals at home who opposed the outdated containment of the Chinese. Even if his rightwing base despised the unreconstructed communist hardliners in Beijing, the President was safe on that political flank because of his reputation as a redbaiter. Nixon would never be soft on communism. In addition, capturing Chinese consumers and using cheap Chinese labor had been a century-long dream of the West. The China market seemed limitless. Not engaging also came with a price, for without rapprochement the PRC would "live in angry isolation," Nixon wrote, a dangerous position for an enemy, potential détente partner, and rising power.[2]

China, too, saw its market as a reason to turn toward the United States. From 1958 to 1962 Mao Zedong had embarked on the disastrous Great Leap Forward to modernize through the genocidal collectivization of agriculture. He industrialized the predominant rural areas and imposed forced labor, leaving the countryside in ruin. Farmers starved in a great famine; the estimated deaths ran from fifteen to fifty-five million people. Worsening the misery by covering up Mao began the Cultural Revolution in 1966, a ten-year effort to purge pro-capitalist thinking from the country. All the while the split widened with Moscow, even escalating into three bloody border clashes in 1969 in which the Soviets considered a preemptive nuclear strike.

China was vulnerable on the border and at home, so the time was ripe to temper communist radicalism. Opening to the United States might steer China toward stability and normal development by attracting American ideas, technology, and exports. And easing tensions with its erstwhile enemy, the United States, might boost China's international status and enhance its security toward Moscow.

Nevertheless, Beijing had long been wary of the United States and the feelings were reciprocated. Each country had such vast political, cultural, and historical differences that their mutual animosity might be impossible to overcome. The stereotypes seemed indelible. In 1950 China judged America as "a nation that is thoroughly reactionary, thoroughly black, thoroughly corrupt, and thoroughly cruel" run by a handful of millionaires, criminals, and fascists who oppressed "countless millions of poor people." Meanwhile, *Time* and *Life* magazines, owned by "American Century" author Henry Luce, himself a child of missionaries in China, portrayed life behind the "Bamboo Curtain" as sterile and dreadful. In American eyes, the Chinese people were like hordes of ants stomped on by treacherous communist overlords. Abroad, they not only

---

[2] Nixon, *RN*, 545.

had attacked Americans in the Korean War but they had infiltrated the United States, or so charged anticommunists like then-Congressman Richard Nixon.[3]

Decades of hostility had hardened positions. Staunch rightwing anticommunists like Ronald Reagan hated "Red" China and cherished Taiwan and its leader Jiang Jeshi, an American ally since the 1930s. China had its equivalent faction in a resolute leftwing led by Lin Biao and supported by Mao Zedong's wife Jiang Qing. For them Nixon's inaugural address was no peace overture but a confession that US imperialists "are beset with profound crisis at home and abroad."[4] Even the dangerous border clashes with the Soviets did not move the extremists toward accommodation. These revolutionary cold warriors urged people around the world to "unite and defeat the US aggressors and all their running dogs."[5]

Détente would be challenging. Once Nixon entered the White House, as historian George Herring notes, both nations "carried out an elaborate, carefully choreographed diplomatic mating dance comprised of signals faint and strong, one step forward, two back."[6] While Beijing hinted at peaceful coexistence with the United States, Washington gave subtle nods through French and Romanian intermediaries. Six months into office Nixon decided to cease travel restrictions to China and withdrew some of the patrols of the US Seventh Fleet in the Taiwan Straits that protected US ally Taiwan from an invasion from the mainland. The next year both countries outlined their views on Vietnam, the future of Taiwan (which the United States recognized as the real China since 1949), and other issues. Nixon learned that for Mao's consumption Zhou Enlai would not abandon revolutionary communist ideology but he would be flexible in talks with Washington.

China and the United States resumed quiet talks in early 1970 at the ambassadorial level but Mao denounced the bombings in Cambodia and suspended the meetings. Nixon would not give up, however. He told reporters that "we must have relations with Communist China."[7]

The interests of Beijing and Washington converged by late 1970 as the Soviets increased their troops at the border and Nixon pulled more of America's out of Vietnam. According to China, US power in Asia seemed to be

---

[3]Margaret MacMillan, *Nixon and Mao: The Week That Changed the World* (New York: Random House, 2007), 107.
[4]Xia, *Negotiating*, 140, also 144. See also Warren I. Cohen, *America's Response to China: A History of Sino-American Relations*, 6th ed. (New York: Columbia University Press, 2019), 148–94, 215.
[5]Herring, *The American Century*, 477.
[6]Herring, *The American Century*, 477, also 476. See also Yafeng Xia, *Negotiating with the Enemy: US-China Talks During the Cold War, 1949–1972* (Bloomington, IN: Indiana University Press, 2006), 136–7; Gordon H. Chang, *Friends and Enemies: The United States, China, and the Soviet Union, 1948–1972* (Stanford, CA: Stanford University Press, 1990), 228–52, 287–9.
[7]Cohen, *America's Response*, 217.

waning while the Soviets were more threatening than ever. Mao needed to speak to Nixon. In October, Nixon became the first president to use the term "People's Republic of China," a phrase of huge symbolic importance to Beijing that legitimized Mao's nation in the eyes of the world.

In a major speech on foreign policy in February 1971 Nixon called for a dialogue with Beijing, conceding that the PRC must have a seat at the United Nations though not by expelling Taiwan. Beijing vehemently opposed America's "two-Chinas" policy UN but Premier Zhou devised a compromise: Nixon would recognize one China (the PRC) and postpone a decision on Taiwan's status to a later date. This would calm US domestic critics, both liberals seeking to normalize relations with Beijing and conservative backers of Taiwan by saying "one China, but not now."[8] The next month the administration ended passport restrictions for travel to China, which Beijing viewed as an insulting infringement on its sovereignty. And then ping-pong entered the picture.

In early 1971, the US table tennis team encountered the top-ranked Chinese team while competing in Japan. An American player made a friendly gesture to a Chinese player that Beijing mistakenly believed Washington had authorized. The PRC jumped at this outreach by inviting the Americans for an all-expense paid visit to play in Beijing. Zhou directly instructed the Chinese players to stress "friendship first, competition second" and, after Mao approved, reiterated that "we must treat [the invitation] as an important event, and understand that its significance is much larger in politics than in sports." In mid-April, with journalists eagerly covering news within China for the first time in two decades, the Americans were soundly beaten by their hosts. That that was not the point, however. In this famous diplomatic episode of "ping pong diplomacy" Zhou proclaimed that the visitors had "opened a new chapter in the history of the relations between China and American peoples."[9] A Chinese official told a US reporter that other Americans should visit, perhaps in an official capacity.

Washington heard the message loud and clear. A few hours after Zhou had met the American ping-pong players in the Great Hall of the People Nixon issued sweeping changes in China policy. He ended the twenty-two-year trade embargo, terminated currency controls, allowed the PRC to trade an equivalent amount of commodities as the Soviets, and expedited visas for Chinese wishing to see relatives in the United States. Soon students, academics, and reporters got invitations to visit. Proclaimed *Life* magazine, "The Great Wall has come down."[10]

---

[8]Cohen, *America's Response*, 218.
[9]Xia, *Negotiating*, 154.
[10]Herring, *The American Century*, 478.

Zhou followed up with an invitation through Pakistani intermediaries for a high-level US government official to visit Beijing for discussions. Nixon called the message "the most important communication that has come to an American president since the end of World War II."[11] In July 1971 Henry Kissinger traveled secretly to China, keeping the State Department, Congress, and anticommunist Taiwan supporters in the dark. Already traveling in Asia Kissinger furtively boarded a Pakistani aircraft headed for Beijing; even the pilots did not know the identity of the incognito passenger who climbed into their plane at 4:00 in the morning.

Upon his arrival in China Kissinger shook hands with Premier Zhou. The handshake was at attempt to correct the infamous slight committed by Secretary of State John Foster Dulles. Dulles had apparently turned his back on Zhou at the Geneva talks on Indochina in 1954.

By all reports, including Kissinger's, Zhou Enlai the pragmatist shrewdly ran the show. Zhou expected concessions from the United States, particularly on Taiwan, an issue that served as a test case of American intentions. Kissinger balked, however, when Zhou insisted that the island was as much the PRC's as Hawaii was America's. Kissinger knew the political fault lines; conservatives at home warned about abandoning Taiwan. He did make some accommodations. Washington would not support a Taiwanese independence movement from China. The NSC Advisor also promised not to support for Taiwanese military action against the mainland.

Additionally, Kissinger offered other goodies. The United States would share information on Soviet troop movements along the Chinese border and inform the Chinese of relevant details in the SALT negotiations. Zhou refused to say directly whether Beijing would help end the Vietnam War but the issue was on the table. Kissinger left the talks basically empty-handed except for one earth-shaking proposition from the Premier: an invitation for President Nixon to visit in 1972, with an assurance that no Democrat would be invited first.[12]

**

Upon Kissinger's return Nixon issued his first Shock. Indeed, the China Shock jolted the diplomatic system. The Soviets got word of Nixon's intentions hours before the announcement, irritated to learn that the President would visit Beijing before Moscow. Rightwinger Ronald Reagan was sent to Taipei to ease concerns there. In Japan the news hit like a typhoon and bungled communications made things worse. Prime Minister Eisaku Sato learned of

---

[11]Chen Jian, *Zhou Enlai: A Life* (Cambridge, MA: Harvard University Press, 2024), 633.
[12]Xia, *Negotiating*, 146–88; Nixon, *RN*, 544; Henry Kissinger, *White House Years* (Boston, MA: Little, Brown and Company, 1979), 734–52.

the China Shock just three minutes before the President addressed the nation while even the US ambassador in Tokyo was unaware of the July 15 address. So disturbed were Japanese voters that the announcement contributed to the fall of Sato's government shortly thereafter.

Continuing his wrecking-ball diplomacy, in October 1971 the President sponsored a motion to seat both the People's Republic of China and Taiwan in the United Nations. It failed. Already sixty-two of some 130 UN members had recognized the PRC, including friends like Canada, Britain, and France. The die was cast. After UN ambassador George H. W. Bush dutifully voted against an Albanian motion to admit the PRC and expel Taiwan, the motion passed overwhelmingly. Washington must conform with the rest of the world regarding Taiwan. Bush understood the reality of admitting Beijing though he did not want to "let a big reality 'muscle out' a smaller reality of Taiwan's existence." The reality was that developing nations in Asia and Africa usually voted against US foreign policy and true to form, they wanted the mainland in and Taiwan out.[13] The PRC's seating allowed Sino-American relations to proceed.

The administration kept the bigger goal in view: the diplomatic gains of opening to China and the domestic political windfall for Nixon himself. The President faced down his own Republican right by calming Barry Goldwater, Reagan, and others who saw the Nixon Shock as treasonous. Even George Wallace accused Nixon of groveling before the communists and of using his announced visit to Beijing as a distraction from the unrelenting issue of inflation. Nixon-opponent George Meany of organized labor's AFL-CIO agreed. Such views concerned Nixon because he sought votes from blue-collar Americans in the upcoming 1972 election.

On the other hand the President rejoiced about the response from Democrats who grudgingly accepted the ground-breaking about-face on China that they had long advocated. The move also might distract from the *Pentagon Papers* dispute; indeed, the timing of the China Shock in the midst of this front page legal issue surprised UN Ambassador Bush. In any case, Nixon believed that his trip, scheduled for February 1972, would play well in the presidential primaries. Like news on Soviet arms control and a peace initiative in Vietnam he expected his Grand Design in foreign policy to have a resoundingly positive political effect.[14] In short, he hoped that his diplomatic agenda made him look good to voters.

***

---

[13]George H. W. Bush, *All the Best: My Life in Letters and Other Writings* (New York: Scribner, 2013), 152, also 153. See also Henry Tanner, "Peking Seating Would Upset Power Patterns in the U.N.," *New York Times*, September 19, 1971, 1.

[14]Herring, *The American Century*, 480; Cohen, *America's Response*, 218; Bush, *All the Best*, 149; Robert A. Wright, "Labor Bids Nixon Restudy Peking Policy," *New York Times*, August 11, 1971, 4.

Nixon orchestrated his week-long trip to China from February 21 to 27, 1972 down to the minute because it represented a historic breakthrough that boosted his image as a preeminent global statesman. The visit piqued the imagination and wonder. Listening to Henry Kissinger describe Nixon's triumphant visit California Governor Ronald Reagan joked that the trip would make a great television pilot and series.[15]

Planning began with a request to Beijing to build a Telstar satellite relay station in the city to allow for live broadcasts of the visit to the United States. Favoring television over print media the administration scheduled major events—from takeoff at Andrews Air Force Base to landing in Beijing—for prime-time viewing. Briefing himself on every topic and person he would meet in China Nixon even learned to use chopsticks.

He had no illusions, however. As he told a gathering on the south lawn of the White House where a Marine One helicopter waited to take him to Andrews Air Force Base for his flight, this might be a "journey for peace" but two decades of hostility could not be whisked away in a week. The President remained optimistic. He concluded that the trip could be compared to the historic moon landing, when astronauts left a plaque saying, "We came in peace for all mankind." The only question was if and when Nixon would meet the "Great Helmsman," Mao Zedong.[16]

The presidential entourage landed in Beijing at 11:30 a.m. on Monday, February 21. Nixon had renamed his plane *The Spirit of '76* to score political points at home but he loved the dual symbolism of both American character and his revolutionary visit. It was Sunday night in the United States, prime television viewing time. Nixon and his chief of staff, H. R. Haldeman, had already decided that the President should be alone to meet Premier Zhou Enlai to maximize exposure back home. As the plane taxied to a halt a burly aide blocked the aisle so that reporters and staff could not exit, and Nixon and his wife, Pat, descended the plane stairs alone. Zhou stood at the foot of the ramp, clapping. Gazing down at over 100 officials and celebrities Nixon also started to applaud.

Once on the tarmac he walked toward Zhou with his hand extended, a "hand for peace" he later noted in what became an iconic photograph that corrected the wrong that Dulles had committed toward Zhou two decades before. Zhou had waited for Nixon to make the first gesture. "Your handshake came over the vastest ocean in the world—twenty-five years of no communication," he told Nixon as they drove from the airport after saluting the national anthems of both countries. The Americans found the welcoming ceremony with the flags

---

[15]Chiang, *Friends*, 200; Kissinger, *White House*, 1093.
[16]MacMillan, *Nixon and Mao*, 3.

FIGURE 4.1. *Two long-time enemies shake hands in Mao Zedong's residence on February 21, 1972. Courtesy: Richard M. Nixon Presidential Library and Museum (National Archives and Records Administration).*

of both countries waving overhead to be a bit too formal, for Nixon understood the drama of the moment. "When our hands met, one era ended and another began," he later noted. With the remedial handshake both he and Zhou agreed that "we have broken out of the old pattern."[17]

As the Americans settled into their guesthouse Mao answered the question on Nixon's mind: when would the Chairman summon him? In the most famous photo of the trip Nixon entered Mao's study and both reached out, grasping hands for a minute. The Great Helmsman had no intention of discussing policy details. After banter about Taiwan's Jiang Jeshi, girls, politics, and Kissinger having assigned Mao's writings at Harvard the two turned to history. Mao set the tone for the visit, demonstrating his broad philosophical and strategic perspective. He also made clear that he was in charge politically and in this diplomatic setting as well. The President of the United States, the "head of international imperialism," had come to listen to his teachings. Nixon readily paid tribute, honoring an ancient Chinese custom.

∗∗∗

---

[17]Xia, *Negotiating*, 193; MacMillan, *Nixon and Mao*, 110. See also Jian, *Zhou*, 640; Nixon, *RN*, 559, 579.

The two superficially ranged over security, economic, and ideological issues. The Chairman apologized for his slow response to the easing of US trade restrictions on China; he realized that the Americans were right to move forward "and we played table tennis." In other words, Mao disarmingly signaled that controversial "internal" issues like the status of Taiwan should not trouble the Sino-American relationship. The Soviet Union was the main threat and China none at all, for its troops did not go abroad (like Russians and Americans). The PRC had no designs on Japan or South Korea, moreover. On ideology, Mao burst out laughing. All of those anti-American slogans were the sound of "a lot of big cannons" and nothing more.

The meeting lasted sixty-five minutes as both achieved their rhetorical goals and Mao welcomed Nixon's efforts. A photo with both appeared in the official Chinese paper the next day. When Mao sent a message that cautious bargaining was ahead if the United States could be trusted, Nixon pledged reliability on his part. "You will find I never say something I cannot do," he told the Chairman, "And I will always do more than I can say." (Indeed, weeks later he ordered the withdrawal of bombers from Taiwan to validate his promise to decrease the US military presence.) Nixon had his diplomatic coup—the first meeting of an American president with Mao Zedong—in his pursuit of détente and reelection. Their initial handshake left the greatest impression.[18] It symbolized the end of a quarter century of Sino-American conflict, at least for over the next quarter century until relations dramatically shifted again.

The rest of the visit was anti-climactic though chocked full of symbolism. At the state dinner of 1,000 people that night, a Chinese military band awkwardly played traditional American tunes like "Oh Susannah," "Turkey in the Straw," and "Home on the Range." The emperors of China oftentimes played music to calm down visiting barbarians. To make a point, however, the band also struck up Mao's favorite from the Cultural Revolution, "Sailing the Seas Depends on the Helmsman." Zhou (Mao did not attend such banquets) spoke of normalizing relations. Perhaps bolstered by fifty-proof mao-tai liquor that had been poured for each guest, Nixon grew emotional as he quoted from one of Mao's poems that they should "seize the day, seize the hour" and move forward in their new relationship.

The next day, February 22, visiting once again the Great Hall of the People with its two-story lobby, grand staircase, and huge chandeliers, the President raised a toast to Mao. Here was Richard Nixon, previously the spokesman for anticommunist hatred of Red China, honoring the leader of communism itself by reciting aphorisms drawn from Mao's Little Red Book. At the end

---

[18]Xia, *Negotiating*, 194, 196, also 197. See also Nixon, *RN*, 561–2.

FIGURE 4.2. *At the opera, Nixon speaks with Jiang Qing (Madame Mao), while Secretary of State William Rogers and Premier Zhou Enlai (on Nixon's right) and Pat Nixon and Kissinger (to Jiang Qing's left) await the performance. Courtesy of Richard M. Nixon Presidential Library and Museum (National Archives and Records Administration.)*

of his stay, he offered another toast with a self-congratulatory but accurate statement: "This is the week that changed the world."[19]

Before leaving for Shanghai and then back to Washington, the delegation visited the Great Wall, the Summer Palace of the emperors, a children's hospital, and the opera. There were more banquets and meetings. The Telstar satellite broadcast images home, revealing China to the world and displaying the new Sino-American relationship. At the Beijing Zoo, Premier Zhou showed Pat Nixon two pandas featured on his package of cigarettes. When she noted how cute they were, Zhou asked if she wanted some. She thought he meant cigarettes! "No. Pandas," he laughed. The placid pandas turned out to be perfect public diplomats. These rare animals had long been given as gifts to other nations, including two sent to the United States by Jiang Jeshi during the Second World War. To the delight of thousands of Americans, Zhou soon shipped two pandas, Ling-Ling and Hsing-Hsing, to the National Zoo in Washington, DC where they became popular mainstays.[20]

***

Nixon and Zhou also negotiated the Shanghai Communique, a diplomatic document that charted the way forward. For their part, the Chinese sought to

---

[19]Xia, *Negotiating*, 197, 189, also 190. See also MacMillan, *Nixon and Mao*, 146–59.
[20]Perlstein, *Nixonland*, 626; MacMillan, *Nixon and Mao*, 148.

protect principles: guarding their sovereignty with an ideology of supporting the proletariat-working class. Zhou gave vague assurances that China would not enter the war in Vietnam, which freed Nixon and Kissinger to negotiate from strength with Hanoi with no fear of PRC military intervention. Both also pledged not to dominate Asia or permit other powers like the Soviets from doing so. Washington remained committed to Japan's defense but would not allow Tokyo to threaten Asia, a critical point for China which remembered Japan's brutality in the Second World War.

Taiwan was the most sensitive topic. Nixon confirmed that the island nation was part of China, which was a status acceptable to Taiwan and that the PRC-Taiwan problem must be solved by Chinese and not Americans. But the United States would only withdraw its military support if tensions eased. There was no mention of revising the Taiwan defense treaty, which could provoke conservatives at home. Zhou assured a peaceful resolution on Taiwan to allow Nixon to secretly pledge the establishment of formal bilateral relations in his second term.

Nixon had achieved his objectives. Policy aside, he had engaged with the formidable Zhou and met Mao. The former was a practitioner while Mao, the visionary poet, was the grand strategist. Both knew where they wanted China to go and Nixon offered to take them there.

The President made clear US interests, especially in protecting Taiwan, yet he also showed that America could be counted on to move forward with China. According to historian Yafeng Xia, Nixon had sought "to gain Chinese confidence, to project firmness, to induce them to cooperate, and to point out the advantages of cooperation." At this early stage in their relationship, noted Kissinger, Beijing demanded American "seriousness and reliability: this litmus test will determine their future policy."[21] Dependability was a promise the United States transmitted to Zhou and Mao, though ideology and emotions soon tested that position.

***

The gains from the approach to the People's Republic of China were substantial although the road ahead was not smooth. Except for conservatives who saw China as the antichrist and threat to Taiwan, the trip won widespread acclaim across the United States. Most observers agreed with noted commentator, James Reston, that Nixon's visit had been a "model of common sense and good diplomacy" despite fears of abandonment by Taiwan and Japan. The President had identified one of the great problems of US foreign policy—

---

[21]Xia, *Negotiating*, 191, also 192–3, 198–212; MacMillan, *Nixon and Mao*, 160–287, 318.

the isolation of China—and patiently solved it. This was, wrote Reston, "Mr. Nixon's finest hour."[22]

In late 1974, George H. W. Bush became the first diplomatic envoy to the PRC. He headed an unofficial embassy, called the Liaison Office, and was determined to cultivate permanent friendly connections to Beijing through personal diplomacy. He largely failed in this mission; Kissinger warned that Chinese leaders cared little about liking somebody. Still, Bush came away from his time in Beijing, a morose capital tainted by the Cultural Revolution, convinced of America's pivotal role in pointing the PRC in the right direction through engagement.[23]

In the wake of Nixon's visit, engagement seemed probable. China established an unofficial outpost in Washington while travel and cultural exchanges multiplied. Masterminding triangular diplomacy, the President leveraged the new relationship with China with the Soviet Union in arms accords, furthering his Grand Design and détente. Tensions eased in Asia though the Vietnam War was a wildcard. Five weeks after Nixon's visit to China, North Vietnam launched the Easter Offensive, driving within sixty miles of Saigon. This posed a political problem for Nixon, who hoped his stunning China policy would supersede the war in the eyes of voters. In the end, it was peace in Vietnam (in October 1972), rather than the opening to China, that helped his reelection.[24]

America's enemies and friends were generally unhappy with the Nixon visit. Sino-American rapprochement was the last thing the Soviet Union wanted. Doctrinaire communist Albania felt sold out by Beijing. North Korea and North Vietnam were both Chinese allies who leaned toward the Soviet camp and were confused and irritated. Asian and Pacific countries with defense treaties with the United States, including Taiwan, Japan, South Korea, Singapore, Thailand, Malaysia, the Philippines, New Zealand, and Australia, wondered about Washington's commitment to defend them. Even the British were miffed that Nixon had not informed them of a move that had implications for the entire world and especially for European security.

Taiwan was thunderstruck. The fanatical support of America's old China Lobby of the early Cold War had faded away, and a new generation apparently either did not recall or care much about backing the unsavory dictator, Jiang Jeshi. While Chinese Americans eagerly looked forward to reuniting with their birthplace—and in the years to come, they welcomed the rapprochement with the "motherland"—the mood in Taiwan itself was glum. The country continued

---

[22]James Reston, "Mr. Nixon's Finest Hour," *New York Times*, March 1, 1972, 39.
[23]Engel, *When the World*, 42–5; Bush, *All The Best*, 215–6, 229, 234.
[24]Herring, *The American Century*, 493–4.

to receive American weapons and ships and trained with the US Navy in joint exercises. But when Nixon went to China, Taipei issued a defiant, unrealistic statement pledging to reconquer the mainland and overthrow the illegitimate communists. Still, the Taiwanese knew that events were out of their control. They felt betrayed, helpless, and angry all at once and feared, above all, that they were expendable in Nixon's larger foreign policy calculations. They felt their very survival was at stake.[25]

A variation of this betrayal typified the Japanese as well. Second to Taiwan Japan lodged the most aggrieved protest. There were questions in Tokyo's business community about the future of involvement in Taiwan's economy. Perhaps Japan should sever relations with Taiwan and recognize the PRC instead. In Tokyo, leaders saw little good that could come from the Nixon visit, which confirmed a "great unraveling" in US postwar foreign policy toward Asia and, perhaps, Japan—America's closest ally in the region if not the world.[26]

Tokyo had made a deal after the American occupation from the Second World War concluded in 1952. In exchange for renouncing militarism and turning away from its natural market of China, Japan joined the US defense coalition in Asia that included Taiwan. Tokyo also conceded the Ryukyu Island chain, most important of which was Okinawa, to US military bases. A more prosperous and confident Japan soon demanded Okinawa returned; the government of Prime Minister Sato determined to make a deal (see Chapter 8).

Suffice to say that when he and the American ambassador to Japan, Armin Meyer, heard the news of Nixon's impending visit to Beijing, they were dismayed. The administration had upended the entire security system. After visiting Washington in January 1972 weeks before Nixon's trip, Sato resigned. His replacement, Kakuei Tanaka, pledged to open relations with the People's Republic of China. After all, reminded a Japanese official, his country was "an Asian nation." This inferred that Japan's loyalties, like America's, could also change.[27]

***

Allies had time to deliberate because relations with China cooled off during Nixon's second term. The road to normalization (or official recognition by both nations) slowed as the administration played its Soviet card as leverage against

---

[25]Nancy Bernkopf Tucker, *Strait Talk: United States-Taiwan Relations and the Crisis with China* (Cambridge, MA: Harvard University Press, 2009), 29–46, 53–68; Kazushi Minami, "Perpetual Foreigners: Chinese Americans and the US Opening to China," *Diplomatic History* forty-seven, no. three (June 2023): 448, 454–60.

[26]Richard Halloran, "Fears of a Great Unraveling: US and Japan," *New York Times*, January 16, 1972, E4. See also Robert Kleiman, "Taiwan Without Tears," *New York Times*, May 8, 1972, 37.

[27]MacMillan, *Nixon and Mao*, 297, also 289–99.

China, which reciprocated in turn. Whereas Kissinger had called China a "tacit ally," linkage provoked tensions; Zhou accused Washington of not being anti-Soviet enough. Like Nixon, the Premier was under increasing pressure at home from hardliners. The Watergate scandal then stalled normalization talks and the Chinese saw Nixon losing credibility. In late 1973, Kissinger's offer of a hotline to Beijing to share intelligence fell flat. The PRC insisted on the one thing Nixon was unwilling to give: severing ties with Taiwan.

Nixon's successor, Gerald Ford, found himself in the same balancing act. Preparing to visit the PRC in December 1975, including paying his respects to an ailing Mao, he also balked on withdrawing America's military presence in Taiwan. Still, Ford determined "to expand upon the dialogue that Nixon had begun nearly four years earlier."[28] He continued the drive toward diplomatic normalization but like Nixon, President Ford depended on support from the Republican right. He had to stick by Taiwan or risk losing a closely fought primary battle in 1976 against Ronald Reagan, the choice of rightwing and staunchly pro-Taiwan conservatives. Nixon had pledged reliability to Zhou; Ford struggled mightily to stick to that stance. Seeking to reassure Beijing Ford and now Secretary of State Henry Kissinger kept sharing intelligence on Soviet movements at the border and approved sales of computers that China could use for weapons development.

All the while hardline Chinese communists got an upper hand to unravel the deals with Nixon. After all, Washington retained its defense treaty with Taiwan and formal recognition of the PRC (and embassy) seemed no closer than Nixon's promises in 1972. By 1974 the question of who would succeed the aging Mao and a terminally ill Zhou preoccupied Beijing. A radical communist faction led by Mao's wife confronted Zhou's handpicked successor, Deng Xiaoping. This so-called "Gang of Four" believed that the United States was a danger to China. When Zhou died in January 1976, the Gang of Four blocked Deng and compelled Mao to choose loyalist Hua Guofeng as Premier. The radicals attempted to purge Deng, but they had to race against the clock, for Mao died in September. The Gang of Four were subsequently exposed as traitors and purged by their moderate rivals in the Communist Party. This meant the rise to power of Deng Xiaoping who re-committed to improving relations with the West.

It took a few more years before Ford's successor, Jimmy Carter, eventually extended full diplomatic relations to the People's Republic of China and withdrew formal recognition of Taiwan. Carter had jumped on the normalization bandwagon until he schooled himself on the Nixon-Kissinger discussions with

[28]Ford, *A Time*, 335.

Beijing. Now he believed that his predecessors had been too conciliatory; Carter's polling showed that Americans opposed abandoning Taiwan. Accordingly, he instructed his secretary of state, Cyrus Vance, to slow down relinquishing official support for Taiwan and insisted on keeping a consulate in Taipei after normalization with Beijng was complete. Deng reacted in fury by denouncing Carter's reneging on prior commitments.

Normalization talks simmered. Eager to sign the SALT II nuclear arms agreement with the Soviets Carter's advisors counseled him that tensions with China undermined US foreign policy. Under pressure at home, worried that his extremist Cambodian friend, Pol Pot, would be toppled by invading Vietnam, and watching Soviet expansionism Deng returned to normalization. He conceded on Taiwan by giving assurances China would not seize the island while he allowed the Americans to sell arms to Taipei. There was still one China but Deng put up with the contradiction that Washington really thought in terms of two. He would bide his time, as part of his slogan of governing. Preparing to invade Vietnam as punishment for its war against Cambodia and angry over a Soviet-Vietnamese treaty of friendship, Deng faced significant troubles so he was doubly focused on US recognition.

For their part, Americans, caught in a vicious cycle of unemployment, high inflation, and a worsening trade deficit looked to the China market as a solution to their economic problems. Trade relations helped with diplomacy. The rightwing defenders of Jiang Jeshi (who died in 1975) groused clearly but not too loudly while Republicans and Democrats joined together to pave the way for myriad trade missions to China.

Diplomatic recognition finally arrived in 1979. Intelligence posited that Taiwan could survive an attack and that the PRC lacked amphibious landing capabilities necessary to invade. The United States withdrew its embassy from Taipei and replaced it with an unofficial American Institute in Taiwan, showing that Washington would not desert its ally. Deng came to Washington to assure the pro-Taiwan lobby that unification would only happen through peaceful means. He traveled the country in a major public relations spectacle. To the delight of onlookers in Houston tickled by the diminutive Chinese leader he donned a ten-gallon cowboy hat to play to the Texan crowd. On March 1, 1979, America extended official recognition to the People's Republic of China just months shy of the anniversary of its founding thirty years before.[29]

---

[29]Cohen, *America's Response*, 220–3.

5

Aftershock

From Engagement to Conflict

The historic opening to the People's Republic of China resonated over the next decades. Diplomatic recognition led to increased engagement through cooperation and competition. However, steps forward could be reversed by steps backward toward conflict. Because the United States and China possessed very different histories, their ideologies and outlooks on the world also varied. Even when engagement appeared to be locked in, the relationship suffered from Chinese suspicions, insecurity, and nationalism that gave rise to American anxieties and recrimination. As a result, crises were common. As time wore on, the two nations increasingly seemed more at odds than in a state of competitive friendship.

* * *

Normalization with the PRC signaled a victory for the democratic West, which compelled Beijing to compromise with Western capitalism as it sought technology and prosperity while enhanced Chinese prospects weakened the Soviet Union. At congressional hearings in 1976, victims of the McCarthyite Red Scare of the early Cold War had scolded US leaders for their anticommunist blinders when it came to China, especially not exploiting the split between Beijing and Moscow. Nixon was one of these red-baiters who had changed with the times.[1]

He had changed the world and then the world changed again. Nixon himself returned to China in 1976 as a former president seeking to continue the normalization process. By the end of the 1970s, the Chinese people generally welcomed the outside world. Students rushed to learn new ideas

---

[1] Herring, *The American Century*, 505–506, 509; Christian Talley, *Forgotten Vanguard: Informal Diplomacy and the Rise of United States-China Trade, 1972–1980* (Notre Dame, IN: University of Notre Dame Press, 2018); Xia, *Negotiating*, 213; Chiang, *Friends*, 290.

and techniques from the West. Exchanges multiplied inside and outside of government; even the ping-pong team returned to China to much acclaim. Members of research agencies in science and technology, acrobats and symphony orchestras, and diplomats traveled between the two nations. These interactions continued despite Beijing's outbursts against Taiwan. Most importantly, thoughts of democracy emerged, however embryonic.[2] History, ideology, culture, and perceptions proved stubborn companions, however.

Economic relations did not proceed smoothly, for instance. Enraged by the possibility that US sales of technology could be used for China's obsolete military, Moscow chafed at Washington's willingness to grant Beijing trade privileges while withholding them from the Soviet Union. For its part, China could not develop without importing US goods but it required this "most-favored-nation treatment" or trade privileges (equal benefits) given to all countries that were party to a commercial agreement, such as low or no tariffs. Under the Jackson-Vanik Amendment to the 1974 Trade Act, US law prohibited most-favored-nation status to communist nations that refused to let their people emigrate. This was directed at Soviet restrictions on Jews, but Jackson-Vanik also applied to China. Beijing wanted an exemption.

Taiwan also plagued the relationship. While Carter worked to shift recognition from Taipei to Beijing, congressional opponents passed provocative legislation that recognized Taiwan as legitimate and sovereign. This Taiwan Relations Act included allowances for military aid for Taiwan's self-defense and an additional provision that a threat to Taiwan would be considered a threat to regional allies and "of grave concern" to the United States.

The law outraged Deng. Carter tried to uphold the normalization agreement as Secretary of State Cyrus Vance explained that China and America would never be allies, but they could be friends. Still, support for Taiwan could be interpreted in a few ways. In 1980, the President authorized the sale of advanced jets to Taiwan. Carter was still cautious, though, soft-pedaling the Taiwan Relations Act and favoring harmony with Deng. He then lost his reelection bid to a staunch Cold Warrior who had long despised communism, détente with the Reds, and the People's Republic of China itself.[3]

***

---

[2]Wang Gungwu, "How Does the Past Serve the Present in Today's China," in *The China Questions 2: Critical Insights Into US-China Relations*, edited by Maria Adele Carrai, Jennifer Rudolph, and Michael Szonyi (Cambridge, MA: Harvard University Press, 2022), 419; Pete Millwood, *Improbable Diplomats: How Ping-Pong Players, Musicians, and Scientists Remade U.S.-China Relations* (Cambridge: Cambridge University Press, 2022), 6, 169, 338.
[3]Tucker, *Strait Talk*, 116–26; Breck Walker, "'Friends but Not Allies'—Cyrus Vance and the Normalization of Relations with China," *Diplomatic History* 33, no. 4 (September 2009): 593–4; Sulmaan Wasif Khan, *The Struggle for Taiwan: A History of America, China, and the Island Caught Between* (New York: Basic Books, 2024), 109–115.

Ronald Reagan resolved to support Taiwan. From the time he was a presidential candidate in 1976, he pledged to uphold the two-China policy and reestablish official relations with Taipei. Reagan unapologetically opposed Carter's normalization agreement and shunned the Shanghai Communique of 1972 itself, the very basis of détente with the PRC. His hardline approach was concerning to those who sought conciliation with China. In Beijing, Deng reassessed whether the PRC should continue to tilt toward the United States.

At first Reagan would not let up in his embrace of Taiwan. He invited to his inauguration a representative from the Taipei government, but who became "ill" en route and did not show so as not to inflame relations. Secretary of State Alexander Haig and Vice President Bush, who had befriended Deng Xiaoping as America's Liaison the decade before, restated that good relations with China were a strategic interest. That logic prompted Reagan to back off his hostility toward Beijing, though ever so slightly. The administration determined to sell arms to its "ally" under the Taiwan Relations Act while also sending some military hardware to Beijing to demonstrate friendship.[4] Deng would not have it. It was one thing to develop an anti-Soviet strategic partnership, it was another to humiliate Beijing by selling arms to Taiwan. There was one China, after all. Deng refused to buy arms if Taiwan got them as well.

Increasing cultural and commercial exchanges as well as a large loan to China did not distract Deng from the pro-Taiwan crowd's hatred. The *New York Times* editorialized that Taiwan was America's ally and that Beijing had no right to tell the United States not to sell arms to the island. Reagan hurled insults that also turned the PRC away from moderation. By the end of 1981 Beijing mentioned America alongside the Soviet Union as a hegemonic threat to world peace. "In one year," writes scholar Warren Cohen, "the Reagan administration had succeeded in undermining the efforts of Presidents Nixon, Ford, and Carter to create a new strategic alignment with a friendly China at America's side."[5]

In 1982, the tenth anniversary of the Shanghai Communique, Deng admitted that relations were lousy even after Reagan backed away from selling advanced fighter bombers to Taiwan. Beijing still looked on arms sales to Taiwan as a betrayal of the normalization process because America had pledged to the one-China policy. China launched press attacks of its own, which signaled a return to the bad old days before Nixon's trip. Relations were at a fever pitch until the two sides reached an agreement limiting arms purchases by Taipei in terms of quantity or quality with the intention of gradually reducing them. Reagan continued to lend vigorous support to Taipei by offering to reduce

---

[4]Engel, *When the World*, 102–4; Bush, *All the Best*, 318.
[5]Cohen, *America's Response*, 227, also 225–6.

arms sales only if China recognized an independent Taipei. He cared little about diplomatic niceties when it came to communist China.[6]

His remarks continued to enrage Beijing to the point that Sino-American relations fell to their lowest in years in 1982. Taiwan was the burning issue but US protectionism toward Chinese textile exports further strained relations. Such sales and imports of technology in return were essential to China's modernization. Beijing found itself blocked by the administration's refusal to license cutting-edge scientific know-how for transfer to China. In the end, however, cooling US-Soviet tensions, influenced by a leaderless Moscow in 1984, renewed bilateral efforts to recover relations from their lowest ebb.

On the advice of his moderate and business-minded secretary of state, George Shultz, Reagan toned down his defiance. Shultz possessed no love for Beijing but he found Reagan's bellicose rhetoric harmful to US strategic ends. Reagan even traveled to China, marveling at the ancient terra-cotta warriors in Xi'an and the vaunted Chinese hospitality. More important the President learned to say less about Taiwan and more about trade, advanced technology transfers, and direct sales of US military hardware. He did insist on "the dignity of each man, woman and child" in the American system, founded on an appreciation of the individual's "special right to make his own decisions and lead his own life." Chinese authorities censored these remarks before broadcasting Reagan's speech throughout the country. Yet he was allowed to urge people to "make your dreams come true" through technology and just possibly, a smidgen of freedom and democracy.[7]

Cold War ice thawed once again. Deng made a surprise endorsement of Reagan's reelection in 1984 because the President's staunch free-trade stance was in China's interests as opposed to the Democrat;s protectionism that aimed to help US labor. During the second Reagan administration ties flourished. Chinese students and academics visited America in greater numbers as universities helped backward Chinese institutions modernize. Exchanges multiplied across fields including nuclear cooperation. The United States became China's top foreign investor by the end of the decade. The two nations also coordinated support for the Afghan mujahadeen rebels against the Soviet invaders.

Pragmatism had replaced drama. To be sure when China suffered economic setbacks or liberalization slowed, Beijing scapegoated the bourgeois, racist Americans. Weapons sales to Taiwan still provoked denunciations. But with the Soviet threat lessened under Mikhail Gorbachev China grew more comfortable with Reagan. More trade, more investments, and more aid had

---

[6]Shelley Rigger, "How Does Taiwan Affect US-PRC Relations?," in *The China Questions 2*, 207.
[7]Quoted in Cannon, *President Reagan*, 460, 461, also 478–82.

turned the crisis relationship to one of engagement. The China dream market remained but so did the dream market of US consumers that the PRC aimed to corner with its exports. Furthermore, expanding trade and investment ties and more travel, tourism, and legal agreements between Taiwan and the mainland hinted at a peaceful future. The election in 1988 of George H. W. Bush, a long-time friend of the PRC in the mold of Nixon, Ford, and Carter, rendered that feeling more concrete.[8]

***

When it came to China, Bush ran counter to Reagan. In a visit to Beijing in early 1989 that included talks with his old friend, Deng Xiaoping, Bush expressed appreciation for how far China had come since his time there in 1974. Chinese leadership remained just as thin-skinned about foreign criticism and general poverty still prevailed, and Beijing was convinced that its brand of communism with Chinese characteristics was the only viable ideology. Yet leaders also understood that China's increasing openness gave people more access to Western prosperity. Indeed, close by Mao's mausoleum in Tiananmen Square sat the world's largest Kentucky Fried Chicken. Political freedoms might be scarce but economics, Bush believed, had opened the door to reform.[9]

The President was also realistic when it came to China. He knew, for instance, that Chinese intelligence spied on the CIA and that American business was not as enraptured with the China market as it had been, as opportunities seemed to be drying up by the late 1980s. The waning of the Cold War brought more scrutiny. And a long-simmering issue seemed to be boiling to the surface: human rights. Beijing's record was appalling with denials of freedom of speech and religion, persecution of dissenters, and forced abortions. Washington had largely ignored these problems, even under the human rights president, Jimmy Carter, and focused on Soviet behavior instead. For his part, Bush did not pester Beijing regarding Taiwan. Chinese openness was a good trend in his eyes (Figure 5.1).

***

Americans dreamed of a liberalizing China that accepted pluralism and less doctrinaire communism as it strived to modernize. The PRC emerged from isolation during the 1980s; perhaps its leaders, along with millions of people, would embrace Western social values and political ideals as contacts between the United States, Western Europe, Japan, and the People's Republic flourished. Even a popular opera that appeared in 1987, *Nixon in China*, explored these

---

[8]Tucker, *Strait Talk*, 127–68.
[9]Bush, *All the Best*, 416; Engel, *When the World*, 110–8.

FIGURE 5.1. *President Bush and his wife, Barbara, visit Tiananmen Square in Beijing on February 25, 1989, four months before the massacre. Courtesy of the George H. W. Bush Presidential Library and Museum.*

possibilities. China's leaders focused on US science rather than American democracy, but the door opened for Chinese people themselves to lobby for certain freedoms. From 1986 onward, intellectuals and students on college campuses initiated waves of pro-democracy protests. Many were arrested and thrown out of the Communist Party, including the influential scholar Fang Lizhi. Led by the nation's old revolutionaries, the repressive Communist Party resisted the calls for reform.

Then a reformer, Soviet Premier Gorbachev, visited China in early May 1989 to coax this old guard into a new relationship with its former adversary. He encountered pro-democracy protesters who Chinese officials first approached with restraint. Deng's heart lay in economic modernization, but he now had a problem with political modernity. Ominously, Deng and company readied to quash the upstart student rebels. Supported by uneasy workers, students occupied Tiananmen Square in central Beijing. When hardline Communist Party members demanded the use of force to clear the Square, Deng declared martial law just days after Gorbachev's visit. Some citizens blocked the entry of soldiers and tanks into Tiananmen Square, and the tension eased. But students erected a "Goddess of Democracy" statue (a near-replica of the Statue of Liberty) just a few hundred feet from Mao's tomb. This "counterrevolutionary" activity supposedly abetted by foreigners now provoked communist authorities.

On the night of June 3 and into the next morning, government troops cleared Tiananmen Square, killing a 1,000 people and injuring and arresting thousands more. Armed only with shopping bags, the famous "tank man" (to this day unidentified) stood bravely in front of the lead armored vehicle along the Square's north side, waving the huge tank to a stop. He then climbed on board, apparently talking to the crew, and then jumped down and blocked its path again. CNN cable television caught the entire episode before friends or arresting officers escorted Tank Man away.

Reports of the Tiananmen massacre circulated rapidly around the world, literally changing overnight the image of China as a reformist regime. This was not a country evolving toward democracy but a government of aging killer thugs who would go to any length to repress people. The "killing fields of Tiananmen left a stain the Communist Party of China could never erase," writes a historian.[10]

What had been a policy of conciliation on America's part shifted toward unbridled criticism, impatience, and conflict. President Bush initially opposed his China advisors who urged him to back the protesters and ask Deng not to persecute the rebel Fang Lizhi. He gently asked the Premier "with a heavy heart" and in "the spirit of genuine friendship" to answer to world opinion by "peacefully resolving further disputes with protesters" and preserving the Sino-American "vital relationship patiently built up over the past seventeen years."[11] Bush prayed as the protests grew larger and larger, not wishing for Washington's interference to exhort hardliners into a military confrontation.

When the Chinese leadership issued its brutal response, though, the time had passed for having faith in democratic rhetoric. Senate Majority Leader George Mitchell called the Tiananmen Square episode a "murder" and Bush's diplomatic pronouncements "outrageous." Cities with big Chinese-American populations witnessed large marches, some displaying Chinese flags with swastikas painted on them. Likenesses of Deng hung in effigy across from the Chinese embassy in Washington. Senator Claiborne Pell, chair of the Foreign Relations Committee, evoked the Nixon Shock period by adding that "China in the past 15 days has pushed back her position in the international community to where it was 15 years ago." The President finally gave way to public frustration and horror.[12]

Tiananmen transformed views of the possibilities in Sino-American relations. Of course, Americans had long been uneasy about China even with the Nixon rapprochement. There were always naysayers to détente. Now the China

---

[10] Engel, *When the World*, 179–80; Cohen, *America's Reponse*, 239, also 233–8.
[11] Bush, *All the Best*, 430–1.
[12] Engel, *When the World*, 176, 179, also 154–80.

haters secured a wider berth in US politics. Believed a growing consensus of protesters, liberals, conservatives, and the press, Nixon had been wrong that engagement would lead to democracy in China. The Tiananmen Square carnage proved quite the opposite. Deng must be resisted and even punished.

***

The tragedy and the ensuing gall of the Chinese government to refuse to apologize prompted a debate on whether to engage or repel Beijing. Deng lashed out at US imperialism and its corrupt liberalism while he removed reformers from the government and even executed some in public. He still sought modernization but that objective was now in jeopardy.

The American public wanted Chinese elites punished. Bush issued sanctions, including a suspension of arms sales. He also gave Fang Lizhi and his wife sanctuary in the US embassy in Beijing. Still, Bush and his national security advisor, Brent Scowcroft, wanted to keep communications open and not return to the pre-Nixon Shock era despite pressure to recall of the US ambassador. Watching in the wings, Nixon and Kissinger advised caution; the administration should consider the "long haul" and not "disrupt the relationship."[13]

While he publicly announced there would be no official contact with China Bush sent a secret mission led by Scowcroft to Beijing three weeks after the massacre. He wanted a modicum of repentance from Deng perhaps by permitting Fang and his wife to leave China. The Chinese Premier offered none, blaming the Americans for Tiananmen because they constantly interfered in China's internal affairs. Communications remained open though tense.

The President never fully grasped the extent of public hostility toward China after Tiananmen Square. As a result Bush's image as a coddler of the "Butchers of Beijing" persisted well into the 1992 election; his Democratic rival, Bill Clinton, wielded the phrase repeatedly against him. Angry Democrats discovered that Bush kept proposing deals with Deng—including an invitation for him to visit the United States—in return for letting Fang go, allowing American broadcasts from China, or stopping the PRC's illicit sale of missiles to the Middle East. Congresswoman Nancy Pelosi proposed a bill to extend the visas of Chinese students in the United States to keep them safe from the Butchers though Bush vetoed it.

Bush's political opponents next tried to suspend most-favored-nation (MFN) trade treatment in Congress' annual renewal exercise. Removing this favorable trade status would hurt by halving the $6 billion in China's sales to the United States. Even the free-trading, diplomatic-minded Bush administration had considered this move though there were fears halting MFN would cause

---

[13]Engel, *When the World*, 181.

a backlash in Beijing, penalize workers, and deny consumers cheap Chinese goods. News of MFN's possible suspension seemed to move Deng who realized the stiff economic cost to China. He also understood that Bush could not stop the anti-Chinese sentiment especially as an election year approached.

As a result of these calculations, in early 1990 Beijing released some dissidents from prison, put in an order for $2 billion worth of Boeing airplanes, and promised to let Fang go if Bush reciprocated by advocating the renewal of MFN. To Bush's dismay Congress would not yield. Not only were legislators unmoved by Beijing's gestures but human rights organizations reported worsening conditions for protesters. If the PRC treated its own citizens so badly it was clear that the rights of Tibetan followers of the Dalai Lama or people of Hong Kong (to be ceded to China by Britain in 1999) would be violated even more. The end of the Cold War made China less important in the eyes of many Bush opponents even if the administration pleaded that a hostile Beijing would cause problems for US interests in Asia. Pelosi tried another tack with a bill that backed MFN if China met certain human rights conditions set by Congress. It failed in the Senate but the message was clear.

Pro-China business lobbyists argued that MFN planted the seeds for expanding a consuming Chinese middle class that would, in turn, push for democracy and human rights reforms. This was the crux of the engagement argument. Anyway, at this time Japan seemed like the more dangerous economic challenger. Besides, Western Europe and Japan backed MFN. Nobody in Deng's circle was going to apologize for the Tiananmen Square incident even to placate foes of MFN. In the end Beijing got lucky when crises elsewhere took attention away from Tiananmen Square and re-jiggered relations with the West.

In Asia, China cooperated in United Nations efforts to bring peace to Cambodia while sharing intelligence with the United States on its menacing client state, North Korea. In the Middle East, when Saddam Hussein invaded Kuwait China voted with other UN Security Council members for sanctions against Iraq. In a bargain brokered with the Chinese foreign minister, Qian Qichen, and Secretary of State James Baker Beijing agreed to abstain on the vote for the use of force against Saddam in return for a visit to the White House that would end China's pariah status. Baker then added in discussion on human rights and trade (he had called out the "slaughter of the innocents" in Tiananmen Square) and Sino-American relations seemed pointed toward normalcy until Congress continued to balk on MFN treatment and the public largely agreed.[14]

---

[14]James A. Baker, Jr., *The Politics of Diplomacy: Revolution, War and Peace, 1989–1992* (New York: G.P. Putnam's Sons, 1995), 103, also 111–3.

Congress rebelled against the Bush administration's conciliation of China. American workers, US diplomats worried about China's missile sales in the Middle East, some investors, and human rights skeptics were alienated by China's trade surplus with the United States and its security policies toward Taiwan, the brutal Khmer Rouge in Cambodia, and weapons of mass destruction. The PRC used prison labor to manufacture goods, cheated on its textile export quotas, and violated American intellectual property rights by ignoring patents and copyrights. Beijing agreed to stop all of these offending policies but it had long pledged to do so. Bush accused Democrats and some Republicans who hated Chinese communism of undermining two decades of Sino-American efforts for peace in Asia. Congress was, yet again, unmoved.

In 1991, Congress proposed conditional or limited MFN treatment but this time Bush's reelection concerns compelled him to stiffen his resolve toward China. Included in a host of issues were restrictions on export licenses and support for Taiwan's accession to the General Agreement on Tariffs and Trade (GATT) before China was admitted. The MFN bill passed the House and Senate. To assure the Chinese Bush sent Baker to Beijing where he heard from hardliner Li Peng that he was lucky even to meet with leaders. America had so insulted the Chinese people that Beijing would grant no concessions. If the United States stopped tourism, student exchanges, imports, and technology transfers, the PRC could find willing takers in Europe and Japan.

Bill Clinton and Bush's Republican challenger, Patrick Buchanan, derided the administration's weakness toward China. Taiwan became an even bigger headache when his national security team advised the sale of F-16 fighters to Taipei. The aircraft were important for national security but also for economic reasons as workers at General Dynamics would be laid off in the current recession without the deal. Neocons demanded the planes to support Taiwan's self-defense. In the midst of the presidential campaign Bush agreed to sell 150 F-16s to Taiwan. Beijing erupted, charging Washington with sponsoring an invasion of the mainland. The China-moderate Bush met defeat at the hands of the moralist liberal Bill Clinton who was clearly ready to take on Deng.[15]

***

Clinton was also pragmatic. He made clear he favored MFN in trade but conditioned it on Chinese behavior on human rights. He appointed a foreign policy team that spoke of freedom and democracy though his domestic advisors wanted more trade with China to aid the ailing US economy. They persuaded the new president to issue an executive order that retained MFN for a year but then set up a big renewal battle in Congress in 1994. This hold gave

---

[15]Cohen, *America's Response*, 239–51; Engel, *When the World*, 181–98.

China time to release prisoners, protect Tibet's heritage, and stop interrupting Voice of America broadcasts. There would also be no linkage to arms sales.

Beijing remained unmoved by the pressure. For example, eight months into Clinton's first term China sold missiles to Pakistan. When the President stopped the sale of satellites to the PRC in response the PRC asked Europeans to supply them. Barred from this lucrative market livid American corporations rushed to the White House and got a waiver so that they could sell to China. Likewise, the Department of Defense wanted to resume contacts with Chinese representatives who provided intelligence on North Korea's nuclear development efforts. In short, business and military constituencies wanted the human rights agenda put to the side and Clinton largely agreed. He supported more political freedom by inviting the Dalai Lama and Hong Kong human rights activist Martin Lee to the White House but admonished that "we needed to stay involved with, not isolate, China."[16]

Such realism ultimately guided the MFN versus human rights impasse. China continued to imprison dissidents, remaining contemptuous of American pleas to ease up on persecution. Even though they cringed at these violations US importers, exporters, and investors looked beyond morality to their bottom line to the extent that economic exchanges boomed by the mid-1990s. In fact, the trade relationship was so successful that the PRC enjoyed a growing trade surplus while the growing US trade deficit incited friction.

Yet most American business leaders wanted more access to the China market rather than protectionism against imports from the country. MFN provided the means to do so; China would open its markets if America opened its in return. Maybe a wealthier China would lean toward democratic change as well. Relenting to pressure Clinton abandoned the human rights campaign and granted China unconditional MFN treatment in Spring 1994. Most Democrats, including Congresswoman Pelosi, went along.[17]

The President still had one more card to play to pursue human rights: the People's Republic of China wanted to join the World Trade Organization (WTO), a comprehensive economic governance association of hundreds of nations that replaced the GATT in 1995. The WTO determined the rules of trade and membership was essential for a developing country like China. Entry into the WTO would give China permanent MFN treatment. Washington did not have a veto power over membership applications but it could persuade other nations to vote against China. Thus, Clinton held out to Beijing the promise of Permanent Normal Trade Relations (PNTR) in return for curbing prison labor,

---

[16]Clinton, *My Life*, 758.
[17]Cohen, *America's Response*, 252–4.

forced abortion, discrimination against Tibetan culture, and the marketing of human organs from executed citizens.

China stalled while American business preferred not to talk about Chinese repression. Deng's cabal had soured on US business due to the human rights campaign as well as the rhetoric from American conservatives who chafed at giving China advanced technology for use surveilling its own people. The Beijing elite was doubly angered when refused entry into the WTO in 1994 even though it had pledged to the principles of the United Nation's Universal Declaration of Human Rights. Of course, the PRC's bad actions spoke louder than promises.

Former president Jimmy Carter explained that Beijing was in an untenable position. China had tried to reform but the Tiananmen Square massacre had set back these efforts. Beijing faced a steady stream of condemnation by becoming ever more resentful. Like many so-called "emerging" nations China defined human rights in terms of shelter, food, healthcare, employment, and education. These basic economic and social rights differed from the West's stress on political and religious freedoms. Carter counseled Clinton to back off or else a "decision you make this year on trade with China may well be irreversible, and a great loss to American business and also to ordinary Chinese citizens."[18]

Clinton ultimately agreed with Carter and the business community that engagement hinged on separating human rights from trade. He weighed whether or not he should reciprocate the visit of the new Chinese president, Jiang Zemin, by becoming the first US president to visit China since the Tiananmen Square massacre. With one-quarter of the world's population and a rapidly growing economy the PRC was bound to have a huge impact on the world. "Greater trade and involvement would bring more prosperity to Chinese citizens; more contacts with the outside world; more cooperation on problems like North Korea, where we needed it; great adherence to the rules of international law; and, we hoped, the advance of personal freedom and human rights," explained Clinton, who decided to visit China in 1998.[19]

The United States did not abandon its campaign for human rights. Clinton scolded President Jiang Zemin about the repression at home yet he also couched such pressure in terms of seeking friendship if only China would behave properly. As usual Beijing brushed aside these remarks, warning Washington not to undercut Sino-American economic relations by belaboring the issue of human rights. An adherent to the notion of a peaceful rise for China, Jiang admitted that much of his government's response at Tiananmen

---

[18] Thomas W. Zeiler, *Capitalist Peace: A History of American Free-Trade Internationalism* (New York: Oxford University Press, 2022), 245, also 243–4.
[19] Clinton, *My Life*, 598.

Square had been a mistake and he even debated Clinton inn public on religious liberty, which was the first time Chinese people witnessed a leader engage on the topic. But that was as far the Chinese leaders would go. In return, Clinton made clear that he favored China's entry into the World Trade Organization.[20]

Monica Lewinsky provided the last drama. Preoccupied with his political survival Clinton thanked protectionist Democrats for their votes against his impeachment by rescinding his offer of Permanent Normal Trade Relations just as Premier Zhu Rongjii readied to travel to Washington in April 1999. After a hasty visit to China by Secretary of State Madeleine Albright and Treasury Secretary Larry Summers negotiations on PNTR resumed. A decisive vote in the Senate followed a close one in the House in October 2000 and Clinton's signature on the legislation gave China clear sailing into the WTO. Beijing joined the World Trade Organization at the end of 2001, followed by Taiwan in 2002.

***

The trade controversies matched dangerous military and intelligence standoffs. Pressure had intensified for Taiwanese independence, for instance, which was best symbolized by President Lee Teng-hui who wanted to assert Taipei's presence on the world stage. Lobbyists had demanded more visas for Taiwanese officials to travel to Washington and in 1994, Lee, the first democratically elected Taiwanese president since 1949, asked for one to transit through Hawaii on his way to Central America. The State Department denied his request according to the wishes of the PRC to not accommodate Taiwanese officials and met with him instead in a lounge at the airport. In May 1995, Lee asked again for a visa to attend a reunion at Cornell University, his doctoral alma mater. The House voted unanimously to grant the visa and the Senate registered only one dissent. Facing congressional unity on the matter, Clinton granted the visa.

Not surprisingly, Beijing reacted in fury and provoked the first Sino-American military confrontation since the Nixon Shock. The PRC recalled its ambassador to the United States, refused the new American ambassador, and terminated reconciliation dialogues with Taiwan. To intimidate those seeking independence the Chinese military conducted exercises in the Taiwan Strait, including launching four nuclear-capable missiles into the surrounding seas. Beijing indicated that it could also strike US cities with nuclear missiles, a reminder that America's support for Taiwan might be costly.

The bellicose measures partially worked as the independence movement waned in popularity and Clinton backed away from supporting sovereignty for Taipei, including reinstating its membership in the United Nations. The

---

[20]Clinton, *My Life*, 793–4. See also Elizabeth Economy, *The Third Revolution: Xi Jinping and the New Chinese State* (New York: Oxford University Press, 2018).

President did not back down from a commitment to defend Taiwan, however. To show his resolve he sent an aircraft carrier task force led by the USS *Nimitz* into the Taiwan Strait in December 1995. Not to be deterred, the PRC massed troops on the mainland across from Taiwan. In March 1996 China fired missiles into the waters around the island.

Clinton doubled down by sending two carrier battle groups near Taiwan but not into the Strait so as not to back China into a corner. Terrified locals feared an impending invasion and war. The emergency ended when Lee was elected and the PRC realized its intimidation tactics designed to prevent Lee from taking power had failed. Beijing returned it troops to base and the Americans sailed away.

Clearly, an era of nationalism replete with military muscle-flexing exhibited China's new assertiveness. But how would the new Sino-American relationship now take shape? Beijing remained adamant, reiterating the "three No's" promise from the United States. The three were no American public support for Taiwan's independence, no Taiwanese admission any other organization in which statehood was a requirement for membership, and no two-China policy. Jiang and Clinton held to the three No's at their summit in Washington, DC in 1997.[21]

Relations simmered into 1998. When Clinton visited China he met quiet disagreement on missile sales, US access to the China market, release of dissidents, and control of North Korea. Substantiated evidence surfaced that China was spying on technology companies for information on advanced weaponry. Still, the trip led to freedom for some well-known prisoners who were transported to the United States before Clinton arrived in China. He placated human rights activists by vigorous denunciations of the Tiananmen Square massacre in broadcasts across China and the United States and asked the Chinese people to hold their leaders to account. Privately, however, Clinton gave reassurances that Washington would not support Taiwanese independence.

The heat rose the next year. Sensing his vulnerability in the Lewinsky scandal political foes accused him of allowing Chinese espionage operations to flourish at home. China's WTO application was also at stake at this time. When NATO forces accidentally bombed the Chinese embassy in Belgrade, Serbia as part of operations to protect Kosovo from ethnic cleansing the Chinese were outraged. The government encouraged demonstrations against the NATO bombings that killed three Chinese as Americans witnessed the force of Beijing-inspired super-nationalism.

***

---

[21] Tucker, *Strait Talk*, 197–230; Khan, *The Struggle*, 126–36.

There had long been engagement with disagreeable regimes like the Soviets in the Second World War or with Mao in the 1970s but Americans generally saw no national security threats that necessitated geniality toward the Butchers of Beijing. Nonetheless, war was unlikely between the two nations regardless of tensions. China had taken its place as the powerhouse of Asia and a budding one in the world by the new millennium. Coddling and conciliating the PRC—Nixon-style—was not necessary anymore.

The China boom was on. The world's fastest growing economy over the past three decades the PRC boasted a gross domestic product exploding 10 percent annually. By 2000, China became the world's third largest economy and readied to eclipse second-place Japan. By 2007, its investments abroad and its huge purchases of energy and raw materials made China a darling of the Global South and North alike. Beijing used the money both for modernization at home and to expand its military. It possessed more than $2 trillion in foreign exchange reserves, the highest amount of any nation. Much of these reserves came in US Treasury notes and mortgage bonds which meant that China floated America's debt. The United States seemed beholden to Beijing, implying that it could disrupt the US economy.

Clinton's realism read like idealism in hindsight for trusting China to change in a democratic direction proved to be folly. In the few years after China joined the WTO its exports around the world surged. The US trade deficit with the PRC multiplied, causing the loss of nearly a million American labor-intensive jobs. The apparel and furniture industries in the South and Midwest were particularly hard hit by cheap imports from China. Nevertheless, in the first decade of the 2000s recessions were blamed on domestic policies rather than on China. Meanwhile, consumers benefited from inexpensive Chinese goods bought at retail outlets like Walmart.

Experts saw China's undervalued currency, the yuan, as the culprit for the burgeoning deficit because it lowered the price of exports. Yet a surge of protectionism did not result, as had been the case when Japanese products had seized US auto and consumer electronic markets in the 1980s. The yuan remained a thorn though Beijing called on the US business community to defend the ballooning trade deficit.[22] There were, however, politicians ready to pounce on China for the hollowing out of old industrial sectors.

Engagement now meant finding a workable relationship that recognized China for the first time as a military threat, a nation with influence, and a market of even greater allure than before but also one bent on surpassing the

---

[22]Zeiler, *Capitalist Peace*, 245–8.

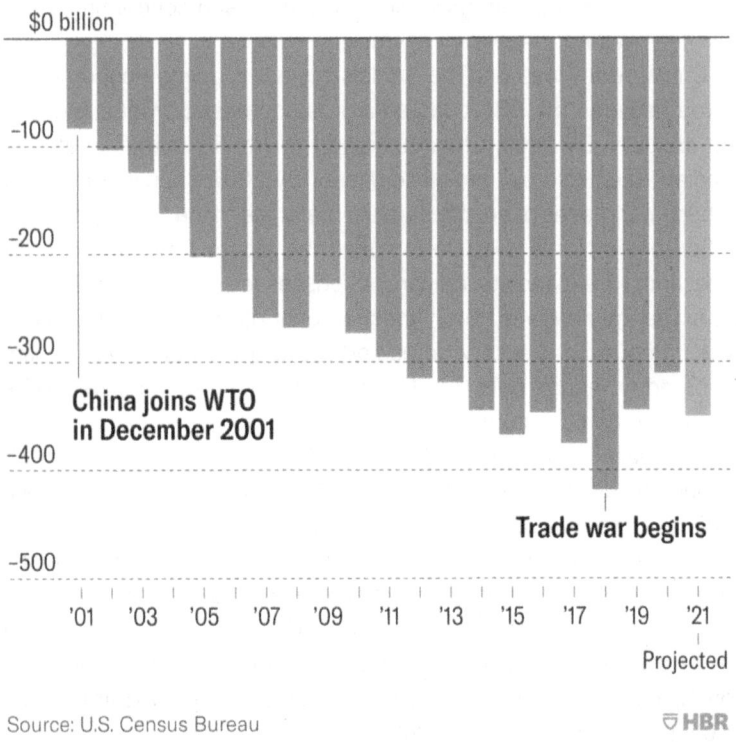

GRAPH 5.1. Thomas Hout, "A New Approach to Rebalancing the U.S.-China Trade Deficit," HBR *(December 20, 2021), https://hbr.org/2021/12/a-new-approach-to-rebalancing-the-u-s-china-trade-deficit.*

kingpin: a somewhat dependent United States. Richard Nixon had predicted a Pacific Century by 2000. It had arrived, led by the People's Republic of China.[23]

The Pacific Century grounded Chinese power in a multipolar world. Even though Washington's so-called "unipolar moment" of US hegemony after the Cold War had steadily waned, Beijing figured it should not provoke the United States, as it did in 1996 over Taiwan. China hoped to garner an image as a responsible member of the international community, so the PRC

---

[23]Cohen, *America's Response*, 254–64.

helped Washington contain North Korean nuclear ambitions, joined security arrangements in Central Asia and tried to manage fair competition for resources in the South China Sea. Worried that America might defend Uighurs or Tibetans, Beijing was careful. A buzzword was "partnerships" with Russia, Western Europeans, Japan, and India. Regarding Taiwan, the new George W. Bush administration required skillful handling because the President believed that his predecessors had been too accommodating toward China. His casting the relationship as a competition rather than a partnership would be tested.

In April 2001 a US reconnaissance plane collided with a Chinese interceptor aircraft, forcing the Americans into an emergency landing on China's Hainan Island. The Chinese plane crashed into the sea and its pilot was never found. China refused to release the US aircraft and its crew, prompting Congress to call for a resolute show of force. At first, Bush endorsed these sentiments, but an outburst of anti-Americanism in China, coupled with warnings from business interests not to undermine economic opportunities, led him to calm passions. Bush came just short of a formal apology over the Chinese pilot's death. Jiang Zemin accepted Bush's retreat while brushing aside his people's resentment. China returned the US plane in July 2001. The event signaled a realization that strategic competition might favor the powerful China, a regional and global player that could no longer be ignored.

Relations generally improved. Bush held to the one-China policy as Beijing protested the shipments of destroyers and submarines to Taipei but did little else. China was awarded the 2008 Summer Olympics, another prestigious development alongside joining the WTO. Beijing even released six men accused of espionage. Importantly, Jiang and Bush also seemed to see eye-to-eye on world events. The Premier, for instance, was among the first leaders to offer condolences and full support in the war on terror after the 9/11 attacks, though he duplicitously associated his suppression of Muslim Uighurs with Bush's effort to defeat the Taliban and Al Qaeda.

In 2002 Jiang and his successor Hu Jintao visited the United States. The next year, unlike Russia and some US allies, China did not contest Bush's decision to invade Iraq. For sure, Congress periodically erupted against China's horrible human rights record. But the Taiwanese independence movement led by President Chen Shui-bian's active pursuit of a modified two-China policy (one China on each side of the Taiwan Strait) actually angered Bush, who rebuked Chen as needlessly hostile. Preoccupied with the war on terror, Washington focused on partnerships and its economy. Patiently waiting for opportunities, Hu also advocated calm in relations with the United States.

Regardless of the administration's preference for solid ties to Beijing, protection of Taiwan fueled the embers of animosity. Hu Jintao, who escalated Chinese nationalism with a slogan of "great rejuvenation," blamed Chen's stubborn resistance on US arms sales and pledges to defend Taiwan. As a result, a surge of troops on the mainland across the Taiwan Straits ensued in late 2004. While Washington insisted that it held to the one-China policy, the belligerence of the Chinese military drove instability in the region. The next year, a Chinese general at the National Defense University warned of a nuclear war if the United States defended Taiwan by attacking the mainland. Two nuclear powers faced off in the Taiwan Straits, rendering it the most dangerous area in the world.

Nonetheless, by 2007 Bush referred to the Sino-American relationship as extremely positive. China continued to manipulate its currency but opened its market and enhanced policing of its intellectual property piracy. Beijing also cooperated to limit nuclear development in Iran and North Korea. Both superpowers' navies even engaged in their first joint exercises while they joined to protect port security and crack down on fishing violations in the North Pacific. Into Bush's final year, the administration focused on "strategic dialogue" with China, doing everything possible to encourage the PRC as a cooperative partner in world events.

As China scholar Warren Cohen has noted, schizophrenia typified the relationship. At times, the Americans and Chinese denounced each other, and at others, they applauded the other side. The superpowers stood eyeball to eyeball in 2008 over Taiwan, waiting on the election of either Chen's faction that sought independence or the old party of Jiang Jeshi, the Koumintang, that wanted improved relations with the PRC. With the latter's victory, tensions eased again. On the economy unfair trade practices by China, such as favoring state-owned enterprises that were inimical to free-market governance, led to America filing complaints in the WTO. Furthermore, the deaths of several American dogs and cats were traced to pet food coming from China. Poisons were found in a range of imports from paint to toys to toothpaste. Beijing promised to double the effort at sanitary regulations but also lashed out at tainted American sardines and meat products.

Schizophrenia persisted as the two quarreled interminably. Human rights remained immune to a remedy yet both nations considered the subject a sideshow that should not disrupt their mutually beneficial relationship. In other words what happened within China's borders mattered less than its engagement beyond them. Both countries' militaries reported increased contact, establishing a military hotline between their defense departments to deal with crises. Americans hoped that engagement would result in a confident and prosperous PRC, one more open and amenable to democratic impulses. By 2009 Washington hoped to further integrate the PRC into the world.[24]

---

[24] Petros C. Mavroidis and Andre Sapir, *China and the WTO: Why Multilateralism Still Matters* (Princeton, NJ: Princeton University Press, 2021), 38–105; Cohen, *America's Response*, 265–83; Khan, *The Struggle*, 141.

Nearly four decades after the Nixon Shock the dream of peaceful Sino-American relations prevailed. Within limits a People's Republic of China joining the rest of the world seemed a reality. The Beijing Olympics of 2008 attested to that notion. On display was a quarter century of modernization in state-of-the-art buildings like the main stadium, the "Bird's Nest," and the "Water Cube" for swimming events. Beijing spent billions of dollars to build these venues and marked expenditures as well for marketing, beautification, transplanting polluting factories, and even exiling people deemed physically unappealing. The unforgettable opening ceremony featured a choreography of light, fireworks, drums in perfect unison, and over 15,000 participants orchestrated by Zhang Yimou, the first Chinese director nominated for an Oscar. Audiences gasped as a gymnast seemingly rose to the heavens to light the Olympic torch. The spectacular show, followed by China finishing first among nations in the gold-medal count, showed the nation's new wealth and national pride.

The old China surfaced as well. Beijing went to great lengths to restrict foreign press movement around the city and to stifle dissent, regardless of its pledge to the International Olympic Committee to promote freedom. Responding to criticism the government set up three zones where protesters could gather but it refused licenses to allow most to assemble there. Police clamped down on Tibetan dissenters who flew banners near Tiananmen Square. China was still a work in progress, believed foreigners though it had come a long way.[25]

***

By the time Barack Obama entered the White House in 2009 there were ominous signs that tensions might worsen. Taiwan, Tibet, Chinese adventurism abroad, North Korea, and other issues had not gone away. The big question mark was which of them the liberal Obama would address. Would conciliation continue or would a new intensity in protesting human rights and promoting protectionism in trade predominate?

It turned out that the answer lay with the PRC as much as with the United States. China had grown more assertive as the new century wore on. After the Great Recession, which hurt America but not China, Beijing saw weakness in the United States. Delays in arms sales to Taiwan and Secretary of State Hillary Clinton's lack of criticism on human rights gave further evidence to Chinese leaders of declining US power. Hearing the Australian prime minister urge a firm stance toward Beijing Clinton replied, "How do you get tough with your banker?"[26] Muscular China seemed to be calling the shots, contemptuous toward the seemingly wounded, incapable, and neglectful rival across the Pacific.

---

[25]Bush, *Decision Points*, 429.
[26]Cohen, *America's Response*, 286, also 284–5.

In a classic case of applied realism Beijing reacted by amplifying its assertiveness through military boldness. Its weak neighbors in the South China Sea could not prevent Chinese occupation of islands they claimed as their own or at least shared. Neglecting their protests Beijing built up the infrastructure on these outposts and militarized many of them. Chinese ships also confronted US vessels around the islands even though the Pentagon swore off any aggressive intentions but did highlight China's violation of the laws of freedom of the seas and navigation.

China even confronted US business. Corporations encountered more restrictions as well as resistance to protests of intellectual property piracy that cost billions of dollars. Beijing offered a deal: more access to its markets if Americans shared their technology secrets. Many US firms balked because they were victims of espionage and they turned to lobbyists in Congress for retaliation by tariffs and other means that might change, halt, or punish China. Despite the establishment of a Strategic and Economic Dialogue to smooth over these conflicts the PRC drifted farther away from being a cooperative member of the international community.

Those in the Obama administration who counseled pushing back against China got the upper hand from 2010 onward, which caused Beijing to grow contemptuous about overtures to maintain good relations. When Obama finally went through with the postponed arms deal with Taiwan Beijing grew irate and suspended military contacts with the Pentagon. Congress continued to blast away at yuan currency manipulation as well though China thumbed its nose at the protest. It also vigorously opposed the Dalai Lama's visit to the White House. China even seemed tired of corralling the North Koreans who torpedoed a South Korean naval vessel with none of the usual insistence by Beijing to apologize.

The PRC also grew more isolated as it occupied the South China Sea islands that it looked on as a top national security interest. When Secretary of State Clinton offered mediation on the issue between the PRC and Vietnam Beijing rebuffed her, saying it was none of her business. Trouble brewed again in September 2010 the Japanese Coast Guard arrested the captain of a Chinese fishing boat that rammed two vessels around the Senkaku Islands.

Japan had gotten administrative control of the Senkakus in 1971 but China claimed them, renaming them the Diaoyu Islands. Clinton again offered to intercede particularly because the Senkakus fell under the authority of the US-Japan Mutual Security Treaty. Tokyo and Beijing exchanged volleys while Clinton insisted that Washington would always defend Japan. The Chinese backed off though they harassed other nations who claimed the islands.

By the end of 2011, Obama announced his "pivot" to Asia and the Pacific. This was a grand strategic objective of turning away from the war on terror but, just as significantly, the notion that engagement with the PRC would make Beijing a responsible partner in Asia and the world stage. The pivot, in other words, meant a willingness to confront China.[27] Now, containing Chinese power would be the focal point.

The President's pivot arose particularly in the economic sphere. He proposed the twelve-nation Trans-Pacific Partnership (TPP), a trade organization conceived in the Bush years. Nations in and on the Pacific—Brunei, Malaysia, Canada, Peru, Singapore, Vietnam, Mexico, New Zealand, Australia, Japan, Chile, and the United States—agreed to remove trade barriers and follow a common set of policies on labor standards, human rights, intellectual property protection, trade and investment, and environmental safeguards. Many of these nations had trouble upholding standards in these categories and the PRC, which was welcome to apply for membership, could not even come close to compliance. At home labor unions denounced the TPP as a greenlight for worker rights abroad to be violated by Vietnam and others.

But both the standards and labor issues missed the point that unity among Asian nations led by the United States was critical. The TPP was an effort to assert America's presence in the region, counter Chinese influence, and enhance freer trade and investment policies. The association was critical to the rebalancing of strategic interests in Asia; in the words of Secretary of Defense Ash Carter the TPP was a US economic "aircraft carrier" in the Pacific.[28]

The TPP was designed with China very much in mind. For Obama the trade agreement was a "very clear signal that America is a Pacific power, that we are going to have a presence there," and that Washington must focus on contesting Chinese power. The pivot to Asia ensured "the security of our allies and the civility of the region," he added pointedly, which included "certain things that are universal, the right to, again, speak your mind, access information, to freedom of assembly." Beijing did not follow any of these principles and it was now a pipedream to think that the TPP would push Beijing to embrace some of them. Rather, the Trans-Pacific Partnership would permit the United States to provide security, prosperity, and democratic principles for those who opposed China.[29]

***

Beijing viewed the pivot as an intrusive attempt to contain its power rather than as a reaction against China's bullying. American accommodation had reached a limit, the Obama administration told Xi Jinping, the apparent successor to

---

[27]Robert D. Blackwill and Richard Fontaine, *Lost Decade: The US Pivot to Asia and the Rise of Chinese Power* (New York: Oxford University Press, 2024), 7–8, 17–22, 239–55.
[28]Zeiler, *Capitalist Peace*, 266. See also Cohen, *America's Response*, 287–90; Khan, *The Struggle*, 145–55.
[29]Zeiler, *Capitalist Peace*, 264–5.

President Hu Jintao. During meetings in early 2012 the two sides saw through the charade of cooperative rhetoric. Vice President Joe Biden gave a toast to Xi in which he listed all of America's complaints from trade to human rights. The Chinese returned the indignity in September by rejecting pleas for Beijing to control North Korea and Iran and expressing the validity of their holdings in the South China Sea.

When Xi assumed the presidency and leadership of the Communist Party in November 2012 there were expectations that he would temper superpower relations. The two nations coordinated on climate change and energy while Xi reportedly got irritated when North Korea refused his demands to cease nuclear missile testing. He also spoke of remedies to Obama's complaints about cyber-hacking into US government agencies though the United States did the same thing to the Chinese government. While Xi exchanged niceties with Obama in 2013 in California, he initiated repressive policies on his own people at a scale not seen since Mao Zedong. So much for engagement to usher in liberalization at home.

Little changed, moreover, in the South China Sea. Xi seized more territory, even declaring an Air Defense Identification Zone 200 miles beyond China's shorelines that included the Senkaku Islands and seas claimed by Japan and South Korea. Planes flying through the zone were to file flight plans with Chinese military authorities, though the United States and Japan rejected the zone as an infringement on their navigation rights. When Obama sent two heavy bombers into the area without following Chinese regulations, Beijing ordered fighter jets into the air. Tokyo scrambled its fighters to meet the Chinese. Tensions ran high before the conflict ended with Obama asking commercial airlines but not the military to file flight plans.

The turn from engagement to confrontation continued when Xi announced the Belt and Road Initiative to develop infrastructure along the old Silk Road to Europe. The endeavor marshaled billions of dollars in investments, much of it going to nations in the Global South that needed the money for development. They also became indebted to China; Xi welcomed the leverage he had over dozens of nations that allowed Chinese tech and industrial companies to dominate world markets. American skepticism tempered some of their marveling over the PRC's grand vision by conceiving of a defensive trading collective with allies to counter Chinese power and reassert the democratic nations' economic and military capacities.[30]

Xi read into relations with the United States what he wanted to see. For instance, he erroneously thought America cared less for Taiwan. Xi also proved

---

[30] Aaron L. Friedberg, "Stopping the Next China Shock: A Collective Strategy for Countering Beijing's Mercantilism," *Foreign Affairs* 103, no. 5 (September/October 2024): 182, 184.

unwilling to condemn Russia's seizure of Crimea from Ukraine in 2014 and had seemingly given up persuading dictator Kim Il-un of North Korea not to test nuclear missiles. Beijing did respond in outrage when Washington announced plans to provide South Korea with an antiballistic missile system.

Xi also thought he had control of the Senkakus but that was false as well. Despite his promises during a visit to the United States in 2015 not to militarize the South China Sea these were just words. His military continued to fortify airfields in the islands. The next year Xi rejected a ruling by a UN tribunal that ruled in favor of the Philippines' claim to Scarborough Shoal and Mischief Reef. Xi grew convinced that the West was hostile to his interests.

Chinese nationalists demanded that the United States vacate its security interests in Asia. The mutual security treaties with South Korea and Japan, they argued, were relics of the Cold War. Asia should be controlled by Asians. The world heard repeatedly about the "Century of Humiliation" that China had suffered at the hands of Western imperialists after the opium wars of the 1840s until Mao (and later, Xi) rescued China from Westerners.

As Obama left office he had failed in many ways regarding China due largely to Beijing's determination to reverse the Nixon Shock engagement strategy and forge out boldly on its own. China had never been cowed by the United States but it had compromised while it sought an expansive economic relationship. Now Xi Jinping reflected a People's Republic of China that had at long last arrived as the hegemon of Asia and as a predominant global power as well.

***

Like everyone else Xi was shocked by Donald Trump's victory in the 2016 presidential election though China had not been particularly central to his campaign. Trump instantly angered Beijing by taking congratulatory calls from President Tsa Ing-wen, the leader of Taiwan's independence party. Such a call had not occurred since Nixon established relations with China. The new resident of the White House then promptly withdrew from Obama's TPP during his first days in office in January 2017. He (and, to be fair, his successor, Joe Biden) then refused to join its replacement, the Comprehensive and Progressive Agreement for Trans-Pacific Partnership of nearly 500 million people producing a combined $13.5 billion.[31] Withdrawing from trade agreements benefited China.

Even proclamations of America First isolationism boded well for PRC's interests in Asia. Trump repeatedly proclaimed his respect for Xi's strongman rule and also applauded other authoritarians like Russia's Vladimir Putin and

---

[31] Blackwill and Fontaine, *Lost Decade*, 247.

Viktor Orban in Hungary. He did so from envy of autocratic power that they possessed and because he liked how they fomented conflict abroad while stomping on critics at home.

The chauvinism might be appreciated by Trump but there was an uneasiness in Western capitals about China. Beijing seemed no longer amenable to compromise or even tolerant of differences. What had been hopes for Hong Kong's democracy, for example, were soon crushed by the Communist Party's contempt for political opponents (the 2024 Hong Kong national security law that labeled dissent as treasonous being a case in point). Xi preferred apologists for his harsh rule; Trump abidingly agreed with this political stance.

Trump preferred to target the huge trade deficit with China. In his cringeworthy words the PRC had been "raping" America for decades. Like Japan in the 1980s China "screwed" and "beat" the United States by stealing trade secrets and jobs. This time around the art of the deal favored America because of Donald Trump, at least in his view. He promised a return to protectionism; that is, an end to seventy years of trade liberalization that had shaped and benefited the American Century. Stacking his administration with protectionist anti-Chinese bureaucrats like trade advisor, Peter Navarro, and the US Special Trade Representative, Robert Lighthizer, Trump singularly focused on the trade deficit and politics rather than human rights, offsetting Chinese power, cooperating with allies in Asia, or reforming the PRC in a liberal direction. He deserved credit for slapping Americans awake to the China threat but his policies of dealing with the predatory Beijing went about things the wrong way.[32]

Americans generally supported such nationalist resistance toward China no matter its ineffectiveness. By 2020 two-thirds had a negative view of the PRC, the highest percentage in fifteen years of surveying about attitudes. Yet Trump's trade war with Xi yielded nothing more than retaliation from Beijing. China even turned the tables in 2018 by using the WTO to issue a grievance against US solar panel tariffs. When Trump visited China that year he insisted that the trade deficit be reduced. He returned with no promises.

In fact, the bilateral trade deficit with China worsened by the time he left office in 2021. Worse, his haphazard tariff policies hurt allies more than China, which kept retaliating by raising tariffs of its own against US products. By mid-March 2020, when the novel coronavirus swept into the United States, the futile trade war became a tragedy if not cruel irony. Americans suffered shortages of medical products that could be procured only from the People's Republic of China. Like it devastated the United States the pandemic hurt China (where it began) but Trump's trade war made things worse at home.[33]

---

[32]John Pomfret, "US-China Relations: How Did We Get Here, Where Can We Go?," in *The China Questions 2*, 22.

[33]Zeiler, *Capitalist Peace*, 274–6; Pomfret, "US-China Relations," in *The China Questions 2*, 23.

Into his second term, because Trump disrupted the old order of liberal internationalism that had so profited the United States his inane approach played right into Chinese hands. That the United States abandoned its moral leadership in the world boosted Beijing's image abroad. Trump also denounced America's own friends with regularity for supposedly not paying their fair share of NATO bills or for undermining the US economy with their exports. This criticism further aided China (and its illiberal allies like Russia) by mobilizing allies—including America's closest trade partners Canada and Mexico—to plan their own protectionist responses. The Belt and Road Initiative developed without vigorous challenges from the indebted (to the PRC especially) United States, whose leader also shunned foreign aid. Furthermore, Chinese cyber-theft, surveillance, subsidies for state-owned enterprises, and forced technology transfers built an unlevel playing field in trade and investment. Trump did nothing to change that system with his ill-advised tariff war and the rhetorical excess that came with it.[34]

***

Joe Biden continued Trump's assertive approach although like his predecessor he met with Xi Jinping to ease tensions. He converted Trump's useless unilateralism into an approach of reengagement, albeit more restricted than in the past. President Biden cast Sino-American relations in a context of democracy versus authoritarianism in an approach that intensified after Russia invaded Ukraine in 2022. He added new human rights sanctions and late in 2022 issued extensive restrictions on semiconductor equipment sales to China. Such coercion seemed not to matter to Beijing but it was clear that engagement was on life support.

China was not about to give up its competitive edge, in fact, quite the opposite. The PRC elevated its goals to outperform America even in the US market and found other markets for China's goods and investments in the Global South and Europe. For instance, by 2024 China processed 85 percent of critical minerals used in high-tech devices while boasting 77 percent of the world's battery-manufacturing capacity. A deluge that escalated beginning in 2023 of cheap and high-value electrified vehicles, produced in China as well as in factories all over the world by BYD and other Chinese automakers, gave China over half of the world market share for electric vehicles. American automakers even faced a future of bankruptcy (Figure 5.2).[35]

---

[34]Paul Bluestein, *Schism: China, America, and the Fracturing of the Global Trading System* (Waterloo: Centre for International Governance Innovation, 2019), 223–66.
[35]Shannon K. O'Neil, "The United States' Missed Opportunity in Latin America," *Foreign Affairs* 103, no. 2 (March/April 2024): 134–5; Robinson Meyer, "China's Electric Vehicles Are Going to Hit Detroit Like a Wrecking Ball," *New York Times*, February 27, 2024, https://www.nytimes.com/2024/02/27/opinion/gm-ford-electric-vehicles.html?smid=url-share (accessed February 28, 2024).

FIGURE 5.2. *Regardless of American efforts to restrain its trade, China was an exporting behemoth from the late 1990s onward. Courtesy: Bet_Noire and iStock.*

As one historian noted, in "what appeared very much like a self-fulfilling prophecy, Beijing's belief that the United States was a hostile force bent on containing it actually became true."³⁶ China expressed its intentions to displace the United States as the world's economic engine by dominating production, trade, and supply chains—and by free or protected trade, subsidies, espionage, and coercion. Special Trade Representative Lighthizer had a credible argument that the People's Republic of China posed an existential threat to the United States as a "lethal adversary bent on [America's] demise" through manufacturing. China aggressively asserted its power by stealing, intimidating, and cooperating and thus waging an economic war against the West. Lighthizer's plan to reset the trade relationship though launching trade wars rather than uniting allies against the People's Republic of China proved counterproductive.³⁷

***

Engagement then competition then conflict had not transformed China in the way Richard Nixon had envisioned over a half century earlier. No longer an extremist communist power, the PRC was not a democracy either. It had

---

³⁶Frank Dikotter, *China After Mao: The Rise of a Superpower* (London: Bloomsbury Publishing, 2022), 294. See also John Pomfret, "US-China Relations," in *The China Questions 2*, 30.
³⁷Robert E. Lighthizer, "After Free Trade," *Foreign Affairs* 103, no. 2 (March/April 2024): 148, 151.

become much wealthier and created a middle class, but those millions of citizens did not enjoy liberal values or a multiparty system. Under Xi, the Chinese military became more adventurous, willing to project power beyond Asia into the Middle East and maintaining its threatening posture in the western Pacific.

No resolution to the Taiwan independence issue appeared. Some experts blamed that impasse on a long-time unwillingness by the Americans to cut Taiwan loose or confront the PRC. Perhaps such inconclusiveness had actually served well in keeping all sides flexible and military conflict minimized. While the Taiwan Straits seemed like a powder keg, in actuality, it was more like a simmering pot within which the temperature had gone up and down according to Chinese dictates but had never boiled over, writes scholar Shelley Rigger.[38] Regardless, Putin's war in Ukraine led pundits to worry about like-minded China invading the island nation.

China had problems of its own, but these only raised the stakes even more. Some million people remain oppressed as ethnic or religious minorities in the PRC, and China possessed an aging population and a large percentage of youth facing unemployment that soured them on the nation's future. The country also suffered from an unequal distribution of wealth, shortages of water, and environmental pollution which made it a more dangerous nation because it might try desperately to solve these dilemmas through conflict.

In economics, by the time Trump launched his trade war and Biden enhanced it in May 2024 by imposing additional tariffs on artificially low-priced electric vehicles, batteries, solar panels, cranes, medical products, semiconductors, steel, and aluminum, China was more immune than before to persuasion or coercion. Trump campaigned against the threat to information security by the 5G network of the Chinese telecom company, Huawei, and tried unsuccessfully to prohibit TikTok, WeChat, and other Chinese apps from the United States. But neither he nor Biden could stop the penetration of Chinese culture.

Xi used soft power to contest the West and the United States. Projecting Chinese "values" throughout the world, he censored Hollywood films (long cherished in China) that portrayed the PRC negatively. In October 2019, when the general manager of the Houston Rockets basketball team tweeted support for the pro-democracy protesters in Hong Kong, Beijing cut off the highly popular National Basketball Association from its lucrative business in the country. The Americans caved. The NBA vocally backed Black Lives Matter and an anti-racism campaign the next year in the United States, but it said

---

[38]Rigger, How Does Taiwan Affect US-PRC Relations?," 204, 210. See also Khan, *The Struggle*, 155–207.

nothing about human rights in China.[39] That was because this superpower competitor—America's major strategic and cultural threat—was also pivotal to US economic fortunes. There was no going back to the pipedream of engagement based idealistically on the notion of peace and mutual prosperity.

In sum, the Nixon Shock had opened a new era and change ensued as China became powerful. As a deputy secretary of state, Robert Zoellick said in 2005, while the United States shut out the Soviet Union for fifty years during the Cold War, "our policy has been to draw out the People's Republic of China" for thirty years after the US-Soviet conflict had ended.[40] Indeed, that Washington (except for Trump) sought to harm the PRC is ludicrous; no nation did more to help Beijing's rise to power than the United States. That welcome persisted among internationalists, though they, too, lost some of their considerable goodwill toward Xi's China.

***

While some talked of applying a new containment strategy to China, others hoped that openness toward the PRC would pay the huge dividend of integrating China into the world economy as an emerging democracy. By 2025, the PRC ranked as the largest trade partner for over 120 countries. Although millions of US jobs were lost due to Chinese import competition, Americans gained from the creation of new employment opportunities and certainly from cheap consumer products. At home, with the world's second biggest economy by 2010, China's meteoric growth lifted over 800 million citizens above the World Bank's poverty line. Engagement seemed to make Beijing a more likely partner in many areas.

In this internationalist-engagement view China simply posed a challenge as a great power rather than a threat to American interests. Because the two Pacific superpowers were so closely linked due to decades of engagement China would be crazy to confront the United States. Worse for growth, stability, and peace would be a China that stagnated or collapsed. Continued pursuit of multilateral and cooperative solutions to global problems would, many believed, deter the PRC from willful obstruction, coercion, and aggression detrimental to all.[41]

Other experts countered that this thinking amounted to the height of naivete. That China would move toward democracy and global responsibility was not borne out by its behavior and policies. In this view the United States

---

[39] Pomfret, "US-China Relations," in *The China Questions 2*, 25.
[40] Peter E. Harrell, "How to China-Proof the Global Economy: America Needs More Than a Strategy," *Foreign Affairs* 103, no. 1 (January–February 2024): 137, also 138–9. See also Cohen, *America's Response*, 291–303.
[41] Thomas J. Christensen, *The China Challenge: Shaping the Choices of a Rising Power* (New York: W.W. Norton & Company, 2015), xiv–xxi, 311.

had traded away its interests. The time of heralding China's membership in the WTO as a transformative event for the better for world trade was long gone. China closed its economy through state intervention that defied the open free-market principles of the West. Even when US business profited, such as in the tech sector, American workers did not. Add in industrial and political espionage against foreigners and expanded repression at home and the picture was bleak. The conflict school believed that only by merging competition into a new cold war would American interests be served.[42]

China under Xi Jinping, quite simply, had regressed. As a specialist of Chinese history explained the Chinese Communist Party never intended to usher in democracy but instead, it resisted that process. The same went for market capitalism, for China was and remained a socialist nation. By definition the state dominated the means of production and exchange. Unprecedented growth and the lure of the supposed China dream market seduced the West into mythologizing China's trajectory toward openness but Beijing merely held capitalist tools in its socialist hands. Seasoned leaders like Jiang Zemin and Xi Jinping remained staunch Marxist who saw American threats all around and determined never to give in to them.[43]

Xi added to super-nationalism to communist ideology. After all, China still followed five-year modernization and development plans like Stalin and Mao had for decades, regardless of the global free market. The Tiananmen Square massacre may have been the most recent mass horror perpetrated by the Communist Party but it drew on a long history dating back to the Cultural Revolution. These tragedies predicted further repression toward the Uighurs, Tibetans, democracy demonstrators in Hong Kong, the vulnerable Taiwanese, and others.

For China the Cold War never really ended but continued without the Soviet Union. From the time of Mao Zedong through Deng Xiaoping and Xi Jinping, China remained an entrenched dictatorship that had always reacted with hostility toward reform and conciliation. Oftentimes, Beijing reacted to the world through nationalism and repression. Yet despite the regulations to control information and ideas under Xi's rule, which revealed a certain insecurity, Beijing also exuded confidence about the future. Its Chinese Dream was as aspirational and achievable as the American dream, fueled by ambitious construction at home and strategic objectives abroad.

---

[42]Matt Pottinger and Mike Gallagher, "No Substitute for Victory: America's Competition With China Must be Won, Not Managed," *Foreign Affairs* 103, no. 3 (May/June 2024): 25–7.
[43]Dikkoter, *China After Mao*, xii–xv, 151.

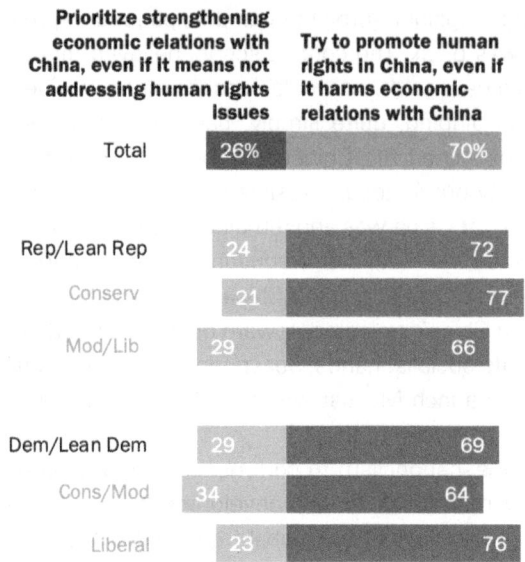

GRAPH 5.2. Laura Silver, "Pressing China on Human Rights—Even if It Hurts Economic Relations—Has Americans Bipartisan Support," Pew Research Center (April 6, 2021), https://www.pewresearch.org/short-reads/2021/04/06/pressing-china-on-human-rights-even-if-it-hurts-economic-relations-has-americans-bipartisan-support/.

Leaders would continue tough measures that were necessary for China's (and Communist Party's) survival and expansion.[44]

***

All presidents to Obama hoped that carrots and periodic sticks would draw out Beijing. They were not necessarily naïve in thinking that China could help maintain US interests. Free-trade multilateralists doubted, however, whether a more united response to the Chinese juggernaut would have much effect

---

[44] Sulmaan Wasif Khan, *Haunted By Chaos: China's Grand Strategy from Mao Zedong to Xi Jinping* (Cambridge, MA: Harvard University Press, 2018), 4, 245; Economy, *The Third Revolution*, 1–54.

either. The era of coercion that followed the era of inducements seemed to bring the same results: Chinese behavior only changed when Beijing wanted it to.[45]

Unlike the thirty-year period from the Nixon shock into the twenty-first century, the next thirty years or so showed that China had lost interest in engagement, and America no longer believed in it. Some likened the mutual nationalism and hubris to "sleepwalking toward war," much as Britain and Germany had permitted rising antagonism to explode into the catastrophe of the First World War. Historian Odd Arne Westad counseled avoiding this scenario by economic détente—dampening regional flashpoints, toning down recriminations, and containing China by energizing the rules-based international system. Circumstances could easily lead to conflict; just on the issue of Taiwan, Beijing's aggressive actions challenged the decades-long strategic balance in the region and gave rise to talk of deterrence on Washington's part. Still, even that issue might not lead to war if both superpowers agreed on a new script in their relationship.[46]

Although China became a national security threat to the United States, it never went to war, and it generally resolved disputes peacefully. Beijing drew on economic and political tools to contain American power in its neighborhood. China remained a member and an active one at that in most international institutions. It engaged in multilateralism.

Thus, when it came to predictions, history was not the clearest guide. Neither optimists about the future of US-China relations nor pessimists had the upper hand. China's expansion might be imperialistic or simply a sign of normal development by a rising power. The opening to China, rapprochement, and then engagement succeeded because both sides correctly perceived the others' domestic political constraints. More recently, uncertainty about the PRC was the rule, and Beijing shared that ambiguity toward the United States. Some combination of waxing and waning engagement, containment, rivalry, and perhaps even conflict spelled the likely future for the two superpowers decades after the hopefulness of the first Nixon Shock.[47]

---

[45]Dikkoter, *China After Mao*, 173–99; Bluestein, *Schism*, 7, 219–21.
[46]Odd Arne Westad, "Sleepwalking Toward War: Will America and China Heed the Warnings of Twentieth-Century Catastrophe?," *Foreign Affairs* 103, no. 4 (July/August 2024): 86–9.
[47]David Lampton, *Living U.S.-China Relations: From Cold War to Cold War* (Lanham, MD: Rowman & Littlefield Publishers, 2024); Elizabeth Economy, "Is Engagement Still the Best US Policy For China?," in *The China Questions 2*, 31, 37; Oriana Skylar Mastro, "Is China a Challenge to US National Security?," in *The China Questions 2*, 177–178, 184; Dale C. Copeland, *A World Safe for Commerce: American Foreign Policy From the Revolution to the Rise of China* (Princeton, NJ: Princeton University Press, 2024), 355–7; Pete Millwood, "(Mis)perceptions of Domestic Politics in the U.S.-China Rapprochement, 1969–1978," *Diplomatic History* 43, no. 5 (November 2019): 890–2.

6

Economic Shock

On Sunday night August 15, 1971, Richard Nixon preempted the popular television Western *Bonanza* with a speech from the Oval Office at 9:00 p.m. Like his China announcement a month before, he once again changed the world. This eighteen-minute address to the nation, the second Nixon Shock, focused on the economy. Seeking to jar America's capitalist allies into reforming trade and financial relations while combating inflation at home, the President upset tradition, core beliefs, and commitments that undergirded the American Century.

Nixon unilaterally took the United States off the gold standard, which meant that friends and allies could no longer convert their sizable holdings of dollars into gold. Actually, the exchange of dollars for gold at Fort Knox, Tennessee, was largely symbolic, but nations could cash out their dollar reserves and possibly bankrupt the United States. Clearly, Washington could no longer shoulder the burdens of the American Century alone. His predecessors had acknowledged this problem, but Nixon was the first to act on it. He did so in a dramatic way that fit his style, political needs, and systemic requirements.

A surprised nation listened as Nixon announced temporary wage and price controls at home to tame inflation, but it was his foreign economic policy measures that prompted anger, anguish, and shock abroad. The international measures promised a more long-term and permanent transformation. To give his message added thrust, Nixon issued an unprecedented tariff hike not seen since the Great Depression forty years before to compel a devaluation of the dollar and reform global monetary affairs. Nixon got the results he wanted. Remarkably, his draconian measures also ushered in an era of growth, integration, and technological innovation that came to be known as globalization.

***

At a gathering of 730 delegates from forty-four nations in Bretton Woods, New Hampshire, in July 1944, American and British economic experts forged a new international monetary system. They sought to stabilize exchange rates that had so dislocated world trade and finance, fluctuating so wildly during the Great Depression. Bankers, merchants, and governments required predictable, stable exchanges of money to expand trade and invest reliably abroad and at home. Unregulated markets in the 1930s undermined that calm scenario.

During that decade countries fixed (pegged) their currencies to gold (the gold "window") to keep them stable in relation to each other's money, but exchange markets were not sufficiently policed. Some nations inconsistently followed the gold standard to inflate or deflate their currencies according to their domestic needs, while others left the gold system altogether. That led to brutal competition in trade through a war for cheap money that made exports more attractive as nations manipulated their currencies to best penetrate foreign markets. This typified the dog-eat-dog approach that destabilized the international monetary system, leading to global economic collapse in the Great Depression.

Making matters worse, nations turned to protectionism against trade partners and further squeezed the flow of money. Most nations unilaterally depreciated (lowered) their exchange rates so they could reduce the price of their exports to make them more competitive. As tariffs (taxes on imports that make a product cost more so that domestic products are more attractive to consumers) reduced imports, seller nations reciprocated by raising tariffs (and quotas, or quantitative limits on imports) in a mutually harmful cycle. Some nations combined into discriminatory trade blocs in which they only exchanged goods at favorable rates with members and penalized outsiders with higher tariffs. The British Imperial tariff system within the Commonwealth was one example, and the United States also engaged in this protectionist practice with Cuba, the Philippines, and others.

The upshot of all of these self-interested, exclusive, and nationalist financial and trade measures were the economically debilitating and politically fraught circumstances of the Great Depression. Protectionism through high tariffs cut world trade by two-thirds, deepening an ongoing economic crisis that had already hit stock markets, farmers, and workers.

The Great Depression endured for twelve years until its end by the outbreak of a horrible world war. Europe, Asia, and North Africa were engulfed in high-tech destruction, including Germany's genocide of the Jews in the Holocaust, mass killings from aerial assault that culminated in the dropping of two atomic bombs, and over sixty-five million mostly civilian deaths across the globe. The trade and currency wars of the 1930s had spilled into politics and society when desperate and angry people turned to fascism and militarism. Leaders in Italy, Germany, and Japan offered solutions to the misery by forging a regulatory and autarchic state, persecuted perceived perpetrators, and eventually took their nations to war.

Officially called the United Nations Monetary and Financial Conference, the Bretton Woods meetings convened to correct these economic and political mistakes and prevent nationalistic extremism from leading to another world war. To assure a prosperous and peaceful postwar, Bretton Woods planners created the World Bank to provide loans and development funding and the International Monetary Fund (IMF). The IMF aimed to create a stable and reliable exchange rate system to allow producers to plan their inventories and sell their food, commodities, and manufactures. Stable money and exchanges would expand trade through liberalization, or lessened barriers to international commerce, so that all nations could prosper under a multilateral trade and payments system.

To stabilize currencies and prices the Bretton Woods system tied the exchange rate to the US dollar which became the dominant financial and trading currency. A government or central bank could trade dollar reserves (money spent on earnings from exports or from US aid) for American gold, a precious commodity that backed the dollar. The IMF facilitated these exchanges at a set price of $35 per ounce of gold based on President Franklin D. Roosevelt's calculation in 1934. This exchange served as the basis of the "gold standard." Again, the vast storehouse of gold in Fort Knox had a totemic role; in reality the gold standard was cherished as a key to stability by bankers, traditionalists, and internationalists.

The fundamental exchange was based on nations cashing in their currencies for dollars at the gold-dollar "peg" of $35/ounce. Other currencies were then linked to the dollar at a fixed exchange rate—that is, one that never or barely changed more than 1 percent. For instance, the British pound valued at $4.04 in 1944 never fluctuated much from the "dollar peg," falling just a penny in 1947 to $4.03. The same went for Germany marks, French francs, Italian lira, Japanese yen, and other currencies that were tied to gold. This gold-dollar "parity" system let capitalist nations expand their trade based on a reliable exchange of currencies.

Bretton Woods "fixed" exchange rates brought enormous benefits. The system stabilized currency markets and helped Europe and Japan recover from the destruction of the Second World War. In fact, their economic progress was unprecedented in world history. Continental Europe enjoyed record-breaking growth in output, employment, consumption, productivity, and investment in the American Century of the 1950s and 1960s. There were recessions and periods of inflation but industrial production compensated for the downturns. Couple that boom with low spending on defense (2–4 percent of GNP for Western European nations) relative to the United States (defense accounted for 12–15 percent of America's GNP) and no wonder that US trade and payments deficits started to grow.[1]

That is, as trade partners recovered, stabilized, and grew richer they converted their currencies into large dollar reserves, cashing them in for US gold. By the late 1950s this process started to drain away US gold stocks. The Americans kept importing from abroad and did not expand exports enough to offset these purchases of foreign goods. Added to this growing trade accounts imbalance US spending on aid such as the Marshall Plan, military assistance programs in the 1950s, and on the Vietnam War in the next decade worsened the American overseas balance-of-payments account. This account amounted to total overseas expenditures and revenue, including exports and imports, aid, investments, and tourism outlays of the country, and it ran increasingly in the red.

That is, the balance of payments evolved into a crisis issue. Buying imports and spending on aid poured more dollars into the coffers of friends and allies, who then cashed them in for gold. The payments deficits grew larger from the late 1950s onward, worsened by the recurring cycle of the dollar-gold exchange under the Bretton Woods monetary system.

There was a basic contradiction built into the Bretton Woods dollar-based regime that eventually undermined it. It was good to stabilize international money exchanges. It was bad, however, that the system did not account for growth in world monetary reserves that matched the massive growth in world trade. As recovering nations expanded their trade as expected, they required more capital. That money came from the United States—in essence, the world's central banker—in the form of dollars. Yet with more dollars in circulation the law of supply and demand made them worth less and less. Inevitably, the piper came calling because the system could not be sustained without the United States ruining itself by dollar expenditures overseas and unsustainable losses of its gold holdings.

Even by the time America's balance-of-payments deficit (higher outflows of capital than inflows and more imports than exports) turned into a crisis in the 1960s policymakers saw no other option but to defend the Bretton Woods gold/dollar peg. Presidents Kennedy, Johnson, and Nixon (early in his administration) pledged to maintain the dollar "as good as gold." As a fundamental support for the Free World's trade and payments system the dollar remained freely interchangeable with gold.

To be sure, defending the dollar-gold link maintained US dominance and power as well as the strength of Cold War alliances founded on the prosperity

---

[1] Robert Solomon, *The International Monetary System, 1945–1981* (New York: Harper & Row Publishers, 1982), 18–85.

of friends. That is why Washington kept going along with a system that was actually detrimental to American economic interests—because it served the Free World. The arrangement came with a hefty price, however. In 1955, the United States had $21.7 billion in gold stocks, enough to cover its $13.5 billion in overseas obligations to foreign central banks and governments. The gold drain eroded that math. By 1971, America possessed $10.2 billion in gold but foreigners held dollars reserves totaling $40 billion. Everyone knew that Fort Knox did not hold enough gold to redeem those dollars but the United States kept spending out of an obligation to defend the Western alliance against Cold War communist enemies.

The problem also seemed too massive to solve. America's friends did not want to rock the boat either by cashing out for gold that the United States did not have or changing the Bretton Woods system that had boosted their recovery and economic expansion. Washington balked at any meaningful overhaul of the system, too. But the possibility that the United States might withhold gold from nations with large dollar reserves struck terror in the minds of traders, investors, and business leaders. As expert Jeffrey Garten explains, the very notion that the United States might sever the gold-dollar link could shut "down the entire global economy" by shattering the certainty that the very basis of stable, predictable exchanges was no more.[2] On August 15, 1971, however, Richard Nixon took that chance.

***

The administration did not take the destruction of Bretton Woods lightly by any means because the second Nixon Shock reflected much more than gradual monetary reform. For several years intense discussions weighed the pros and cons of slamming shut the gold window entirely. Experts around the world had debated ways to tinker with the monetary system, even coming up with additional funds for the IMF to support international exchanges and relieve the American financial burden. But the US payments deficit continued to erode and the threat to gold persisted. This is why chief advisors gathered with Nixon at the presidential retreat at Camp David for three days starting the Friday before his announcement. They pondered, plotted, and perfected options well beyond mere reform of Bretton Woods.

It was clear why they were present at the mountain retreat in Maryland. They were going to make a confession to the world that America's outright hegemonic leadership over the international economy had ended. The United States could no longer sacrifice on its own at such a scale of expenditures on

---

[2] Jeffrey E. Garten, *Three Days at Camp David: How A Secret Meeting in 1971 Transformed the Global Economy* (New York: Harper, 2021), 10, also 4–9; Niall Ferguson, *The Ascent of Money: A Financial History of the World* (New York: Penguin Press, 2008), 305.

aid and imports for the sake of its allies' prosperity. Since the Second World War America had opened its markets to imports oftentimes without insisting on reciprocal action by trade partners to buy its exports in return. The United States had also spent billions upon billions of dollars in a disproportionate effort to provide for the Free World's military defense. Nixon would now ask—no, require—them to share that burden. The Camp David meetings drove home the key point that trade partners must stop relying on US unilateralism and adopt, instead, a truly multilateral, multinational system of trade and finance.

The President did not necessarily like the fact that he was giving away US power. Of course the United States—its trade and the dollar—still reigned in the global economy. Yet like the arena of nuclear weapons in which the Soviets had gained parity with the United States, so had Western Europe and Japan cut into America's global economic standing. They were now trade competitors. Neither not supplicants nor dependents they were rich nations capable of shouldering North Atlantic Treaty Organization (NATO) and economic aid obligations. Nixon determined to do something to preserve, as much as possible, US power, prosecute the Cold War, and direct the world economy into a new era.

Just as important for him—as much or more than his grand strategic objectives abroad—he could also shore up his political standing at home. The international arena was linked to the domestic economy. His measures could clamp down on inflation and boost business and jobs, with the significant addition of portraying the President as a vigorous, farsighted leader. The second Nixon Shock played into his overall foreign policy image that undergirded détente abroad and, he hoped, would get him reelected in 1972.[3]

***

By 1969, when Nixon took office, the American economy was in trouble. Domestic markets were overheated by spending on the Great Society social welfare programs and the Vietnam War. Inflation (rising prices and labor costs) spiraled upward. Inflation also made exports more expensive and thus less competitive, worsening the balance-of-payments deficit. In addition, imports of consumer goods like electronics and clothing became more appealing due to inflation, slowing sales from US factories and workers employed in them. Inflation also meant that the dollar would be worth less on currency markets; foreign banks and governments would seek to unload their dollar reserves for more stable and precious gold.

---

[3]David P. Calleo, "Since 1961: American Power in a New World Economy," in *Economics and World Power: An Assessment of American Diplomacy Since 1789*, eds. William H. Becker and Samuel F. Wells, Jr. (New York: Columbia University Press, 1984), 415–9; Garten, *Three Days*, 11.

The specter of an inflation-driven recession troubled the administration as did confidence in the dollar, which had hit bottom. The United States simply lacked the gold reserves to save the Bretton Woods system. Furthermore, industrial competitiveness had so deteriorated that the once solidly positive trade balance headed for its first deficit of the entire twentieth century in 1971. Protectionist pressures mounted as a result. Staying the course meant admitting to the main cause of inflation and the payments deficit: overspending. The American Century depended on robust expenditures, however. Nixon decided to take a brave (and brazen) course, one that he believed would both help him politically and overhaul the world economy, to solve these profound challenges.

At first, he pursued austerity to fight inflation by cutting spending through an approach he called "gradualism." This was prudent but it increased unemployment and debt for the business community. Inflation barely receded to the irritation of voters who were sick of high prices and businesses forced to pay more for capital goods in construction and other sectors. In regard to prices and inflation in 1971, White House counsel Charles Colson reportedly said that hamburger meat "seems to be the one item that is highly visible and meaningful to the housewife." Ground beef prices had skyrocketed in the late 1960s and had not come down. Sexism aside Colson's meaning was clear: Nixon must get prices under control or risk an electoral backlash.[4]

Indeed, Nixon's political concerns largely dictated his economic policies. He had lost the presidential election of 1960, he believed, because of a recession during the late Eisenhower years. The Republicans likewise did badly in the 1970 congressional midterm elections because of economic woes. The administration had options, preferring to reflate the dollar (and thus boost export revenues) by raising interest rates to slow inflation but the President would not take the more unpopular route of wage and price controls—yet. As political scientist Joanne Gowa later noted unilateralism abroad and the 1972 election at home guided Nixon. He focused much attention on foreign policy, of course, but he showed no "inclination to swim against the prevailing current of political opinion." Such risk-taking imperiled his presidency.[5]

Still, something had to be done about the dollar-gold pressure. Dollar appreciation led to a wave of speculation in Spring 1971 that enlarged foreign

---

[4]Quoted in Paul Donovan, "The Economic Indicator We Need? A Candy Bar," *The New York Times*, January 20, 2024, 9, https://www.nytimes.com/2024/01/18/opinion/inflation-rate-election-voters .html (accessed March 2, 2024). See also Diane B. Kunz, *Butter and Guns: America's Cold War Economic Diplomacy* (New York: The Free Press, 1997), 192–7; Arnold R. Weber, *In Pursuit of Price Stability: The Wage-Price Freeze of 1971* (Washington, DC: The Brookings Institution, 1973), 3–5.
[5]Joanne Gowa, *Closing the Gold Window: Domestic Politics and the End of Bretton Woods* (Ithaca, NY: Cornell University Press, 1983), 68, also 21–6, 163–70.

dollar reserves once again. American banks paid more than $3 billion into their branches abroad. Germany then revalued its mark and when the Dutch followed with the gilder there was even more speculation against the dollar. This worsened the US international payments balance. Meanwhile, the American trade surplus had headed into deficit.

Former governor John Connally, the secretary of the Treasury who Nixon had appointed in February 1971, announced in May that the United States would not devalue the dollar or change the price of gold. Three months later this audacious, nationalistic, and wily Texan furthered this gradualism by announcing his "four No's": no wage and price review board, no wage and price controls, no tax cut, and no increase in government spending. Such resistance fed into Connally's image as a tough cowboy, which Nixon loved especially in gauging the effect abroad. The President conferred upon his Treasury secretary "1-man responsibility" for the international economy as the "lead man."[6]

Regardless of Connally holding the line into July 1971 it was clear that something had to give. Nixon was getting fewer kudos for his China Shock than he was questions about the economy.[7] For selfish reasons nations with surplus dollar holdings were not going to revalue sufficiently to help the dollar. In any case, the Bretton Woods system did not compel them to do so; America would always pay up. Inflation remained stubbornly high with interest rates rising and the trade balance worsening. Experts talked of a dollar crisis.

***

Nixon held steady for the moment. He still refused wage and price controls, tax cuts, and spending increases despite the persistence of higher prices and a slow recovery from recession. Throughout July speculation against the dollar continued. Countries captured even more dollar reserves, threatening US gold stocks. France and Japan considered appreciating their currencies to help but that would make their exports more expensive, which was not in their national interests. American labor unions asked for import restrictions while half of the public supported government controls to freeze wages and prices temporarily.

By early August, as the stock market continued to tumble, the prime interest rate rose to 6.5 percent and joblessness inched back over 6 percent after a decrease in the months before. Nixon indicated he would consider a wage-price board to get inflation in order. That danger seemed particularly acute when major steel companies announced a price hike of 8 percent and a wage agreement to give workers a 30 percent raise over the next three years. Meanwhile, John Connally and Nixon discussed dollar devaluation while the Europeans refused revaluation (appreciation) of their currencies.

---

[6]Sargent, *A Superpower*, 108.
[7]Nixon, *RN*, 517–8.

The allies knew not to blackmail the United States by cashing in their dollars for American gold though they also understood that they could instill such a fear of a run on gold that the Bretton Woods system might collapse. On August 8, France announced its intention to buy $191 million of gold from Fort Knox to repay loans from the IMF. A congressional committee then recommended that the dollar be devalued or foreign currencies appreciated to resolve the current recession and monetary crisis. If this did not happen then the United States should unilaterally "float" the dollar downward against other currencies, thereby suspending the fixed Bretton Woods rate of $35/ounce of gold. Connally and the Treasury would not go that far right now but the secretary did not oppose the move farther down the road either.

The outflow of dollars and gold over the next few days reached such a tremendous level that exchange markets made headlines all over the world. Paul Volcker, the undersecretary of the Treasury for monetary affairs, told senior officials that the dollar crisis had reached a climax and something had to be done. On August 12, Nixon, Volcker, Connally, Federal Reserve Chairman Arthur Burns, Paul McCracken, Chairman of the Council of Economic Advisors, Secretary of Labor George Shultz, Caspar Weinberger of the Office of Management and Budget, and various White House advisors retreated to Camp David to consider their options.

As they departed Washington, the time for gradualism had passed and so had hopes for collaborative maintenance of Bretton Woods' dollar/gold exchange regime. The administration readied to liberate its foreign policy from the weaknesses imposed on it by the international financial system. The President's speechwriter, William Safire, was informed on his way to Camp David that "this is the most important weekend in economics since March 4, 1933," the day of President Franklin Roosevelt's inauguration and the advent of the New Deal revolution of government activism.[8] Now Nixon primed for his own activist revolution.

***

At Camp David the outlines of Nixon's so-called "New Economic Policy" (ironically, the name for Soviet leader Vladimir Lenin's communist economic plan of the 1920s) took shape. Some in the administration feared that a drastic change in Bretton Woods currency exchanges would disrupt the

---

[8]Harold James, *International Monetary Cooperation Since Bretton Woods* (Washington, DC: International Monetary Fund, 1996), 219. See also James Reston, Jr., *The Lone Star: The Life of John Connally* (New York: Harper & Row Publishers, 1989), 406; Garten, *Three Days*, 26–44; Kunz, *Butter*, 197–203; Allen J. Matusow, *Nixon's Economy: Booms, Busts, Dollars, and Votes* (Lawrence, KS: University of Kansas Press, 1998), 55–131, 123–31; Daniel J. Sargent, *A Superpower Transformed: The Remaking of American Foreign Relations in the 1970s* (New York: Oxford University Press, 2015), 106.

world economy and not provide enough relief to the US payments imbalance. Connally and Nixon overruled them because they wanted a "big play." Nixon prized football and he loved making history.

At multiple meetings over two days Treasury's Connally, who Nixon called his quarterback, took charge while being coached by the President. Tellingly, the team of foreign policy advisors were absent, including Secretary of State William Rogers and National Security Advisor Henry Kissinger. This scrimmage was intended to remedy the domestic and global economies with an eye cast downfield at the 1972 election. Nixon cared less for the details of the decisions than for their political effect. That is, he eagerly awaited the reception at home and abroad once his dramatic Hail Mary pass to win the game of devaluation and inflation control reached the endzone.

Camp David discussions about wage and price controls revealed near unanimity even though this would be the first time they were imposed in peacetime—they were used to tame inflation in the Second World War. This conservative administration detested the intrusive bureaucracy required to oversee the freezes so advisors sought a temporary ninety-day term for them. A voluntary phase would follow guided by a Cost of Living Council chaired by Donald Rumsfeld, a respected official best known for his service four decades later as secretary of defense in the George W. Bush administration. The administration reinstated a 10 percent investment tax credit that Nixon had canceled in 1969 to spur business and also advanced tax reductions by a year. In addition Camp David advisors repealed a 7 percent excise tax on new automobiles. So as not to inflate the economy further Nixon pledged to cut expenditures. These domestic measures, especially the wage and price controls, grabbed much attention.[9]

The international measures sparked controversy. Closing the gold window accompanied by a 10 percent import "surcharge" or "border tax" (a tariff) designed to hold other nations' feet to the fire to appreciate their currencies was the most dramatic play Connally called as advisors huddled at Camp David. The decision prompted substantial debate.

"Fed" Chair Arthur Burns and monetary advisors like Volcker worried about the historic importance of gold as a bulwark against inflation. Holding Burns in high esteem Nixon, too, understood the political implications of ending the gold standard so cherished by conservatives and bankers. After all the populist Democrat William Jennings Bryan had run for president four times and lost on a campaign to free the dollar from gold. The experts also warned of a contradiction. Slamming the gold window would depreciate the dollar and make exports more competitive but a tariff hike would reduce demand

---

[9]Matusow, *Nixon's Economy*, 149–51.

FIGURE 6.1. *At Camp David, "Coach" Nixon conferred with his "quarterback," the nationalist Treasury secretary, John Connally. Courtesy Richard M. Nixon Presidential Library and Museum (National Archives and Records Administration.*

for imports and appreciate the dollar. Admitting to that inconsistency Connally also steadfastly replied that upholding economic principles was not the point of the big play.

***

Rather, closing the gold window served US interests and the border tax was a cudgel to force countries to accept currency realignment. As the Texan repeated, "this cowboy knows that you can ride a good horse to death, and the world has been riding a good horse to death in the post-war years."[10] If trade partners refused to appreciate their currencies, then the administration would continue to prevent the dollar's convertibility into gold and US imports would remain protected by a 10 percent tariff wall. The time for action was now. Look at the British, pointed out Connally. They wanted Washington to cover all of their dollar reserves; that is, they wanted to exchange $3 billion for 40,000 tons of gold at Fort Knox. "Anybody can topple us—anytime they want—we have left ourselves completely exposed," he grumbled. It was imperative to end the dollar-gold drain madness. With the appropriate revaluation of currencies relative to the dollar, Bretton Woods itself might even be saved.

Would not such a shocking move as unilaterally severing the tie to gold be looked on as "a Pearl Harbor in reverse" to Japan in particular, asked Burns? By suddenly ending decades of generous support, allies would be traumatized. Washington might bring down the entire economic structure so painstakingly built during the American Century, and thus escalate diplomatic tensions within the Western alliance.

So be it, answered Connally. "We'll go broke getting their good will. So, the other countries don't like it, so what?" But the Soviets would cackle about the disintegration of the capitalist world, especially when NATO allies retaliated with their own protective tariffs, others warned. "Let 'em," Connally rejoindered, unmoved by complaints about his America First approach. In reality, allies had to bow to American wishes. "What can they do," asked Connally rhetorically, but toe the line and revalue? White House advisor H. R. Haldeman summed up, "that we have too long acted as Uncle Sugar and now we've got to be Uncle Sam."[11]

The potential rewards of hardline nationalism were substantial. Waiting in the end zone after the administration's big play could be a new monetary regime, dampened-down inflation, and reelection success. Or there could be a total overhaul—a new paradigm. In any event, in recent years, insufficient attention was given to the economic part of US foreign economic policies. A Marshall Plan mode of thinking toward Europe—of letting trade partners enjoy the benefits of a high dollar and open access to the American market—must change abruptly.

---

[10] Matusow, *Nixon's Economy*, 173. See also Nixon, *RN*, 519.
[11] Matusow, *Nixon's Economy*, 152, 153; Zeiler, *Capitalist Peace*, 178; Haldeman, *The Haldeman Diaries*, 342. See also Garton, *Three Days*, 73-4; Francis M. Bator, "Mr. Connally's War. I," *New York Times*, November 29, 1971, 39; Perlstein, *Nixonland*, 599.

Boldness spoke to Nixon's inclinations as a fighter with a reputation for unpredictable decision-making who surprised friends and enemies alike. The President himself worried about looking weak by changing his mind on wages, prices, and on the dollar-gold link. Fed Chair Burns noted in his diary that political motives governed Nixon's decision to act.

That is why speechwriter Bill Safire might have initially drafted the announcement, but the President wrote most of it into the early morning of Sunday, August 15. Four drafts later, Nixon himself named his program the "New Economic Policy." He then told Safire to modify the speech with "gutsy rhetoric," preferring "brutal and effective" to "beautiful" language on the topic of explaining his economic revolution to the American people and shocking the international community in the process.[12]

Above all the President needed to explain why he had reversed from gradualism to the sudden big play. Recent circumstances facing the United States and the health of the dying Bretton Woods system guided the shift. Nixon contested the notion that the declining dollar meant failure and humiliation abroad or that Americans should fear that their money would be worth less. With an eye on the ballot box, he argued that dollar devaluation really meant prosperity and power in the long run. Simply, the United States required a radical departure from its historic permissiveness abroad. Through boldness, Nixon planned to turn failure into an assertion of US international strength and action against inflation at home.[13]

The problem was that nobody knew what kind of monetary system would replace the discarded Bretton Woods and the gold standard. In this sense, Nixon was reckless. In addition, he deviated from the market economics that conservatives so cherished, adopting instead government controls that were anathema to them. Nixon also exhibited his usual cynicism. He sold voters a plan that implied American weakness relative to the rest of the world but couched it as a means of saving the United States from greedy speculators who took advantage of American goodness. He did not mention, however, America's role in its own demise through overspending and hegemonic policies.

Just minutes before Nixon went on television, Secretary of State Rogers informed the unwary Japanese of the impending bombshell. The United States was Japan's closest friend, its security blanket and main foreign source of economic livelihood. As the *Wall Street Journal* had predicted before the Camp David weekend the administration "is getting ready for a new cold war

---

[12]Haldeman, *The Haldeman Diaries*, 345.
[13]James, *International Monetary*, 219.

against the rest of the free world."[14] It certainly seemed that way to Tokyo. Japan called the speech the second Nixon Shokku.

***

Facial makeup applied Nixon sat at his Oval Office desk in a gray suit and tie and a white shirt with an American flag to his right and the presidential colors to his left. He held seventeen easy-to-read triple-spaced pages divided into outlines with big page breaks and lots of white spaces. The President had worried about interrupting *Bonanza*, the second longest running western on television, but "the big one" necessitated the interruption. In ordinary times Nixon might give a mundane address but this was no normal occasion. Some 46.2 million Americans, or one-quarter of the nation's population, tuned in.[15] All three networks broke into their scheduled programming as the world's attention turned to Richard Nixon.

Detailing the wage-price freezes, tax cuts, the 10 percent tariff surcharge, and the end to the dollar-gold link the President painted a picture of challenges facing the country and the world in broad strokes. He led off the announcement with his goals of cultivating peace and prosperity without war. Such objectives required "bold leadership ready to take bold action" through more jobs, less inflation, and protection of the dollar from international speculators.

He would not proceed timidly nor in a piece-meal fashion; every part of his plan fit with the others and the agenda's domestic and international parts were inseparable as well. His domestic proposals also addressed a theme of returning to the prosperity of the American Century when foreign competition presented few challenges, US productivity and fuller employment ruled, and inflation seemed beatable. Nixon knew his audience: American voters.

His final topic addressed the dollar "as a pillar of monetary stability around the world." He talked of repeated monetary crises over the past half decade or so that benefited not "the workingman; not the investor; not the real producers of wealth." Rather, the enemy of the average American were greedy money wheeler-dealers who held the dollar hostage. Their day was over, however, when he closed the gold window.

Nixon reminded allies of American munificence since the war—$143 billion in foreign aid, an open world (and United States) economy for their trade, and headquarters in the United States of the International Monetary Fund, the World Bank, and the United Nations. These were pillars of prosperity and security only because of American sponsorship behind them. Washington's policies had succeeded by enriching friends but with their recovery also came a responsibility "to bear their fair share of the burden of defending freedom

---

[14]Matusow, *Nixon's Economy*, 131, also Solomon, *The International Monetary System*, 176–87; Calleo, "Since 1961," 420; Garten, *Three Days*, 212, 214–5; Perlstein, *Nixonland*, 601–3.
[15]Garten, *Three Days*, 220–1, 238.

around the world." It was time "for exchange rates to be set straight and for the major nations to compete as equals." The era had passed "for the United States to compete with one hand behind her back."

Economic partners received a resolute message. Seeking "fair competition around the world," Nixon assured transatlantic and transpacific allies that America "has always been, and will continue to be, a forward-looking and trustworthy trade partner." But the Bretton Woods had outlived its primary purposes and he would now "press for the necessary reforms to set up an urgently needed new international monetary system." To fuel efforts at restructuring he imposed the 10 percent border tax surcharge that was directed not at any one nation and intended to be temporary. This import fee would be removed when "unfair exchange rates" no longer disadvantaged the United States.

***

The second Nixon Shock aimed to instill confidence, prosperity, opportunity, and freedom in the international community. Rather than shrinking in fear behind "a protective wall around ourselves" as "the rest of the world moves ahead," he implored Americans to recapture their "competitive spirit." Only in this way could the country balance between stability at home and involvement abroad. He believed that Americans could "shape the world of the future."[16] That future would be globalized.

Issued by an avowed internationalist, the speech was a lightning bolt. Nixon's backers believed he had electrified the nation by offering a solution to economic woes that was both dramatic and countered the wearisome pessimism of voters. He got solid marks at home, even from Democrats, although their progressive wing moaned about the lack of help for workers or too much aid to employers. Liberals lamented that Nixon had stolen their thunder on the economy. To be sure, Democratic National Chairman Larry O'Brien chided that "no wonder the President wants to run off to China. Faced with that kind of an economic mess, who wouldn't?" Organized labor applauded the cheaper dollar and import surcharge, though unions criticized the wage freeze as amounting to a reverse Robin Hood of robbing the poor to pay the rich.

Surveys showed the popularity of Nixon's agenda at home. Veteran pollsters found a level of unanimity not seen since the anger over the Pearl Harbor attack thirty years before. As Nixon exclaimed a few months later since the Second World War, "the United States has not bargained hard for a better

---

[16]Address to the "Nation Outlining a New Economic Policy: The Challenge of Peace," American Presidency Project, August 15, 1971, https://www.presidency.ucsb.edu/documents/address-the-nation-outlining-new-economic-policy-the-challenge-peace (accessed March 4, 2024). See also Garten, *Three Days*, 222–38.

FIGURE 6.2. *Nixon poses after his televised economic address on August 15, 1971. Courtesy Richard M. Nixon Presidential Library and Museum (National Archives and Records Administration).*

position in world trade, the goddamn State Department hasn't doesn't the job. We're changing the rules of the game."[17] Americans of all political stripes agreed with his assessment and response.

Conservatives generally liked the President stepping up in a bold way to battle inflation, though the business community did not like government

---

[17]Matusow, *Nixon's Economy*, 173. See also Perlstein, *Nixonland*, 603.

meddling in the economy. The Dow Jones stock index registered its biggest one-day gain to date—a historic 32.9-point rise—on the Monday following his address. Business leaders also wondered about the gold and surcharge measures, fearing that they might set off a trade war. Surely, with trade liberalization slowing over the past half decade, this was no time to hint at protectionism. Still, most of the business community and economists appreciated Nixon's plan, even if it was risky.

Observers understood the political brilliance as well. The *New York Times* predicted that, like Nixon's upcoming historic trip to China, the economic Shock could multiply votes in his favor in 1972, should the economy heal. Wielding the football metaphor, radio commentator Paul Harvey called Nixon a "gutsy quarterback" who had previously called plays into the line that went nowhere in defeating inflation. Now he had tried a big play on fourth down that even risked his reelection.[18] The gamble seemingly paid off, at least in its immediate political impact.

In fact, Nixon scored brilliantly in the 1972 election. Deficit spending for workers, tax cuts for business, rising interest rates that gratified bankers, and a lid on prices for consumers boosted his candidacy. In one of the rare successes by presidents to manage the business cycle, the second Nixon Shock temporarily helped the economy by boosting growth and lowering unemployment without a long-term turn to protectionism or an excess of government spending. Normalcy soon replaced Nixon's revolution just months after the Shock. The odd man out—mercantilist John Connally—left this internationalist administration in May 1972, replaced by the conventional liberal George Shultz at Treasury.

The economy stabilized to serve Nixon's political purposes in the campaign of 1972. He later rebuffed his chief aide, H. R. Haldeman, who tried to brief him on the course of various currency revaluations. "I don't care about it," retorted Nixon. "Nothing we can do about it." Even with speculation, say, about Italian currency, the President replied, "I don't give a shit about the lira" because "there ain't a vote in it."[19] Monetary, trade, and fiscal policies served electoral politics.[20]

As a side note, once Nixon relaxed wage and price controls, inflation exploded in the United States and the rest of the world, with the first oil crisis deepening and exacerbating the woes. Consumer costs doubled in 1973, then doubled again the next year to over 12 percent. Interest rates hit record highs, making 1974 the worst year for the US economy since the Second World War. The rest of the 1970s experienced only periodic improvement. The decade

---

[18]Zeiler, *Capitalist Peace*, 180–1. See also Matusow, *Nixon's Economy*, 156.
[19]Calleo, "Since 1961," 421.
[20]Matusow, *Nixon's Economy*, 180–1.

became infamous for stagnation and a loss of confidence in government to the extent that a backlash against postwar liberalism ensued. As a result, a neoliberal free-market revolution gained momentum.[21]

* * *

In contrast to the generally favorable domestic reaction to the second Nixon Shock, foreign observers were far less supportive. The visibly agitated managing director of the IMF who had been watching the announcement innocently with Connally and other Treasury officials quickly headed for the door, humiliated both by the message and the ambush. When it came to the international community laughed Connally, "there's no question that [Nixon's speech] shook them up."[22] This signaled the opening round of a few years of a difficult relationship between the International Monetary Fund, allies, and the United States.

Individual countries protested the closure of the gold window out of form because fixed exchange rates had rooted the monetary system for a quarter of a century. Now that stability could be lost. America's partners believed Nixon pinned the burden to adjust on them while avoiding his responsibilities as the leader of the capitalist system. The United States seemed to be avoiding concessions even though Washington's mismanagement of its economy, as well as inflation and unemployment, were as much to blame for the Bretton Woods crisis as their undervalued currencies.[23]

In Japan and Europe, the second Nixon Shock rudely interrupted vacations. When Nixon spoke it was morning in Tokyo. Officials were summoned from golf courses to deal with the crisis as Japanese markets began to tumble. Western Europe had still not awakened when the President finished his address and besides, it was a holiday in many countries so markets were closed. But Georges Pompidou, the French president, left the Riviera for Paris and the Canadian prime minister, Pierre Trudeau, rushed back to Ottawa from a cruise off Yugoslavia.

The economic reaction rang alarm bells. Once the stock markets opened on Tuesday on the European continent they promptly crashed. Wisely, European central bankers and finance officials ordered financial exchange markets closed for two weeks after which they carefully monitored their currencies. They allowed a float upward against the dollar, though slowly and incrementally. In Japan, the stock market lost 20 percent of its value over the week while Tokyo also struggled to keep its currency markets open. The finance ministry bought dollars and sold yen at a frenetic pace for two weeks, hoping to maintain the traditional Bretton Woods 360 yen/dollar rate. That effort failed, compelling the

---

[21]Calleo, "Since 1961," 421–2.
[22]Reston, *The Lone Star*, 411. See also Garten, *Three Days*, 238.
[23]Garten, *Three Days*, 254–5.

government to buy about $4 billion with little to show for its efforts but a sinking yen. No nation could stop devaluation because ultimately the dollar ruled global markets.

***

Nations now asked the key question: what next? Nixon seemed hypocritical as a principled proponent of the free market while he advocated change by nationalist-mercantilism exhortations in practice. This dualism required a balancing act on his part. As desired he rocked the entire monetary and trade system while Washington still committed to maintaining a liberal multilateral order of free trade and capital flows. In fact, the administration made clear that it sought to adjust rather than abandon the Bretton Woods monetary regime. So did this mean that once currency revaluation occurred Washington would return to the gold standard and fixed exchange rates?

Nations wondered. Having already revalued its currency the key industrial engine of Europe, West Germany, resigned itself to a new regime. Bonn understood that the dollar needed to be fixed or a trade war was imminent. The Japanese, though, fought yen appreciation. Tokyo was truly shocked because the 360 yen/dollar fixed rate had endured for two decades. For all allies the despised tariff surcharge conjured up memories of the economic warfare of the 1930s. Foreign policy officials and economists in the administration knew that Washington must lead negotiations to put to bed the fear of economic warfare.[24]

Over the next few months the internationalists and national security team converged on the nationalist John Connally. He would likely storm into negotiations like a bull in a china shop, recklessly creating chaos with no mutually acceptable resolution to the dollar exchange issue. Indeed, Connally knew very little about economics but he deeply understood politics. His philosophy of the international arena was simple: "foreigners are out to screw us. It's our job to screw them first."[25] Nixon was in accord, for this nationalist moment at least.

At initial talks with European Community nations in London in September 1971 just weeks after the second Shock, the high stakes "economic poker game" as one journalist called it witnessed Connally's refusal to devalue the dollar alongside appreciation of foreign currencies. The burden was on the allies, not the United States. He also told them that their revaluations must swing the US trade balance in a positive direction by a massive $13 billion. "We had a problem and we are sharing it with the world, just like we shared our prosperity. That's what friends are for." The Europeans refused Connally's terms and the meetings deadlocked.[26]

---

[24]Garten, *Three Days*, 248–50; Sargent, *A Superpower*, 116.
[25]Sargent, *A Superpower*, 108.
[26]Leonard Silk, "Economic Poker Game," *New York Times*, September 15, 1971, 61; Garten, *Three Days*, 262, also 255, 258, 260–1.

Trade partners were unmoved. At an IMF meeting of finance ministers at the end of September they sought a deadline for the import surcharge's removal. Connally gave them two conditions. First they must allow their currencies to float cleanly on the free market against the dollar. This would, hopefully, lead to depreciation of the dollar and thus a boost for US exports to correct the trade deficit. Second they must open their markets, granting specific trade concessions to American exports. The finance ministers balked. They did not want to abandon their so-called "dirty" floats—exchange rate changes by government intervention rather than market forces. And they certainly refused to make trade deals under compulsion with the Nixon-Connally 10 percent border tax gun held to their head. America's friends went home as monetary reform stalled.[27]

The reaction was understandable. The second Nixon Shock left trade partners holding the bag of hundreds of millions of dollars that they could no longer convert into gold. They were also miffed by protectionism from the alliance's leader that had built the General Agreement on Tariffs and Trade (GATT) liberal trade regime as one pillar—alongside those of Bretton Woods (IMF and World Bank) and the NATO military pact—as the foundational props for containing international communism. Nixon's measures recognized that the allies' recovery from the Second World War was now complete but those same allies did not like the implications.

***

Eventually negotiations moved forward after two months of debate and strategy sessions within the administration. Many of Nixon's economic and foreign policy advisors criticized Connally's aggressive stance, which they predicted would obtain no concessions from allies, result in no real reform of Bretton Woods, precipitate a global recession in the process, and undermine cooperative relations among NATO members.

Henry Kissinger in particular worried about fracturing the Western alliance at this delicate moment when the President neared his China trip and engaged in arms control in Moscow. The European Community might coalesce into a trade bloc to protect itself from US trade penetration. Meanwhile, Japanese sensitivity could call into question Tokyo's long history of dependent security and trade agendas with the United States. By November 1971, Kissinger urged Connally to offer constructive plans rather than smash the system. He then confided in Nixon that "Texans don't really have a diplomatic touch," warning that "[i]f we screw everybody in the free world . . . we will then undermine the whole structure of free world competition."[28]

---

[27]Garten, *Three Days*, 269–70.
[28]Garten, *Three Days*, 275, 277, also 271–4.

Nixon decided to calm down Connally's saber-rattling. Business leaders told him to cool it because the Texan had unsettled stock markets. Besides, the chaos over exchange rates impeded the President's preferred focus on his Beijing mission. Connally understood the wind had shifted. Nixon could not speak for the Free World if squabbling undermined the capitalist alliance. So the secretary offered a deal to the group of ten nations, America's top trade partners, at IMF meetings in Rome and Washington in late 1971.

Surprisingly, Connally proposed to devalue the dollar against gold, which represented a willingness to compromise that stunned other nations and ended the logjam. Broached as well in talks between Nixon and French President Georges Pompidou at meetings in the Azores this modest devaluation realigned currencies. The administration, in short, had crossed the rubicon of dollar devaluation. The dollar would depreciate by 8.7 percent while the Europeans and Japan agreed to substantial appreciation of their currencies, namely 14 percent for West Germany and 16.9 percent for Japan. The allies also agreed to launch major trade negotiations under GATT to expand markets for US exports.

Under the follow-up Smithsonian Agreement signed in Washington, once realignment provided for a new dollar exchange rate currencies could float up or down within a range of 2.25 percent (or 4.5 percent overall) from the fixed rate of $35/oz of gold. The administration then dropped its import surcharge. Nixon served notice that the United States had to accept a new world economic order of shared power. Dollar devaluation epitomized that reality.

More shocks to the system ensued in the months to come. The Smithsonian "parity" of 2.25 percent below or above the fixed exchange rate soon fell apart as the British devalued below it in April 1972, within four months of the Smithsonian conference. As another dollar crisis grew more severe it was clear that no nation intended to stop speculation by revaluing currencies. Out of habit they still counted on the United States to support the Bretton Woods system. The new neoliberal internationalist Treasury secretary, George Shultz, counseled a diplomatic solution to the crisis that hinged on the free market.

It took some time but by February 1973 the United States devalued the dollar 10 percent, which was well below the Smithsonian parity. The Japanese, Italians, and Swiss followed with currency appreciation as well and a month later all nations of Western Europe had floated their currencies. By 1974 floating exchange rates were the norm. Two years later the Jamaica Accords abolished an official price for gold itself. The gold standard was no more; like currencies the price of gold would float according to the demands of the market.

Ten years later, in 1985 under the Plaza Accord named after the hotel in midtown Manhattan, the major industrialized nations agreed to push down an overvalued dollar once again. This agreement successfully coordinated currencies though crises erupted periodically, including during the Great

Recession of 2008–2010 and the COVID pandemic-induced financial collapse of 2020.

* * *

As economic policy devaluation failed to cure inflation. Currency depreciations repeated themselves. For his part Nixon believed the second Shock ultimately "was wrong. The piper must always be paid, and there was an unquestionably high price for tampering with the orthodox economic mechanisms," including the gold standard. He was satisfied with deregulating international capital markets though he disliked angering allies. He grasped the reality of intervention in markets, however. He noted that "the *politics* of economics has come to dictate action more than the *economics* of economics."[29]

The second Nixon Shock represented a significant transition in the world economy. Grand economic strategy had transformed from America's American Century hegemony to the modern era of multilateral competition. Nations shared the burden of the world economy with international institutions like the IMF becoming more central to that effort. Nixon envisaged a future of a "five-fingered" world economy in which the United States' dominance over Europe, China, Japan, and the USSR had waned. That said Nixon's big play paid off for the United States. Dominance over the world economy prevailed through the central role of the dollar regardless of American challenges within the Western alliance.[30]

The continuation of the Cold War ensured Washington's leadership position. Nonetheless, the new system, wrote Peter Peterson, Nixon's chief advisor on international economic policy and the author of an influential report in 1971, entitled *The United States in a Changing World Economy*, "fully recognizes, and is solidly rooted in, the growing reality of a genuinely interdependent and increasingly competitive world economy whose goal is mutual, shared prosperity."[31] The second Nixon Shock "advanced that vision," writes scholar Jeffrey Garten.[32] It birthed the end of the dollar/gold fixed exchange system, a development that converted markets from local and national entities to those regional and global in scope.

---

[29]Nixon, *RN*, 521, 522. See also Sargent, *A Superpower*, 126–7.
[30]Sargent, *A Superpower*, 101.
[31]Peter G. Peterson, *The United States in the Changing World Economy, Volume 1: A Foreign Economic Perspective* (Washington, DC: U.S. Government Printing Office, December 1971), v.
[32]Garten, *Three Days*, 323, also 276–311. See also Calleo, "Since 1961," 421, 435; Matusow, *Nixon's Economy*, 176–7; Solomon, *The International*, 188–234, 298–315; Kunz, *Butter and Guns*, 221–2.

7

Aftershock Globalization

American-induced monetary reform under the second Nixon Shock stimulated a remarkable phenomenon. Financial exchanges boomed over the long term. Despite the bullying by an administration desperate to shore up US power and get reelected, Nixon inadvertently launched a process of economic integration and vast expansion the world over that launched the modern era of globalization that shaped history over the past half century and more.

***

A mutually acceptable definition of globalization eludes experts. Some believe the phenomenon is purely economic; others posit that it is multidimensional as well as unprecedented and revolutionary, and skeptics counter that it is a temporary and easily reversible phenomenon. All agree, though, that a transformation occurred in the world economy after 1971 that began integrating nations and people into larger communities, bringing people, business, and nations together by dissolving time and distance that promoted greater awareness and, supposedly, reduced hierarchies of power. Globalization converted markets from local and national entities to entities that are regional and global in scope. It theoretically incorporated national and regional networks into a vast, borderless, multilateral, and mutually profitable global economy. These elements define globalization.

The term best expressed the dynamism of the world economy, its booms and crises, and new forms of governance by global and civil society, especially after the Cold War. Globalization may have been a child of the 1970s, but there is only one mention of the term in the Library of Congress database of book titles prior to 1983. It matured in the 1980s and roared into dominance in the

1990s.¹ For the three decades after the second Nixon Shock, it became not only a buzzword but a defining theme of the post-Cold War era.

Globalization threw off the chains of history and geography leading, through free markets and technological innovation, to an expanding and more level playing field in global commerce for all competitors. Market capitalism, corporate growth, economic and cultural interdependence, the diffusion of state power by intergovernmental networks, and transnational trade and financial linkages flattened or equalized the world, according to journalist Thomas Friedman.²

The second Nixon Shock seems like a minor player in this gargantuan process but by freeing the dollar from gold and curbing controls on currencies that Shock injected trillions of dollars into the world economy as capital flowed into the Global South and around the Global North. Markets in Europe expanded as did new money markets fueled by petroleum exporters who, after the first oil crisis, poured their huge profits into offshore accounts and lent funds from them to oil importers. Such "petrodollars" blossomed in these extraterritorial money markets. To boot, these markets and oil exports themselves were denominated in dollars, so the United States remained the king or at least ran the court.

In short, skyrocketing inflation was the result, in the words of economist Harold James, of the "negative supply shock" of the oil crisis. Curiously, though, the negative turned into a positive. The Nixon Shock, coupled with the first oil crisis, as James further notes, catalyzed the integrative forces of globalization as the world searched for alternatives to supply problems.³

As American banks worked with the Nixon administration, the dollar soon accounted for roughly 60 percent of all foreign exchange reserves in central banks. Through the deregulation of the economy and neoliberal consensus, US bankers and administrations minimized government interference by relying on market forces to direct trade and investments. They capitalized on the growing interdependence of national economies, which meant no nation could adopt employment, income distribution, or trade and financial policies without sacrificing the welfare of its people in the global marketplace.

---

¹Richard W. Mansbach, "The Many Meanings of Globalization," in *Introducing Globalization: Analysis and Readings*, eds. Richard W. Mansbach and Edward Rhodes (Los Angeles, CA: Sage, 2013), 2–8; Martin Albrow, *The Global Age: State and Society Beyond Modernity* (Stanford, CA: Stanford University Press, 1997), 119–62; Alan M. Taylor, "The Global 1970s and the Echo of the Great Depression," in *The Shock of the Global*, 100.
²Thomas L. Friedman, *The World is Flat: A Brief History of the Twenty-First Century* (New York: Picador, 2007).
³Harold James, *Seven Crashes: The Economic Crises that Shaped Globalization* (New Haven, CT: Yale University Press, 2023), 15–8, 24–5, 167–78.

There was still substantial competition for jobs and capital, but nations could no longer close themselves off from the outside. Nations were better off renouncing nationalism, even though the "negative supply shock" of the oil crisis heightened inflation and pressured the world toward protectionism.

Globalization differed from traditional concepts of interdependence among nations. Capital flows, migration, technological innovations, trade liberalization, and even cultural contacts were of a scale far more immense, dense, and rapid than ever before. Globalization also promised greater benefits than interdependence, which targeted particular societies rather than the entire world. A modern, functioning, and open capitalist order that extended production and exchanges across borders and oftentimes ignored territorial domains (countries) epitomized the globalizing world economy.[4]

Before then, as the Bretton Woods system demonstrated, financial liberalization was essentially nonexistent while trade liberalization and multinational corporate expansion occurred at a growing but constrained pace. Liberalization or openness to capital and trade flows did not spurt even in the 1970s. It took decades before many European nations dropped capital controls that protected their exchange rates. The advent of the single-currency regime under the Euro finally brought widespread financial liberalization in Western Europe. And while initially slow on the uptake, the developing nations came around to the financial boom.

***

Transnational or multinational corporations led the globalization charge. Under the General Agreement on Tariffs and Trade, tariffs fell on industrial goods within the Global North but it was not until the GATT Uruguay Round of negotiations from 1986 to 1993 that the developing nations (as new members) had a significant role in trade liberalization, which was a foundation of globalization. Multinational corporations had long earned the hostility of poorer host nations because of their exploitation of resources, influence on politics, and blind eye toward oppression by national elites who ruled in their favor. The US labor movement also despised the effects of low-cost imports on wages that the free-trade regime encouraged. By the late 1970s, with a need for more foreign investment in the struggling Global South and rising foreign investment in the United States itself, the image of multinationals began to change.[5]

---

[4]Alfred E. Eckes, Jr. and Thomas W. Zeiler, *Globalization and the American Century* (Cambridge: Cambridge University Press, 2003), 1–2, 183; Sargent, *A Superpower*, 129–30; Charles S. Maier, "'Malaise': The Crisis of Capitalism in the 1970s," in *The Shock of the Global: The 1970s in Perspective*, eds. Niall Ferguson, Charles S. Maier, Erez Manela, and Daniel J. Sargent (Cambridge, MA: Harvard University Press, 2010), 43–4.
[5]Taylor, "The Global 1970s," 100–6; Vernie Olveiro, "The United States, Multinational Enterprises, and the Politics of Globalization," in *The Shock of the Global*, 155.

The emergence of the Organization of Petroleum Exporting Countries (OPEC) reordered the world power structure because oil prices lay at the heart of global trade, so intertwining oil production and with the process of globalization. Long a moderating voice in Arab politics, friendly with the United States, and home to one-third of known petroleum reserves, Saudi Arabia pulled the American, Japanese, and European economies toward growth or recession, bankrolled the world economy, and demanded a new economic order with redistributed political power. Under their oil minister, Ahmed Zaki Yamani, the Saudis maintained stable though steadily rising oil prices that calmed markets and countered revolutionary forces in the Arab-Islamic Middle East. Oil shortages in America gave Yamani and OPEC leverage until the mid-1980s when oil supplies overtook demand.

The combination of more energy efficiency and energy independence in the Global North and conflict between OPEC nations led to plummeting prices, and Yamani found himself out of a job. OPEC experienced the effects of globalization; it could not sustain a commodity cartel in a world of geographically dispersed suppliers—from the Arab world to Africa to Venezuela to North America—with different interests, alliances, and objectives.[6] Globalization had no national or regional loyalties that could restrain multinational firms increasingly unfettered from regulations.

As for multinational corporations the tremendous opposition to them at home and abroad in the Global South, especially after revelations of business collusion with unsavory regimes in Chile, South Africa, and elsewhere, did not slow down the expansion of US business abroad. The value of US direct investments abroad (what multinational corporations do) rose 122 percent from 1973 to 1985 from over $103 billion to over $230 billion. By 2000, these global investments stood at nearly $1.3 trillion. The thirteen-fold increase over a quarter century included investments in the developed nations by Western Europe, Japan, and Canada in real estate, manufacturing, transport, banking, and insurance. Ventures in the Global South lagged though they still rose substantially in Latin America and the Middle East due to petroleum.

Investors also drew on more international associations. Chief among them was a group of European business leaders who began meeting in Davos, Switzerland in 1982. This meeting of elites and the wealthy expanded throughout the decade to include politicians and other luminaries who networked, negotiated deals, and discussed policy issues at the World Economic Forum that gathered annually in January.[7]

---

[6]Eckes and Zeiler, *Globalization*, 188–94.
[7]Robert Gilpin, *The Challenge of Global Capitalism: The World Economy in the Twenty First Century* (Princeton, NJ: Princeton University Press, 2000), 163–92; Eckes and Zeiler, *Globalization*, 195,

Economic dynamism multiplied globalized cultural icons starting in the takeoff 1980s. Disney, McDonald's, Mary Kay cosmetics, and VISA epitomized the phenomenon. The Disney corporation entered into a joint venture with Japanese investors to build a theme park in Tokyo identical to those in California and Florida. In its first year of operation in 1983, Tokyo Disney attracted ten million visitors, many of them familiar with films, products, Mickey Mouse, and Cinderella whose Castle completed the park. Tokyo Disney became an iconic part of Japanese culture; even Emperor Hirohito occasionally wore a Mickey Mouse watch. Across Asia enthusiasts flocked to Disneyland, including Kim Il-un, the son of the North Korean dictator, who tried to enter Japan on a fake passport so his kids could visit the park in 2001.

Japan's embrace of McDonald's also led to booming expansion. The food service giant opened a restaurant abroad in Canada in 1967 and then put one in Tokyo in 1971. Promoting hamburgers and fries to make the Japanese tall, white, and blonde the managing director of McDonald's Japan, Den Fujita, proclaimed that "the reason Japanese people are so short and have yellow skins is because they have eaten nothing but fish and rice for two thousand years."[8]

Globalization of food promised change. With a keen awareness of local culture McDonald's adapted to local tastes. In Japan visitors could get a Teriyaki Burger while in Chile they ordered a McNifica. The results were stunning. The more profitable a country's McDonald's the more outlets saturated the market. By 1980, McDonald's added 1,000 restaurants abroad to its fast-food arsenal at home of 6,000 stores. Seven years later it had 10,000 restaurants serving twenty million people in forty-seven countries. The chain soon opened in Moscow and Beijing. By 2000, McDonald's served burgers in 26,462 restaurants in 119 nations, some 14,000 of those in Europe, Asia, and Latin America.[9]

Some critics chafed at McDonald's supposed cultural imperialism of adapting to local tastes while others called its reach crass Americanization. Still, pop culture spread through the process of creating unified world markets by the convergence and standardization of tastes, customs, and ways of life. Some even associated peace with globalization and McDonald's. This "Golden Arches" theory held that nations with McDonald's outlets would never go to war against each other because their mutually profitable business ties incentivized efforts to preserve peace.[10]

204, 213–4.
[8]Eckes and Zeiler, *Globalization*, 214–5.
[9]James L. Watson, ed., *Golden Arches East: McDonald's in East Asia* (Stanford, CA: Stanford University Press, 1997).
[10]John Tomlinson, *Globalization and Culture* (Chicago, IL: The University of Chicago Press, 1999), 83; Thomas L. Friedman, *The Lexus and the Olive Tree: Understanding Globalization* (New York:

Mary Kay Ash also successfully exported services—in this case cosmetics. Battling sexism in the corporate hierarchy, she worked tirelessly to persuade women to sell beauty products. By 1979, her company based in Dallas, Texas, reached over $100 million in sales, with 50,000 directors. Consultants oftentimes drove around the country in the Mary Kay trademark pink Cadillac, leading to an exclusive contract with General Motors to paint some 100,000 special Mary Kay cars. She motivated consultants with cars and also profit-sharing schemes and bonuses.

Mary Kay joined together three faiths—God, family, and women entrepreneurship. By the 1990s that combination skyrocketed the company into upscale markets worldwide. She not only took on the cosmetics powerhouse, Estee Lauder, but as the Cold War ended Mary Kay sold $10 million worth of products in Russia and pursued the China market as well by opening a factory in Hangzhou. By the turn of the century (she died in 2001) Mary Kay cosmetics boasted 600,000 direct sales consultants in the United States and nearly forty nations, grossing $2 billion in sales.[11] Cosmetics had become globalized.

Rather than appeal to a youth or women's market VISA sold to everyone by simplifying travel and consumption. Labeled the first truly transnational corporation in 2001 the credit card company owned 57 percent of the worldwide market through a full-service payments network owned by 21,000 member financial institutions around the world. In 2022, it still controlled roughly 57 percent of the global credit card market. The brainchild of a former Seattle bank officer VISA established a global brand beginning in 1968 with computer centers and leased telephone lines that required five minutes for authorization for each transaction. By 1970 the company had issued thirty million cards; thirty years later VISA credit card holders numbered over one billion. Some 82 percent of Americans spent with credit cards by the mid-2020s, using them in over 130 nations to the tune of $2.1 trillion in annual transactions that took just five seconds for approval.[12] Richard Nixon never conceived of such an explosion in business and cultural integration when he announced his second Shock in August 1971.

***

Multinationals like VISA, Mary Kay, McDonald's, and Disney benefited not only from technological progress but also from changes in economic thought and policy that greatly influenced the acceleration of globalization. In the 1970s,

---

Farrar Straus Giroux, 1999), 195–8.
[11] Mary Kay Company, "Quick Facts," February 2, 2017, https://www.marykay.com/en-us/about-mary-kay/company-and-founder/company-quick-facts (accessed March 12, 2024); Eckes and Zeiler, *Globalization*, 215.
[12] Eckes and Zeiler, *Globalization*, 215–6.

ideas turned from government intervention to promoting fair labor standards and employment, social justice, and stable business cycles. Ironically, Nixon's wage and price controls served as the peak practice of the active government. Neoliberal thinkers like Milton Friedman of the University of Chicago issued attacks on such statist approaches, advocating instead for entrepreneurship, reliance on the Federal Reserve and monetary policy, fluctuating exchange rates and free trade, competition in the labor market (minimizing union power), lower taxes, and deregulation. To various degrees, these all became elements of globalization.

Neoliberal ideas captured the White House when Ronald Reagan took office in 1981. His predecessor, Jimmy Carter, had worked with Congress to lessen regulations on the airline, trucking, railroad, and financial industries. Reagan went further by not distinguishing between anti-trust regulations that promoted competition and regulations designed to protect the health of Americans. Instead, he saw government as the problem, complaining that the federal government had "overspent, overestimated and overregulated."[13] He immediately slashed taxes by 25 percent and pushed for trade liberalization. Reagan's pro-industry position undermined the social safety net and led to major scandals in housing, the savings and loan banking sector, defense contracting, and environmental safety oversight. Nevertheless, market policies became dogma in the Reagan 19803 and beyond.

Voters rallied around Reagan's simple message: freedom depended on American leadership. That meant freedom abroad not only in the context of prosecuting the Cold War but freeing the economy at home and overseas through regulatory reform, free trade, and privatization. Tax cuts necessitated issuing high-yield treasury bonds to foreigners and Americans to plug the gap between federal spending and declining revenues. That process made for a stronger dollar which, in turn, made exports more expensive and foreign goods cheaper. That was good for US consumers but bad for the trade deficit, which grew sharply.

As a result, by 1985 America once again became a debtor country. Foreign investments in the United States surpassed the nation's assets abroad, a trend that persisted for decades. By 2025, Japan, China, and the United Kingdom held roughly $8 trillion or a third of America's globalized $34 trillion debt. In 2000, the United States' external debt exceeded $2 trillion; by 2025, it reached nearly $33 trillion, accelerated by Reaganomics, neoliberalism, and recovery programs from the Great Recession and the COVID-19 pandemic.

***

---

[13]Cannon, *President Reagan*, 819, also 820. See also Eckes and Zeiler, *Globalization*, 205; Schaller, *Reckoning*, 99–118.

Freedom came at a cost though debt, a high dollar, and trade deficits also brought vast changes under globalization. As the US economy deregulated and internationalized and the country's dependence on trade multiplied during the 1970s–1990s, imports and exports surged to over one-quarter of gross domestic product. Old industries like footwear and apparel saw their plants shipped abroad, exposed by free-trade policies that showed they could not compete with low-wage foreign labor in the globalizing economy. Established in New England in 1908 Converse athletic shoes, for example, declared bankruptcy after falling victim to cheap imports. Typically, unions and companies were weakened or bypassed by the neoliberal policies of globalization.

Another shoe company, Nike, took a tack more in line with globalization. The Oregon-based manufacturer looked abroad for low-income workers in developing countries, some of them with abysmal conditions of sweatshop labor. Nike also aggressively branded itself in sports around the world when National Basketball Association (NBA) superstar Michael Jordan became the poster child for the globalized reach of sports.

The sports/globalization link was a profitable mix of global money and culture and boxer Muhammad Ali had shown the way in the 1970s. Ali held the first ever heavyweight bout in Africa, defeating George Foreman in Zaire before an international audience that watched on television and in movie theaters thanks to satellite technology—itself a driver of globalization. He then became one of sports' most beloved citizen when, with hands shaking from Parkinson's disease, he stunned a worldwide audience of millions by lighting the Olympic torch in Atlanta in 1996.[14]

Nike took its marketing cues from Ali and others, and through the merger of athletics with big business boosted profits for the company, Michael Jordan, and professional basketball. In one of the most famous advertisements of all time "the man who could fly" was pictured in midflight with a basketball above a caption that read, "Just Do It!" Nike's share of the sneaker market rocketed from 18 percent when the ad first aired in 1988 to 43 percent of the market ten years afterward. The so-called "Jordan Effect" on commercial culture including sports, advertisements, the media, and movies doubled Jordan's worth to Nike to over $10 billion by 2000. Fully one-quarter of Nike's sales went to Europe by the early 1990s while Japanese teenagers bought up Air Max shoes for $1,000 a pair and up. The company competed by adding value through design and marketing, outsourcing contracts to cheap-labor countries that often exploited their labor, and drawing on celebrity endorsements. After

---

[14]Eckes and Zeiler, *Globalization*, 198.

Jordan retired Tiger Woods took his place in the marketing pantheon, in his case building on Nike's $200 million a year golf business.

Jordan's star quality joined with the global reach of satellite television to establish a worldwide following for his team, the Chicago Bulls. American sports leagues drew on talent abroad as they marketed overseas as well. Athletes from eastern Europeans entered the National Hockey League while Europeans, Latin Americans, Australians, and Chinese played in the NBA. In 2008 alone-, eighty-one players from thirty-five countries were on NBA squads, up from a mere four players drafted into the league in 1994. In Major League Baseball in the new millennium, a quarter of the starting lineups were foreign-born players.[15] Such was the reach of globalization.

***

Perhaps the most impressive effects of mighty mix of free-market neoliberal thought arose from technological change. Faster, cheaper, and expanded communications and transportation systems—the internet, efficient supply chains, massive container ships, jet travel and freight—reduced shipping, port, storage, and wait-time costs as factors in production. All were drivers of globalization. Research shows that innovative and widely adopted technology "enabled unprecedented movement of persons, things and ideas" that have made people more interdependent and made more porous traditional territorial and geographic boundaries.[16]

Consider shipping. Air freight's share of trade rose nearly doubled from 1980 to 1997 as transportation by plane surged for high-value products. The increase also dropped the cost of air shipping from sixty-eight cents per mile in 1930 to a paltry eleven cents sixty years later. Furthermore, with a six-fold increase in ship tonnage from 1955 to 1998 the unit cost to carry freight by sea dropped by 70 percent. By 2010, international seaborne trade included more than 50,000 vessels belonging to 10,000 shipping companies which multiplied the tonnage of products carried. That trend grew even more dynamic as internet-based companies like Amazon took over consumer markets and delivered their goods over the next decades.[17]

---

[15]Miguel Korzeniewicz, "Commodity Chains and Marketing Strategies: Nike and the Global Athletic Footwear Industry," in *The Globalization Reader*, eds. Frank J. Lechner and John Boli (Malden, MA: Blackwell Publishers, 2000), 163–5; George H. Sage, *Globalizing Sport: How Organizations, Corporations, Media, and Politics are Changing Sports* (Boulder, CO: Paradigm Publishers, 2010), 128–30; Walter LaFeber, *Michael Jordan and the New Global Capitalism* (New York: W.W. Norton & Company, 2002), 54–76, 143–51; Andrei S. Markovits and Lars Rensmann, *Gaming the World: How Sports are Reshaping Global Politics and Culture* (Princeton, NJ: Princeton University Press, 2010), 89.
[16]Mansbach and Rhodes, *Introducing Globalization*, xvii.
[17]Marc Levinson, *The Box: How the Shipping Container Made the World Smaller and the World Economy Bigger* (Princeton, NJ: Princeton University Press, 2006), 266–71; Eckes and Zeiler,

Based on innovation, information, deregulation, and high-skilled services the new globalized economy swept over the world. VISA, as previously noted, pointed to this trend, boosted by advances in data processing and communications. Other examples abound. From 1970 to 1990, the cost of a three-minute phone call between the banking centers of New York City and London dropped by 90 percent. As astounding, in 1956, eighty-nine phone calls took place simultaneously through the transatlantic telephone cable. By 2000, one million conversations occurred at the same time through satellite and fiber optics, a number that does not even count emails and faxes that further magnified the speed and volume of communications. Prices for computers and the cost of compiling, storing, and analyzing financial data and conducting transactions also plummeted.

The boom in technology led to a phenomenal expansion in capital flows within the Global North and from North to the Global South. Cross border transactions of equities and bonds rose to 164 percent of the US gross domestic product in 1996, up from just 9 percent in fifteen years before. These were dominated by private and voluntary transnational capital flows rather than government sources. Such financial operations had millions of globalized investors at their core.[18]

***

The enormous scale and scope of transnationalism—or exchanges of goods, services, money, and people migrating across permeable borders—represented the essence of globalization unleashed by the second Nixon Shock. To give an idea financial globalization is a good case. Over a ten-year period from 1986 to 1996 the assets of US-based international and global mutual funds climbed from $16 billion to $321 billion. The velocity of exchanges spiraled upward as well. At the time of the move asway from the Bretton Woods fixed exchange rates in 1973 business on foreign exchange markets amounted to $15 billion. Twenty-five years later floating exchange rates spurred the daily turnover to $1.5 trillion. Electronic trading integrated financial markets even more, allowing money in and out according to market conditions. For instance, foreign investors sent $100 billion into Asia in 1996 and during the ensuing Asian financial crisis the next year they withdrew the same amount.

The transformation in work and communications also reshaped the world. Many people worked in low-skilled secretarial positions but others were lawyers, accountants, engineers, business consultants, educators, designers,

---

Globalization, 245; Vaclav Smil, *Two Prime Movers of Globalization: The History and Impact of Diesel Engines and Gas Turbines* (Cambridge, MA: The MIT Press, 2010), 159.
[18]Eckes and Zeiler, *Globalization,* 216, 245.

and information specialists. They integrated into the Information Age by producing ideas, data, and innovative technologies rather than manufactured and agricultural goods. By 1998, the information technology sector had doubled its share of gross domestic product to 8.2 percent and expanded thereafter. Previously, the domain of academics and the military the internet in the 1990s transformed into a tool for the masses.

In the 1990s, "virtual" transactions by individuals skyrocketed as people visited distant locations around the globe through email, networking with business associates and sharing photos. They had access to affordable personal computers and programs thanks to Apple Computers, IBM, and Bill Gates at Microsoft. Fewer than forty million people worldwide, enjoyed connections to the internet in 1997; a year later, the number reached over 100 million. By 2024, over $5.3 billion people, or 65 percent of the global population, connected to the internet. Growth was most substantial in the Global South.[19]

The virtual world led to a burst of gaming, sports betting, and sharing of data through computers and then cell phones. The overall growth in social media sites and usage, moreover, seized the attention of billions of people. The video service YouTube began in 2005 and soon became a standard viewing platform for 100 million videos per day. Facebook, which changed its name that year, grew to over three billion users by 2023. Facetime started in 2010 and shortly became ubiquitous for phone conversations. A Chinese company launched TikTok in 2016. Two years later it was the most downloaded social media "app" in the United States and by 2022 TikTok had a billion worldwide active video users a month.[20] There might have been an "attention economy" without globalization but it certainly would not have been planetary in scale with the billions of viewing platforms as a commodity themselves.

＊＊

Globalization had a historic role in international affairs. The Cold War ended for several reasons though clearly the Soviet Union went out of existence in part, due to the information revolution. Moscow could have either embraced new information sources, thereby opening up its closed society and undermining communist authority, or further entrenched the Soviet economy in obsolescence. As his empire disintegrated between 1989 and 1991, even Mikhail Gorbachev resorted to the fax machine to stay in power when hardline communists tried to oust him. The public turned off Russian television and

---

[19] Eckes and Zeiler, *Globalization*, 217, 245.
[20] Daniel Ruby, "TikTok User Statistics (2022): How many TikTok Users Are There?," *Demandsage*, October 16, 2022, https://backlinko.com/facebook-users; https://www.britannica.com/topic/YouTube.

tuned into Radio Liberty, the BBC, the Voice of America, and Cable News Network (CNN) for the truth about politics. The information age moved power from centralized government bureaucracies to transnational networks of people and activist groups. This doomed Soviet communism.[21]

That downfall converted the Reagan Doctrine of supporting freedom around the world into an even more optimistic view of the world that made globalization mantra in the Clinton years. In the late 1980s, gloom and doom about US economic prospects in the face of Japanese competition ruled academic hallways. Such declinism gave way to euphoria at the end of the Cold War, however. Reflecting victory culture scholar Francis Fukuyama proclaimed the "end of history." He meant that centuries of world conflict had been replaced by globalization's universal liberal elements that spread democracy and capitalism around the globe.[22]

There were holes in that argument yet this dogma seemed logical as well. Russia would quickly transform its socialist economy to a private one through "shock therapy," or a minimal transitional period. Shock therapy had worked in Bolivia and Poland but the former Soviet Union was different. It turned out to have mixed success; not even McDonald's could save the average Russian citizen from struggling for a living despite the wealth of oligarchs around them. They turned to the determined would-be dictator, Vladimir Putin, who took advantage of the disillusionment and economic toil. America could also engage China with capitalist trade and investment though the Tiananmen Square massacre called democratic hopes into question. Neither the gift of pandas nor the Beijing Olympics convinced communist leaders that capitalist democracy was a good option for their country.

Such setbacks defied the buoyant view of globalization's impact. Experts believed that the presence of the CNN, which drew seventy-five million viewers, assured the end of history. Owner Ted Turner gifted the United Nations $1 billion to support internationalism against nationalist impulses in the hope that CNN would be "a positive force in the world, to tie the world together." Indeed, globalization's prophets in the media seemed to preempt dour diplomats in forging the new liberal democratic order.[23]

As a template globalization captured Washington. In the 1990s, Bill Clinton looked to "the consolidation of market democracy" throughout the world as a means of winning the presidency by untying the Democratic Party from its

---

[21] Eckes and Zeiler, *Globalization*, 218–9.
[22] Francis Fukuyama, *The End of History and the Last Man* (New York: The Free Press, 1992), 39–50.
[23] Eckes and Zeiler, *Globalization*, 223; Royce J. Ammon, *Global Television and the Shaping of World Politics: CNN, Telediplomacy, and Foreign Policy* (Jefferson, NC: McFarland and Company, Inc., 2001).

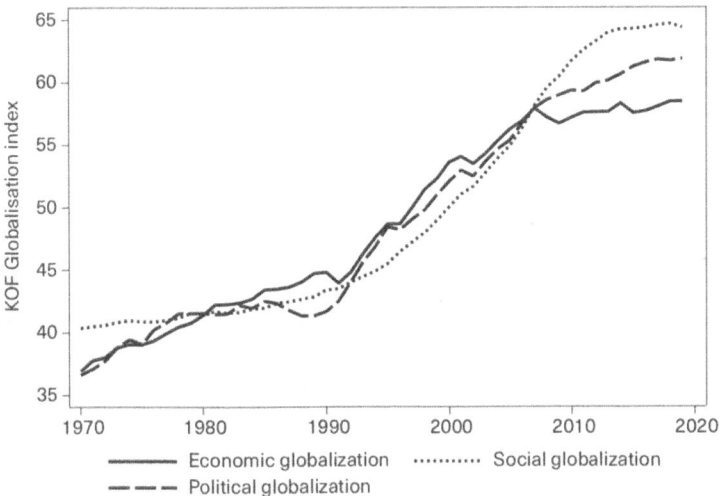

GRAPH 7.1. *Jonas Tallberg, Karin Backstrand, Jan Aart Scholte, and Thomas Sommerer, "Global Governance: Fit for Purpose? SNS Democracy Council Report 2023," SNS (May 2023), https://www.sns.se/en/articles/sns-democracy-council-2023-global-governance-fit-for-purpose/.*

big-government traditions. The process also guided world affairs. Some called Clinton the first "globalist" president who was a believer that the Information Age and free-trade would strengthen the economy and assure democratic transitions throughout the world. As opposed to internationalists globalists had faith in the primacy of economic affairs over political relationships. American security and military policies may have contested communism and tough diplomacy toward enemies remained essential. Yet the linkage of economic liberalism to democracy, undergirded by deregulation and free exchanges among the capitalist nations, helped bring down the Soviet Union. It could also reform China's communist state and transform other autocracies into democracies. The transnationalism of private financial, trade, technological, and cultural innovation and integration won the day, at least until September 11, 2001.[24]

Government officials changed as well by seeking greater access to foreign markets for the high-tech service sector and more rules to create a fair and profitable playing field abroad for business. In fact, anti-monopoly rulings and eager foreign investors holding billions of dollars turned the US telecommunications market from an export surplus sector into a massive trade deficit by the mid-1980s. Part of the problem arose from the relatively open American market as compared to most state-subsidized industries in

---

[24]Klein, *The Natural*, 78–9; Eckes and Zeiler, *Globalization*, 220, also 221–3.

competing countries. In response, trade negotiations at the Uruguay Round of GATT included the new sector of services to address the issue.

Unfairness also arose from the theft of ideas and technology. Safeguards of intellectual property could not prevent piracy in the consumer electronics markets. People around the world illegally copied audio and visual material as well as cassettes, computer chips, books, and television broadcasts without compensating the owners who held patents and copyrights. Developing nations like China, Mexico, and India favored the practice to appropriate technology, provide jobs, and catch up with the industrialized world. Pirating spilled over into all sorts of consumer goods—authentic-looking Reebok running shoes or Louis Vuitton handbags—that sold for a fraction of the price of the real item. Foreign movies came out on unauthorized videocassettes and later on DVDs. Pirated drugs might be unsafe or ineffective but many were made in the very same factory from which the legitimate product exited. By the late 1980s the US government estimated losses from intellectual property theft at upward of $61 billion a year.

Successive administrations from Reagan onward aggressively pursued sanctions on nations that stole computer programs, biotechnology, and satellite signals and pursued international agreements to protect creative works and expand copyright protections. Again nations turned to the GATT for enforcement mechanisms and to persuade developing nations to adhere to international intellectual property standards with the intention of facilitating a globalized free market of ideas while compensating creators.[25]

American officials, business leaders, and producers and workers wanted the trade system to provide a remedy to these problems as well as guide globalization. This need, in part, could be fulfilled by new regional and global economic associations. Nixon had envisaged the continued preeminence of US power within a multilateral global framework in which other nations competed with America. This is what he meant by big power parity that maintained the dominance of the dollar but recognized shared leadership. New groupings of economic and political associations shaped by the elements of globalization underscored this vision.

***

After the Cold War Europeans from both east and west looked across the iron curtain that had divided them with a desire to re-integrate the continent. For starters, the former Soviet bloc nations believed that their entry ticket into the world economy hinged on joining the European Community (formerly the European Economic Community or Common Market). In 1973, the addition of Denmark, the United Kingdom, and Ireland raised the number of Community

---

[25]Eckes and Zeiler, *Globalization*, 209–10, 212–3.

member states to nine. During the next decade, Greece, Spain, and Portugal joined and, in 1995, Austria, Finland, and Sweden became members.

Meanwhile, in 1992, Hungary, Poland, and the Czech and Slovak Federal Republic established a Central European Free Trade Area with sixty-four million people that grew through internal market-based cooperation but also pointed toward Western Europe and the process of globalization. Multinational corporations poured investments into these countries and Russia to develop oil and gas, food processing, machinery, and catering industries though tensions arose over agricultural protection and migration from east to west. Nevertheless, the European Community promised to integrate the former Soviet empire into the rest of Europe.

The European Community merged its major institutions into the dynamic European Union (EU) that proved revolutionary. Its biggest enlargement occurred in 2004 with ten new nations, most of them in Eastern Europe. Bulgaria, Romania, and Croatia brought the total to twenty-eight EU members until the United Kingdom left in 2020 under "Brexit." Turkey waited in the wings for entry as Christian and democratic Europe balked at membership for this Muslim, culturally conservative semi-autocracy.

With a gross national product at over $6 trillion (bigger than America's), the EU strived for its full integrative potential as a single market without borders. In 1986, these nations passed the Single European Act to harmonize product standards, eliminate all internal trade barriers (like the fifty United States enjoyed), and enhance labor and educational mobility around the region. The Maastricht Treaty of 1992 that renamed the bloc as the European Union called for a common currency—the Euro—by 1999. The EU comprised only 6.4 percent of the world's population but 42 percent of global exports and imports. Behind the North American Free Trade Area (NAFTA) it was the second largest economic bloc in the world. While the United States housed 345 of the top 1,000 companies and Japan another 310, the EU accounted for one-quarter. The EU juggernaut competed particularly against its key partner, the United States.

Indeed, despite the power of regionalism that many experts believe supplanted globalization in importance, the European Union intertwined with the United States. One-fifth of US imports came from the region and a quarter of its exports went to the bloc. By 2022, American exports to the EU totaled over $553 billion and imports reached nearly $351 billion. Two-fifths of US foreign investments, including in key sectors like commodities, financial services, and cable television, flowed into Europe while the EU's financial interest in America's economy concentrated in manufacturing, wholesale trade, and petroleum. EU companies and subsidiaries employed over three million Americans in the 1990s, a figure that blossomed over the next decades. The European Union and the United States controlled 55 percent of all direct foreign investment in the world. Trade and investment ties cemented together the two economies into a prosperous transatlantic community.

There were squabbles that revealed tensions in globalization. For instance, Euro Disney outside of Paris provoked controversy as critics perceived it as a threat to European culture. A French journal called it "Mousewitz" due to its prepackaged meals and initial prohibition on alcohol that smacked of barbaric American puritanism and mind control. Still, the US-EU relationship was sound, profitable, and nourished globalization in the rest of the world.

The EU clearly rivaled the Pacific Rim in dynamism in the decades after the Cold War though Asia also flourished. The so-called "Four Tigers" of South Korea, Taiwan, Hong Kong, and Singapore (perhaps Five, with Malaysia) joined Japan as sources of trade and investment that promoted their industrialization and integration into the world economy. Their export-led growth multiplied savings and income. Hong Kong and Singapore equaled EU nations in per capita incomes while South Korea and Taiwan joined the ranks of middle-income countries. They were also hubs of high technology that produced computer chips, superconductors, and other cutting-edge goods. Regionalism fueled globalization in Asia and Europe alike.

That trend led to an era of trade integration as business and government sought to sustain growth by deregulating national markets and connecting them to each other. To encourage economic cooperation countries established ASEAN—the Association of Southeast Asian Nations of 500 million people. At its founding in 1967 ASEAN was a collection of low-income countries. A quarter century later many of its members had moved to middle-class status. In addition, a high-level meeting in Canberra, Australia, in 1989 united about two dozen diverse Asian nations and the United States under the Asian-Pacific Economic Cooperation (APEC) organization to leverage regional interdependence.

Across the globe globalization stimulated regional groupings. In the Americas long-time rivals Brazil and Argentina set aside their differences, especially after the military government was overthrown in Buenos Aires in the mid-1980s. They established the MERCOSUR economic bloc in 1991 that aspired to a customs union like the European Union, which Paraguay and Uruguay later joined. Central American nations followed with their own economic arrangement. For North America, the culmination of competition from the EU and a post-Cold War era sense of American hegemony—the "unipolar" moment of the 1990s when the United States had no geopolitical rival—resulted in Washington tabling a regional trade bloc of its own.[26]

***

---

[26]David Marsh, *The Euro: The Politics of the New Global Currency* (New Haven, CT: Yale University Press, 2009); Gilpin, *The Challenge*, 193–226; USTR, "European Union Trade and Investment Summary," 2022, https://ustr.gov/countries-regions/europe-middle-east/europe/european-union#:~:text=The%20U.S.%20goods%20trade%20deficit,(%2415.8%20billion)%20over%20

In 1987, the Reagan administration negotiated a free-trade agreement with Canada, at the time America's largest trade partner. It did so in part because the Uruguay Round of GATT was deadlocked, thus denying progress toward liberalization, and in part to coax both the European Union and the United States toward openness. The US-Canada pact went beyond tariffs to include other trade barriers, government procurement, and dispute settlement.

A few years later Mexico, America's third largest trade partner, sought a similar free-trade deal with the United States. This was a dramatic move. For seventy years, Mexican nationalism had kept the imperial colossus of the North at arms' length yet the economy was mired in stagnation and corruption. Millions of its citizens had migrated north across the border in search of low-skilled jobs, opportunities for their children, and safety. In doing so, they provoked a wary segment of outraged and scared anti-immigration Americans.

The time seemed ripe for a novel answer to Mexican struggles and American fears. President George H. W. Bush and Canadian Prime Minister Brian Mulroney leapt at the opportunity presented by the Harvard-educated president of Mexico, Carlos Salinas, to mold a sweeping regional accord that covered trade in goods, services, and investments. They also planned for mechanisms to settle disputes when they arose. This NAFTA was quickly negotiated.

Brought before the Senate as a treaty NAFTA instantly sparked opposition. Labor unions feared manufacturing jobs would flee to Mexico. Indeed, in 1992, independent presidential candidate Ross Perot heard a "great sucking sound" from across the border that mercilessly absorbed US business and workers. Furthermore, environmentalists worried about Mexico escaping from strict US regulations on clean air and water. Democrats, moreover, largely opposed this free-trade accord as detrimental to their constituencies in the labor and environmental movements.

Like his predecessors the Democrat's president, Bill Clinton, advocated for NAFTA for economic and foreign policy reasons. He was a free trader who did not think America would lose manufacturing jobs but instead gain a lot of them. Clinton also thought that NAFTA would help the long-term stability of Mexico and the hemisphere and even curb immigration into the United States

---

2021 (accessed March 15, 2024); Shannon K. O'Neill, *The Globalization Myth: Why Regions Matter* (New Haven, CT: Yale University Press, 2022), 95–122; Eckes and Zeiler, *Globalization*, 224–8; Daniel Yergin and Joseph Stanislaw, *The Commanding Heights: The Battle Between Government and the Marketplace That Is Remaking the Modern World* (New York: Touchstone, 1999), 157–60, 169–91, 302–30; Baker, *The Politics*, 610.

by boosting the Mexican economy, anti-corruption efforts, and democracy. That is, with better prospects Mexicans would decide to stay in their country rather than flee from it.

Ronald Reagan and especially George H. W. Bush had projected a sweeping vision of a "united hemisphere" from Tierra del Fuego to Alaska. Not only would such a farsighted vista reshape investment strategy and boost confidence in the Mexican economy but it would transform geopolitics with a continental imagination, as the EU was doing in Europe.[27] For all of these presidents, North American regionalization was a stepping stone in the process of globalization.

The globalization lobby of business and free traders and, because they favored free trade, most Republicans joined Clinton in supporting NAFTA. American auto dealerships, banks, insurance companies, telecommunications outfits, and others in the service sector would benefit from the markets more easily accessed without the burden of costly border restrictions like tariffs. These lobbyists joined with neoliberal politicians to win the day.

NAFTA passed Congress in late 1994 and Clinton signed it. Most of its extravagant claims about creating tens of thousands of jobs did not materialize while immigrants also continued to flow northward. NAFTA did aid Mexico with factories called maquiladoras that expanded employment along the border. Furthermore, the association made it more acceptable for Washington to bail out Mexico from its debt crisis of 1995 with a $40 billion rescue loan. Mexican exports also flourished as did those from Canada, and the inflow of goods from both worsened the US trade deficit and took jobs away from Americans. Undeniably, though, US consumers benefited from cheap goods and services and NAFTA remained a bloc with great potential. The free-trade area amounted to a tremendous market of 407 million consumers by 2000 with $10 trillion in gross domestic product, though most of that largesse came from the United States.

The hope of stimulating a burgeoning middle class in Mexico persisted and was partly realized. In later years, American tourism to Mexico expanded and provided dollars to the country. The EU also felt compelled to negotiate with NAFTA nations or risk being shut out of the large North American market. This was, in short, the tough bargaining side of globalization. That is, global competitors now had to produce in the cheapest places and build supply chains and marketing networks that connected each of the world's three main economic regions: NAFTA, the EU, and ASEAN.[28]

***

---

[27]Baker, *The Politics*, 609.
[28]Clinton, *My Life*, 432; ds Eckes and Zeiler, *Globalization*, 231–5.

In a larger sense, globalizers believed that the way to promote prosperity, access to markets, protection of intellectual property, freedom (including capital movement and legal immigration), and democracy lay in a complete overhaul of the international trade system. The General Agreement on Tariffs and Trade dealt with a myriad of issues by moving beyond solely tariff negotiations though it still lacked authority as a trade forum, rather than a treaty, to deal with the increasing and complex array of problems that affected world trade, finance, and investment. In other words, GATT was inadequate for the globalizing economy.

During a difficult and protracted Uruguay Round of GATT from 1986 to 1994, negotiators proposed a new comprehensive institution to address a host of issues and oversee the global economy. This World Trade Organization (WTO) managed trade liberalization, rules on protective measures, dispute resolution, standards and coordination on everything from tariffs to copyrights, and development for a Global South that had long felt excluded from the GATT free-trade system.

The WTO eventually numbered 164 member states and 24 observer nations along with several intergovernmental institutions like the United Nations. As of 2025, only two dozen or so countries in the world remained outside of the WTO. It also became a symbol of the very essence of globalization under the leadership of the United States. This institution was poised to usher in an era of unified worldwide markets across sectors for developing

FIGURE 7.1. *WTO headquarters in Geneva, Switzerland. Courtesy of the World Trade Organization.*

and developed nations alike, harmonizing behavior, mediating politics, and pursuing democracy.

The WTO and its sister financial institutions, the International Monetary Fund, and the World Bank, provoked opposition but they also represented the new era of globalization that addressed mutual wealth, human rights, and democratic reform at the so-called end of history. In short, these bodies countered narrow-minded and divisive nationalism (like the second Nixon Shock) that had provoked hot and cold wars during the past century. While the internet empowered individuals in the globalized world, the WTO and IMF governed the world economy through the expertise of elite bureaucrats.

Many decried the power of these unelected leaders who found themselves under attack from activists, governments, and politicians running from left to right across the spectrum. Others protested the so-called neoliberal "Washington Consensus" under the IMF that granted aid and loans to nations in need on free-market terms. The neoliberals insisted on free trade, open markets, and austerity measures like cutting social spending as well as tax cuts to attract investors. The economic purposes of the globalization institutions, like the IMF and WTO, were to boost growth and reduce poverty, and they did that.

Despite its disruptive, unrelenting, and sometimes exploitative impact, globalization spread world governance and progressive norms that improved many lives, curbed abuses by authoritarian regimes, publicized reprehensible traditional practices like female genital mutilation, caste systems, and religious persecution, slowed environmental degradation, and promoted peace and democracy by reducing nationalism and encouraging interdependence among nations. This was a tall order—and an impressive list of accomplishments. Many nations and groups succeeded because free trade, free flows of investment, deregulation, and market competition raised living standards and global awareness.[29]

Globalization remained a powerful force even after the tragedy of 9/11 and the reassertion of the national security state. To be sure, globalized entities in business and finance turned to the nation-state rather than transnationals or multinational corporations to provide safe marketplaces. Safety, prosperity, and democracy required more than privatization and free trade. As historian David Landes notes, even Adam Smith, the guru of laissez-faire economics,

---

[29]Richard W. Mansbach, "Globalization: Love It or Loathe It?," in *Introducing Globalization*, 302, 305–6; William Greider, *One World, Ready or Not: The Manic Logic of Global Capitalism* (New York: Simon & Schuster, 1997), 11–25; Eckes and Zeiler, *Globalization*, 235–47; World Trade Organization, "Countries 2024," https://worldpopulationreview.com/country-rankings/wto-countries (accessed March 15, 2024).

believed that "the state can (will) do some things—defense, police—better than private enterprise."[30]

The craze over globalization ended in the early part of the millennium. The term no longer served as an idealistic, heady buzzword of the ages but was viewed, rather, as a process requiring pragmatic reform and even muzzling. Globalizers adopted intergovernmental cooperation, such as joint efforts to suppress terrorism and an assault on world poverty under the WTO that had been chastised by poor nations for not prioritizing their interests. Political leaders remained wedded to globalization; even denialists and nativists like Donald Trump had investments overseas.

Globalization also linked to geopolitical concerns. Encouraging Western unity in the war on terror in 2002, for instance, President George W. Bush told the French president, Jacques Chirac, that "globalization in trade has to go hand in hand with globalization of solidarity." Seven years later, President Barack Obama thought beyond economics by asserting that even the military surge of troops in Afghanistan in 2009 would indirectly make the world safe for globalization by raising living standards and reducing the cost of goods in the country, thereby "bringing the world closer together."[31]

In the first quarter of the new century, leaders were more attuned to principles that spoke to justice and opportunity as well as order and wealth, no matter if these norms served American hegemonic interests. George W. Bush believed fervently that "our economy, our security, and our culture would all be weakened by an attempt to wall ourselves off from the world." Thus, "Americans should never fear competition" through free trade.[32] As President Obama wrote in 2020, in the opening pages of his memoirs, nations had a choice in dealing with "the relentless march toward an interconnected world, one in which peoples and cultures can't help but collide." They could "learn to live together" in a world "of global supply chains, instantaneous capital transfers, social media, transnational terrorist networks, climate change, mass migration, and ever-increasing complexity," or they "will perish."[33]

This was a warning and a hope, perhaps even a faith, in the good of globalization. Many economists saw globalization here to stay, for there was no putting back together the Humpty-Dumpty of the previous non-globalized era of the government-heavy regulatory state. Besides, the United States was

---

[30]David S. Landes, *The Wealth and Poverty of Nations: Why Some Are So Rich and Some So Poor* (New York: W.W. Norton & Company, 1999), 520.
[31]Zeiler, *Capitalist Peace*, 253, 261.
[32]Bush, *Decision Points*, 306. See also Andrew J. Bacevich, *American Empire: The Realities and Consequences of U.S. Diplomacy* (Cambridge, MA: Harvard University Press, 2002), 217–8.
[33]Barack Obama, *A Promised Land* (New York: Crown, 2020), xvi. See also Eckes and Zeiler, *Globalization*, 238, 259.

a winner from the process of globalization and like the rest of the world, largely a loser from economic nationalism. Even more than benefits globalization seemed to have reversed America's much-touted decline.

Declinism was proved wrong. Donald Trump pushed to make America great again by nationalism while progressives argued for ending free-trade globalization and overhauling the entire world economic system. Despite the polls that showed most Americans just as pessimistic the globalizers held that like Mark Twain, the reported death of the American-led neoliberal ethic itself was much exaggerated. They even spoke of a renewed and even the American Century.[34] What Richard Nixon wrought in 1971 history modified into a positive force for interdependence and harmony—at least in theory, with much grounding in reality, and even more potential in the future.

---

[34] Edward Goldberg, *Why Globalization Works for America: How Nationalist Trade Policies are Destroying Our Country* (Sterling, VA: Potomac Books, 2020), 43–66, 155–80; Joseph S. Nye, Jr., "Is the American Century Over?," *Political Science Quarterly* 130, no. 3 (Fall 2015): 393–400.

8

Trade War

On September 21, 1971, Richard Nixon invoked the Trading with the Enemy Act of 1917 against the closest of allies, and a dependent one at that—Japan. The Trading with the Enemy Act gave the president authority to regulate international transactions in a declared national emergency. As its title indicated, resorting to economic warfare was directed at wartime enemies like Germany in the First and Second World Wars. That a state of emergency existed regarding Japanese textile exports seemed absurd.

Nixon's threat was also hypocritical. He was no protectionist, and he supported Japan's stability by allowing the country to prosper through exports to the United States. He was also a cold warrior who cherished the close US-Japan relationship and the Western alliance in Asia on which Japan depended. Strong-arming Japan just did not make sense—except, that is, in a political sense. Protectionism was often good politics, and as in the China and economic Shocks that preceded this one, an electoral strategy guided Nixon's actions.

***

This third Nixon Shock anticipated an America First approach of later years. Of course, the economic Shock had indicated his willingness to truck with nationalism. Nixon had encouraged the "overwhelming majority of Americans who buy American-made products in America" not to worry about his measures.[1] Yet the economic Shock had inadvertently led to globalization. This trade Shock against Japan paved the way for an eventual backlash against that very process. This culminated in the nationalist-populism that captured the Republican Party a half century later, though the fracturing of the United

---

[1] Address to the Nation Outlining a New Economic Policy: "The Challenge of Peace," The American Presidency Project, August 15, 1971, https://www.presidency.ucsb.edu/documents/address-the-nation-outlining-new-economic-policy-the-challenge-peace (accessed April 18, 2024).

States itself in ways that undercut liberalism and globalization had already appeared at the end of the American Century.[2] Nixon sowed the divisiveness, and so did a few of his successors in the White House.

***

The crisis with Japan arose from two major changes at the end of the American Century. The first was disenchantment with free-trade policies, especially within the labor movement. Growing opposition to imports as supposed giveaways to foreign producers led to protectionist opposition by contingents of both political parties—progressives and midwestern populists among the Democrats and southern textile manufacturers who supported Republicans. They doubted that low tariffs (free trade) created jobs, consumer satisfaction, higher standards, more democracy, less bureaucracy, and a peaceful world.

In particular, the Kennedy Round of GATT from 1964 to 1967, which cut industrial tariffs to next to nothing, spurred a backlash to trade liberalization at home by the election year of 1968. Exporters complained that they still did not get enough access to markets abroad, especially in the new rival European Economic Community's agricultural markets. As spending on the Great Society, the Vietnam War, and aid commitments around the world stoked inflation, the overheated economy spurred a demand for imports. By the late 1960s, though the United States still ran a trade surplus, it was sinking fast.

A rash of import quota bills in 1968 and organized labor's nascent defection from the postwar free-trade coalition signaled the uprising by protectionists against a generation of Washington's free-trade leadership since the Roosevelt years. Even if questionable as economic policy, protectionism was oftentimes good politics. Progressive Democrats joined many Republicans in calling for fair, not free trade by complaining how Americans, in the words of Connecticut moderate internationalist Abraham Ribicoff, had gotten "screwed" at the Kennedy Round. While President Lyndon Johnson might denounce the protectionists, the legacy he left in the trade arena was one of rebellion everywhere against the postwar order of free-trade law and practice. Even his vice president, Hubert Humphrey, the Democratic nominee who contested Nixon in the 1968 election, sought to curb competitively harmful imports in the vulnerable auto and textile industries. Nixon engaged these protectionist rebels as well.[3]

A key component of his campaign focused on winning the South, which was a traditional Democratic stronghold. Nixon skillfully played the trade card there

---

[2] Daniel T. Rodgers, *Age of Fracture* (Cambridge, MA: Harvard University Press, 2011), 1–14.
[3] Zeiler, *Capitalist Peace*, 167, also 164–70; Jagdish Bhagwati, *Protectionism* (Cambridge, MA: The MIT Press, 1989), 43–59; Tim Lang and Colin Hines, *The New Protectionism: Protecting the Future Against Free Trade* (New York: The New Press, 1993), 33–57, 73–114.

alongside other elements of his so-called "Southern Strategy" that included a slowdown on civil rights under a banner of law and order. He needed an answer to the populist threat from former Alabama governor George Wallace, an independent seeking white middle-class conservative, racist, and working-class voters who could take support away from Nixon throughout the country.

These groups related to Archie Bunker, the main character of the popular sitcom, "All in the Family," that debuted in January 1971. A bigoted, xenophobic lower-middle-class stiff in the Queens borough of New York City, this paragon of the end of the American Century struggled against the market dictates of educated elites. Liberals understood the satire, but Archie expressed the frustrations of many average Americans, in the Midwest and South as well as the Northeast. Said one worker, "You think it, but ole Archie he says it, by damn."[4] Nixon saw an opportunity to wean blue-collar voters from the Democrats and perhaps turn the South toward his own party (indeed, the region became a bastion for the Republicans from the 1980s onward) by an emphasis on trade protectionism.

The key to this approach lay with the powerful senator from South Carolina, Strom Thurmond. The American textile (cotton, woolen, and synthetic apparel) industry comprised one-eighth of all manufacturing labor in the country, employing 2.4 million workers in mills and factories across the United States and particularly concentrated in the South. In that region its dominion lay in the Carolinas, which made Thurmond a major political force. He had left the Democratic Party in 1948 to run as a Dixiecrat who opposed Truman's civil rights measures and then he joined the Republican Party in 1964. Thurmond cared about slowing civil rights and supporting the textile industry, which accounted for 40 percent of South Carolina's industrial jobs even though the state had low wages and was historically hostile to unions.

The Senator demanded import restraints on Japanese textiles that threatened employment and employers in his state. If Nixon adopted textile protectionism, Thurmond pledged in return to head off Republicans in the primaries and convention of 1968 from endorsing the upstart governor from California, Ronald Reagan. He could also help contain George Wallace in the general election.

Nixon eagerly took that deal and Thurmond made good on his promise. The Senator convinced the American Textile Manufacturers Institute, a powerhouse lobby with access to politicians and government policies, to donate to Nixon's campaign. Having prevailed in the Republican primaries, Nixon the presidential candidate then blamed Democrats for not protecting

---

[4]Patterson, *Grand Expectations*, 740. See also Judith Stein, *Pivotal Decade: How the United States Traded Factories for Finance in the Seventies* (New Haven, CT: Yale University Press, 2010), 32–9.

the industry from predatory import competition. Wallace won most of the Deep South in the 1968 general election though Nixon picked off the Carolinas.

Once in office President Nixon hoped to keep disaffected white southerners in his camp and he needed Thurmond's help in doing so. Thurmond had helped "make" Nixon in 1968 and he could just as well destroy him in 1972, at least in the South. He could also hurt Nixon on the Vietnam War, which he supported—for now. Also up for reelection in 1972 the Senator again demanded that the President deliver on textile trade protectionism. So did the powerful Wilbur Mills, the Democratic chairman of the pivotal House Ways and Means Committee who warned that unless Nixon acted quickly, the congressman would push a textile import quota bill through Congress. Mills had already proposed quotas on textiles and shoes. He was the dominant Democrat on Capitol Hill and also a political rival to Nixon, with aspirations for the presidency.

Once again, Nixon acted on the politics of trade in his Southern Strategy. He succeeded. In 1972, he captured 70 percent of the votes in the region, a percentage equal to his and Wallace's total in 1968.[5]

Nixon endorsed freer trade but the politician in him oftentimes overwhelmed his internationalism when it came to trade. During his presidency he shied from big multilateral rounds of tariff-cutting under the GATT rubric though he would send legislation to Congress to engage in negotiations in the Tokyo Round beginning in 1974. He preferred bilateral deals to advantage US producers and workers and when it came to two-way trade, Japan became his main target.

Tokyo seemed a perfect scapegoat for the international monetary mess and runs on the dollar, the declining US trade surplus that would soon fall into deficit, inflation at home, and any tensions over a détente strategy predicated on opening to China. Furthermore, memories endured of Japan's devious surprise attack on American soil at Pearl Harbor on December 7, 1941, that precipitated the United States' entry into the Second World War. That Japanese Prime Minister Eisaku Sato failed to deliver textile quotas over nearly three years of negotiations made Nixon resentful of Japan; he took this textile trade wrangle personally.

On trade/textiles and finance Nixon saw the Japanese as arrogant and stubborn, especially toward an American ally that had been so generous in

---

[5] I.M. Destler, Haruhiro Fukui, and Hideo Sato, *The Textile Wrangle: Conflict in Japanese-American Relations, 1969–1971* (Ithaca, NY: Cornell University Press, 1979), 56, 58–9; Earl Black and Merle Black, *The Rise of Southern Republicans* (Cambridge, MA: Harvard University Press, 2002), 32–4; Joseph A. Fry, *The American South and the Vietnam War: Belligerence, Protest, and Agony in Dixie* (Lexington, KY: University Press of Kentucky, 2015), 260; Matusow, *Nixon's Economy*, 120; John Egerton, *The Americanization of Dixie: The Southernization of America* (New York: Harper's Magazine Press, 1974), 130; Schaller, *Altered States*, 216.

the postwar years. Henry Kissinger conveyed even more contempt by once denigrating the proud Japanese as "little Sony salesmen" with no long-term vision or grand philosophy in international affairs. Unlike Chinese leaders like Zhou Enlai the Japanese were supposedly "prosaic, obtuse, unworthy of his sustained attention," carped Kissinger, and he wondered if they were even critical to US national security. Launching volleys of nationalistic diatribes and policies against Japan seemed a sure bet politically for an administration focused on the 1972 elections.[6]

***

Relatedly, the second change the Nixon administration faced at the end of the American Century addressed bilateral foreign policy and geopolitical strategy with Japan, the closest of allies. Ever since he had served as vice president to Eisenhower and then as a representative of Pepsi-Cola and other companies in the 1950s, Nixon's relationship with Japan was positive and comfortable. Visiting the country frequently confirmed for him that defending Tokyo against communist China's regional ambitions was paramount. He even decried the limits on Japan's rearmament built into its constitution before America ended its occupation of its former enemy in 1951.

Once in the Oval Office Nixon sought a reassessment of policy toward Japan, particularly regarding the island of Okinawa that the United States had occupied with military bases since the Second World War. He hoped to return this largest island in the Ryukyus chain to defuse rising criticism of American rule; indeed, much of Okinawan population disliked the US presence there. The nation had also experienced two atomic bombs and suffered from a "nuclear allergy" in which just 12 percent of Japanese felt safe because of the US nuclear "umbrella." They wanted these weapons banished from Japan and Nixon was willing to oblige. Nonetheless, the political stresses might lead to the loss of all US bases in the country, a dangerous possibility because they were used to defend Taiwan, South Korea, and South Vietnam from aggressors in the region.

In return for handing over Okinawa, Washington insisted on treaty rights to retain the bases there, as the US military insisted. And regarding removal of its nuclear arsenal the administration sought an option that gave Washington the freedom to reintroduce them in an emergency. These were all sensitive issues for Prime Minister Sato and the Japanese Diet (parliament), and for Nixon, the US military, and Congress particularly, because the Americans aimed to keep their security commitments in Asia and the Pacific despite the pullout of troops from Vietnam. By 1969, the United States had already returned thirty-

---

[6]Schaller, *Altered States*, 212, also 211. See also Zeiler, *Capitalist Peace*, 170; Destler, *Textile Wrangle*, 7.

two bases to Japan while holding on to ninety-eight installations. It was no surprise that some 2,400 street protests erupted that year alone against the US military presence.

In sum, Washington wanted operational control over its bases but would accept limited Japanese oversight. For its part, Japan wanted its sovereignty restored over Okinawa, the right to impose conditions on the use of bases, and the WMDs removed—though the United States could use them for regional security. Nixon invited Prime Minister Sato to Washington to discuss the deal in November 1969. Sato's prime focus was on Okinawa so he was eager to talk with the President.

Running underneath their discussions was an insistence that American allies must share the burden of their common defense, including financing it. Japan argued that its exports and trade surplus with the United States were instrumental to generating the revenue to meet this commitment. The problem, however, was that American industries and their legislators clamored for protection against this surge of imports from Japan. That is where economics met politics and where textiles entered the picture of the Okinawa treaty discussions.[7]

***

The linkage of textile exports to Okinawa reversion provoked anger, hostility, consternation, and confusion within and between the two nations. Agreement hinged on Japan's willingness to tighten restrictions on its textile exports. Sato, however, had as much domestic pressure on him as Nixon faced from Thurmond and Mills. Japanese producers and their political representatives insisted on expanding sales abroad while the Americans, conversely, wanted to protect their markets. By the Nixon years Japan accounted for roughly 15 percent of total US imports and America absorbed nearly one-third of all Japanese exports to the tune of $7.3 billion by 1971. Most of these exports from Japan were manufactured goods, such as textiles, steel, electronics, and, increasingly, automobiles.

Statistics told only part of the story. In 1961, Japan had bent to pressure and instituted voluntary export restraints on cotton textiles sent to the United States. Yet Japan was a different country a decade later. Postwar guilt and repentance had largely given way to a new confidence and self-respect due in large part to spectacular economic achievements. For Japan textiles were an expression of a new nationalism celebrated by the press and politicians. In short, the country resolved to stand up to Washington's demands.[8] Tokyo

---

[7]Schaller, *Altered. States*, 213–5; Walter LaFeber, *The Clash* (New York: W.W. Norton & Company, 1997), 348–50; Herring, *The American Century*, 485.
[8]Destler et al., *The Textile Wrangle*, 87.

wanted Okinawa returned and its textile exports multiplied in the coming years.

By the end of 1971, the ballooning US balance-of-payments deficit (higher expenditures than revenues from trade, aid, investments, and tourism) reached negative $29 billion, worsened by America's first trade deficit in a century of $2.27 billion. That is, imports exceeded US exports for the first time since 1893. Japan accounted for $1 billion of that deficit in 1969 and by 1971, its contribution to the shortfall swelled to $3.2 billion on a bilateral trade of nearly $11.5 billion. Japan had penetrated the US market and its success incited outcries.

The structure, not just the size, of the trade deficit also bothered Americans. They saw industries like televisions, steel, and shoes driven to extinction by foreign competition like radios had experienced years before. In addition, US exports to Japan did not enjoy the reciprocal access that the Japanese had in American markets even though Japan was America's second biggest purchaser of export goods after Canada. The United States exported mostly capital goods not made in Japan and also unprocessed food and industrial raw materials. These were cheaper products than the manufactured ones Japan sent to America—thus, the US trade deficit. These terms of trade amounted to a total US export balance of $4.1 billion as contrasted to Japan's whopping $7.3 billion in exports solely to the United States.

American business, politicians, and experts blamed the deficit imbalance on collusion by Japanese politicians, bureaucrats, and elite producers who they ominously nicknamed "Japan, Inc." This supposed predatory juggernaut threatened the US economy and perhaps American society itself. It was easy to take play on the image of wartime Japan; US politicians exploited the memory of the imperial marauder responsible for the lives of so many Americans, not to mention the dastardly secretive attack on Pearl Harbor.

Tokyo also served as a scapegoat for deeper failings. Although there were complaints about the trade deficit with Canada and an impending one with the European Community few voices reached such a fever pitch against them like Japan provoked. And while Japan might have a heavy-handed bureaucracy the country also supported an educational system that graduated more high-tech engineers than the United States, invested much more in productivity, and encouraged a cooperative labor force. Even the nationalist Treasury Secretary John Connally admitted that America's relative decline could not be completely blamed on foreigners. "The simple fact is that in many areas other nations are out-producing us, out-thinking us, and out-trading us," and he grudgingly singled out the Japanese. They were "more industrious than we are, and they work harder than we do, they save more than we do" as well.[9] Some even called on Tokyo to teach the United States a thing or two about modernization and management styles though few believed rigid and interwoven Japanese business culture could be transferred to US soil.

There was also a darker nationalistic side to the criticism. Tokyo's rapacious image remained, complemented by mysterious behavior indecipherable to Westerners that encouraged lurid, even paranoid explanations. The more belligerent, sensationalist, and occasionally racist views voiced even by respected mainstream publications like *Time* magazine argued that Japan's "Oriental history and psychology" dictated its mighty industrial economy. In the words of Maurice Stans, Nixon's secretary of commerce and a major protagonist in the looming textile trade war, this outlook had converted Japan's "shooting war" at Pearl Harbor to an "economic war" thirty years later. Connally expressed similar views in May 1971 during the buildup to the monetary Shock by charging that the "Japanese are still fighting the war, only now instead of a shooting war, it is an economic war." They seek to "dominate the Pacific" in the short-run and "and then perhaps the world."[10]

American consumers were actually part of the problem because they wanted Japanese imports. On the other hand, pundits and politicos zeroed in on Japanese trade and domestic policies. They increasingly called Japan's unfair exporting practices abroad, protection of its home market, and monolithic trade structure orchestrated by the impenetrable Ministry of International Trade and Industry (MITI) a "business invasion" of the United States.

In the more moderate assessment of a widely circulated report, "The United States in the Changing World Economy," issued by Nixon's chief economic advisor, Peter Peterson, "the structure of Japanese foreign trade, the practices which regulate it and its asymmetrical distribution have contributed to major imbalances in Japanese international economic relations." The Japan of 1971 was "impressively different" from the Japan of 1951 at the end of the US Occupation. Above all, the Western nations of Europe and North America could not simply turn their backs on Japan and undercut its economic viability. Doing so would destroy the Free World. Unlike the Europeans, though, the Japanese had not accepted an increasing share of responsibility for maintaining the Western alliances' security and economic order. Nor had Japan opened its markets to suppliers from around the world, which was an expected course for a nation that had recovered from the war and had grown so strong.[11]

---

[9]Matusow, *Nixon's Economy*, 135. See also William Bywater, "Letters to the Editor: Damage From Trade Deficits," *New York Times*, February 19, 1972, 30.
[10]Schaller, *Altered States*, 232, also 231; Zeiler, *Capitalist Peace*, 172; Matusow, *Nixon's Economy*, 135.
[11]Peterson, *The United States in the Changing World Economy*, iii, 4, 10, 25–6.

Much of this unbalanced trade pattern was by design due to Cold War imperatives. To help Japan rebuild in the postwar years into an economically stable and politically reliable ally, Washington had long accepted that US markets must be sacrificed to Japanese exports. That had been acceptable when Japan was not so competitive but as early as the mid-1950s some US producers (the textile industry, for one) had begun complaining about these imports. Their protests intensified in the next decade.

Combined with the US payments deficit that was compounded by Vietnam War and overseas aid spending, a Bretton Woods monetary system that allowed for nations like Japan to undervalue their currencies and thus compete even more effectively with cheap exports, and rising inflation at home Nixon felt compelled to act. Japan served as a somewhat deserving foil and also as a scapegoat for American problems that placed domestic politics front and center. Nixon's demand was simple: he wanted Japanese textile export restraints before he agreed to hand over the island of Okinawa.

***

The textile wrangle consumed two presidential summit conferences, two top-level ministerial meetings, and nine separate negotiations over three years. In March 1969 the President appointed Commerce Secretary Stans to lead the talks. He had been Nixon's campaign finance director in 1968 so he knew the importance of fulfilling political promises. Stans determined to reassert the power of the Commerce Department that had waned since Herbert Hoover's leadership in the 1920s. For his part Nixon cared less about Okinawa than he did about satisfying Strom Thurmond and the textile industry; he tapped Stans to deliver the Senator. The Secretary decided to visit Tokyo and "lay down the law" to Prime Minister Sato and the Japanese textile industry by demanding their "unconditional surrender."[12]

Off Stans went in May 1969 to Tokyo, where he received a frosty reception. Japan's foreign ministry wanted negotiations on textiles delayed pending a resolution on Okinawa. Meanwhile, manufacturers and MITI officials scoffed at complaints that Japan's 1 percent of the US synthetic (nylons, acrylics, polyesters) textile market justified export quotas. Indeed, foreign man-made textiles accounted for only 4.2 percent of American consumption. Furthermore, export quotas on cotton goods had been in place for nearly a decade. Labor-intensive factories specializing in inexpensive sweaters and children's clothing in the United States might justifiably claim injury but that was a narrow part of the industry. The Japanese were willing to negotiate on that specific sector

---

[12]Schaller, *Altered States*, 216. See also Destler et al., *The Textile Wrangle*, 44–5.

but they would not agree to voluntary quotas across the board. Japan's resolve stiffened. American manufacturers wanted comprehensive coverage, though, and they pressured Nixon. Negotiations hit an impasse.

Japan's media grew even more resistant by calling on Sato to stand up to Stans and end Japan's postwar subservience. Contrary to Nixon the Prime Minister cared less about textiles than about retrieving Okinawa. Nonetheless, he was known for being fervently anticommunist and pro-American, a leader who appreciated US friendship and consistently upheld the bilateral military alliance. Sato was also a realist in domestic politics, being nationalist enough to respond to growing public pressure on the reversion of the Ryukyus.

Stans left Japan complaining about his rude treatment and stunned by the "un-Japanese" reception. He had expected some resistance before submission but he got a lot of the former and not an ounce of the latter. The Japanese called him vulgar. Tokyo believed it demeaning to make concessions to unreasonable US demands.

For the rest of the year neither MITI nor Commerce could even agree on how to measure Japanese exports much less come up with the beginnings of a compromise. Tokyo finally assented to talks under GATT rules in Geneva to save face. Officials wanted to avoid a total breakdown that might poison the upcoming Nixon-Sato summit of November 1969.[13]

Henry Kissinger, the national security advisor who cared little about the Japanese and the "low politics" of economics, now intervened behind the scenes. Tokyo preferred this method of secret back-channel negotiations, so when Nixon told Kissinger to get a deal done before the summit there was hope for a resolution of the textile wrangle. Quietly consulting with Japan's go-between, a "Mr. Yoshida" who was one of Sato's friends, Kissinger hammered out a tentative deal a few months before the summit. They agreed that progress must be made on textile export restraints through self-imposed quotas by the Japanese for five years in return for Nixon's public announcement on Okinawa reversion. Sato rushed to embrace the agreement by not even informing MITI or Japanese textile manufacturers.

Excluding Japanese producers caused the quick demise of the Kissinger-Yoshida deal. Just two days before Sato arrived in Washington Mr. Yoshida frantically informed Kissinger that there could be no announcement of a textile export quota at the summit. A textile deal was off the table though a security agreement salvaged the remnants of a bilateral accord. In it, the United States would withdraw nuclear weapons from Okinawa with the proviso that they could be reintroduced in an emergency. This just required Sato's sign-off.

---

[13]Destler et al., *The Textile Wrangle*, 94, also 40, 88–95. See also Matusow, *Nixon's Economy*, 120–2.

The summit beginning November 19, 1969, included an agreement on the reversion of Okinawa to Japan by 1972. Indeed, the Senate voted for a treaty, and the United States turned over Okinawa on May 15, 1972. The Americans retained military bases in the Ryukyus to defend the region, and Nixon acknowledged the Japanese people's anti-nuclear sentiment by withdrawing these weapons of mass destruction. Sato signed the emergency reintroduction agreement that the American military desired in case of a crisis.

The President also asked Sato to meet with Kissinger and him in a room off the Oval Office, out of view, to discuss textiles. The American public, Congress, and the Pentagon had accused Nixon of a giveaway on Okinawa. Fully cognizant of the political ramifications of this view, Nixon asked Sato for compensation by an official agreement on textile export restraints based on the informal promise of Mr. Yoshida. Sato pledged to do his best to get such an agreement once he returned home. Kissinger and Nixon believed Sato had made a clear, firm, and definite commitment. The President and the Prime Minister shook on a deal that Nixon took as done but that Sato believed was still fluid.

The Prime Minister went back to Tokyo, triumphant over the fact that he had rid Japan of the foreign occupier through the Okinawa agreement. He did not possess the courage to admit, however, that he had made a deal on textiles. Thus, he reneged on his promise to Nixon to convince Japanese producers to accept voluntary export restraints.

Sato definitely knew he had agreed to a deal with Nixon and for the rest of his time in office he tried to fulfill it. At the same time, he also tried to conceal it for domestic political reasons. Sato actually had much more pressure on him at home regarding textiles than Nixon did. In any case, using the momentum of the summit deal, he called a snap election and stormed to victory at home. Convinced that the Okinawa agreement would bring Japan out of its isolationist shell and into world responsibility, Nixon soon realized his mistake of trusting the wily Sato's vague promise on textiles.[14]

***

The textile trade war plummeted downhill from there. The five-year accord on textile export restraints hammered out between Kissinger and Mr. Yoshida was sent to Geneva in early 1970 to provide cover for Sato that he had sold out the Japanese industry for the return of Okinawa. Mr. Yoshida assured Kissinger that Sato would honor the textile deal under the multilateral GATT rubric in Geneva and thus agree to Maurice Stans' tough terms on restraints. Still, Sato

---

[14]Destler et al., *The Textile Wrangle*, 121–49.

FIGURE 8.1 *Nixon welcomes Prime Minister Eisaku Sato to Washington, DC for US-Japan summit talks. Courtesy Richard M. Nixon Presidential Library and Museum (National Archives and Records Administration.*

could not acknowledge it had been part of the summit accord with Nixon. Nobody in Japan—not manufacturers, MITI officials, nor Japan's ambassador to the United States—would fess up to an agreement. As a result, when the State Department presented the rather harsh terms in Geneva, the Japanese rebuffed them. That answer confused and disappointed American diplomats, who had been kept in the dark by Kissinger and Nixon.

Despite attempts to break the logjam by emissaries from the United States, like Nixon's friend and free-trade lobbyist Donald Kendall of Pepsi-Cola, American protectionists now got the upper hand. The Japanese tried to assuage Washington with modest proposals of selective export controls but Stans had reached "the end of the line."[15] He issued an ultimatum that either Tokyo accept the quotas as previously agreed to or Nixon would turn the matter over to a Congress chafing to impose import restraints. Stans argued, correctly, that trade policy had been guided by geopolitical and military factors that subordinated economic and financial considerations. Now he put Congress on notice to reverse course by elevating the economics and politics of textile trade over foreign policy.

Indeed, Congress signaled a green light on protectionism. Senator Thurmond suggested that Nixon not turn over Okinawa until Japan met American demands. Then in April 1970, Chairman Mills of the Ways and Means Committee introduced a quota bill on both textiles and footwear, though it exempted nations that voluntarily limited their exports. Mills really did not want quotas but he backed himself into a corner by pledging to limit textiles. Nixon, too, preferred voluntary compliance, particularly because he feared that in the eyes of voters, Congress would share credit with him for taking care of the industry and that would undermine his reelection strategy. He was already in a bad mood about the domestic outrage over his recent secret bombing of Cambodia. Japanese textiles seemed a symptom of stormy weather hovering over his domestic political standing.

Stans then tried his own hand at diplomacy. He worked through a business contact to the MITI minister, Kiichi Miyazawa, who was an English-speaking expert on economic affairs allied closely to Sato. Miyazawa offered a one-year export restraint plan that at least met Nixon's political requirements. Intrigued, the secretary of commerce insisted on the original five-year timetable. He invited Miyazawa to his Watergate apartment decorated with big-game trophies that Stans had shot on safari. The Japanese minister considered dead animals unclean; when Stans served lunch amid his trophies the mood deteriorated. Things got worse when Stans pulled from his pocket a supposed "Sato memo" from the 1969 summit that pledged export controls. This ploy humiliated Miyazawa who knew nothing of such a document. He bolted from Washington, receiving a hero's welcome back home for standing up to the Americans—a first in Japan's new postwar independent foreign policy posture.

---

[15]Destler et al., *The Textile Wrangle*, 178.

Nixon both backed down and grew angrier. When Miyazawa refused to negotiate with Stans ever again Nixon, worried about US-Japan relations, replaced him as his chief textile negotiator. In Stans place stepped White House aide Peter Flanigan, an assertive loyalist close to the American business community who was more amenable to compromise. He drafted a three-year deal hinged to the growth in the US textile market; should that market expand so could imports from Japan.

But Nixon had also sent Stans to Congress where Chairman Mills' draft quota law to reduce textile imports 40 percent below their 1969 level unless Japan voluntarily restricted its exports awaited. The President then imposed limits on Japanese television imports as a veiled threat that more constraints were pending. The good cop/bad cop routine seemed to work. In late October 1970, when Nixon and Sato met again, the Prime Minister agreed to settle the dispute along Flanigan's terms. Once again, though, Sato had left his textile industry in the dark. Upon his return to Tokyo leaders rejected voluntary export controls.[16]

Nixon was beside himself. The textile wrangle had gotten out of hand, seeping into domestic politics and the high politics of diplomacy. The 1970 midterm elections had not gone well for Republicans who lost seats in Congress. So, Nixon endorsed passage of Mills' quota bill in mid-November and promised to call Congress into a special session when some senators balked at the legislation. By the Christmas break, however, the Senate killed the textile bill. In January 1971, Flanigan received a compromise plan from Japan but two months later Nixon renewed his call for stringent export restraints. He called the entire textile fiasco "the Jap betrayal" that made him look weak and foolish.

Just as bad for Nixon, Congressman Mills negotiated a voluntary textile restraint accord with Japanese textile industry representatives who preferred to remove the matter from the clutches of bureaucrats and let the private sector solve it. The press proclaimed this deal as a grand achievement for presidential hopeful Wilbur Mills and Nixon responded in fury. In his eyes, Sato had failed to deliver on two promises and to boot, then inadvertently boosted the reputation of Mills, a potential Democratic rival in the 1972 presidential campaign. The President denounced the Japanese industry plan and appointed a new negotiating team headed by aide Peter Peterson and David Kennedy, a former secretary of the Treasury. Unfortunately, the agreement on Okinawa, due for Senate consideration, now intruded on the textile tug of war.

---

[16]Destler et al., *The Textile Wrangle*, 240, 158–222.

Senator J. William Fulbright, the powerhouse chair of the Foreign Relations Committee, insisted that any accord on Okinawa's reversion be submitted to Congress as a treaty. Nixon agreed. So did Strom Thurmond, who in June 1971 linked the impending signing of the Okinawa treaty to textiles. He wanted a quid pro quo. President Nixon actually took the higher road of national security by separating textiles from Okinawa. Nonetheless, he was not unhappy with Thurmond's remarks that both issues were interrelated and that America was doing Japan a big favor on the Ryukyus. He liked the pressure on Sato because he was growing frantic over the textile impasse as the 1972 election approached. Mills and Thurmond were watching.[17]

***

The textile tussle took an even more severe turn by July 1971. After Nixon rejected the industry proposal Sato reshuffled his cabinet, naming two presumptive successors to work on a solution from their perches as foreign minister and MITI minister. He signaled a willingness to conclude the squabble but then the President kicked in the door of resistance entirely. His twin Nixon Shocks stunned Japan. By opening the door to China and cutting the dollar loose from gold and demanding yen revaluation he disregarded Japanese sensibilities and interests.

Nixon relished the impact on Japan. Indeed, when Sato was notified minutes before Nixon's shocking demand on August 15 for Japan to revalue its yen the Japanese leader shook his head. He was heard to mutter "not again"—reference also to the first Nixon Shock when Tokyo listened in disbelief to the news that the President would visit Beijing.[18] Nixon now expected an imminent resolution on textiles. David Kennedy, who had much experience with Japanese officials and businessmen, negotiated with the Japanese through the summer.

Amazingly, no progress ensued. Nixon grew apoplectic. Kennedy told him the future of trade policy with Asians and Europeans hinged on a textile deal and he well knew that not only was his Southern Strategy in jeopardy heading into the election year of 1972 but so was his reputation as an effective leader. Peterson warned him that without an agreement US textile producers would turn to Mills for restrictions. The congressman then might win Democratic primaries and oppose Nixon in the upcoming election. And there was the novel trade deficit and persistent payments problems. Something had to be done to stop the bleeding of dollars overseas, Japanese trade advantages, and Nixon's worrisome political fortunes at home.[19]

---

[17]Destler et al., *The Textile Wrangle*, 223–74.
[18]Matusow, *Nixon's Economy*, 168.
[19]Destler et al., *The Textile Wrangle*, 275–94.

At cabinet-level economics meetings in Williamsburg, Virginia in September 1971 the Japanese and Americans talked past each other on textiles. The Japanese stated that both the import surcharge of the economic Shock and the threatened textile quotes were "totally barbarian." In fact, Tokyo countered that if Nixon did not immediately end the surcharge Japan would end its modest general export restraint policy begun a few months earlier. This despite even a friendly State Department warning to Tokyo that export limits were needed to bring the global balance of payments into equilibrium. It was clear there was a widening gulf between Tokyo and Washington over a host of issues—China, Taiwan, textiles, and even the final push toward Senate approval of Okinawa reversion. Things might get nasty in the months to come. Nixon might become an "undependable, capricious, and utterly inscrutable ally," warned the respected commentators, Rowland Evans and Robert Novak.[20]

***

Political rivals in Japan questioned the need for export restraints though they agreed to reopen textile talks especially after David Kennedy warned that without a signed agreement by October 15 President Nixon would impose unilateral quotas under the authority of the Trading with the Enemy Act. The new MITI minister and expert in both bureaucratic and party politics, Kakuei Tanaka, planned secret negotiations to deliver Sato's twice-pronounced promises. He would try to extract concessions from the Americans and then make a show of bowing to their overwhelming pressure. Kennedy told Nixon of the pending deal, contextualized in the usual theater of fist-banging and anger by the Japanese.

The unprecedented possible resort to the Trading with the Enemy Act, however, leaked to the press. American newspapers called this strong-arming a sad day in a downward spiral of relations with a close ally. Nixon placated the critics in part by sending the Okinawa treaty to the Senate on September 21 with a message that discouraged the linkage to textiles. He and his wife also met Emperor Hirohito in Alaska a week later in a historic event for a sitting president. He hoped to smooth relations between these two postwar friends.

Meanwhile, Tanaka expended every effort to win approval from the Japanese textile lobby for voluntary textile export restraints. After promising them aid to compensate for lost business, the most powerful Japanese federation relented and accepted the deal. Industry leaders also insisted that

---

[20]Rowland Evans and Robert Novak, "Tokyo Finds U.S. Inscrutable," *New York Times*, September 30, 1971, A19.

the import surcharge from the second Nixon Shock end; the President soon obliged. Just hours before the Trading with the Enemy Act quotas were to be imposed Kennedy and Tanaka initialed the agreement on October 15 to limit wool and synthetic textiles exports for three years and factor in annual market growth in export quotas thereafter.[21]

The pact actually allowed the Japanese to double their exports in the first year but Nixon and US producers hailed the agreement as a victory. Economic advisor Peter Peterson put on a good face by arguing that the accord prevented permanent walls of protection and showed that "competitors in the free world can cooperatively work out their differences." The Japanese disagreed, saying they would not forget the "bad, very bad" treatment and that the compulsory (read) voluntary export restraints came at a cost to America's long-term foreign policy interests. Japan soon found itself outcompeted by other Asian nations who could produce textiles more cheaply yet the immediate damage was considerable. Editorials in the major newspapers recognized the danger of the America First approach to US international political and diplomatic positions especially in relations with Japan.[22] In the game of electoral politics, however, Nixon and Southern textiles producers had triumphed.

***

Protectionism indeed paid off politically. In April 1972, the textile industry—led by southern mills—sent a big check to Stans (who had left Commerce to run Nixon's reelection fund-raising campaign) for $363,000. Another $150,000 poured into the coffers in November just before the election. Nixon won the South in 1972 and stormed to reelection. No doubt the textile wrangle's outcome aided his cause.[23]

As the American trade position deteriorated US leaders started to reexamine their free-trade stance. For his part, according to historian Allen Matusow, Nixon increasingly sounded like "the average congressman" who took a nationalistic position on trade policy. The President spoke of "the facts" that America had lost comparative advantages in trade except for agriculture and advanced technologies. It was time to reassess free-trade internationalism.[24]

***

For the remainder of the 1970s, US-Japanese relations remained important but secondary to the strategic battle against the Soviet Union and oil diplomacy in

---

[21]Destler et al., *The Textile Wrangle*, 294–314.
[22]Schaller, *Altered States*, 239. See also "U.S.-Japan: Summit or Nadir?," *New York Times*, January 11, 1972, 36.
[23]Schaller, *Altered States*, 217–25, 231–40; Destler et al., *The Textile Wrangle*, 45–6.
[24]Matusow, *Nixon's Economy*, 123.

FIGURE 8.2. Sato (left, with translator) listens as Nixon speaks at the Western White House in California on January 7, 1972. Looking on, left to right, are Secretary of State William Rogers, John Connally, US Ambassador to Japan Armin Meyer, and a contented Commerce Secretary Maurice Stans. Courtesy: Richard M. Nixon Presidential Library and Museum (National Archives and Records Administration).

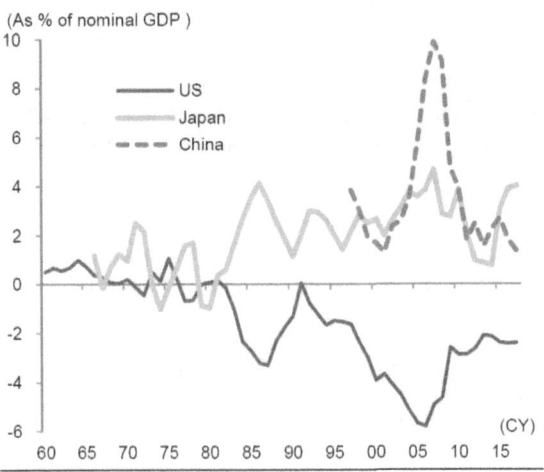

GRAPH 8.1. Takashi Miwa, "What Can We Learn from the History of Trade Wars," Nomura (August 2018), https://astonishingceiyrs.blogspot.com/2022/10/history-of-trade-wars.html.

the Middle East, despite both Presidents Ford and Carter complaining about the growing trade deficit. By Gerald Ford's tenure in 1974 the US trade deficit with Japan stood at $1.8 billion; by 1980, it hit $9.9 billion. Becoming the first sitting president to set foot on Japanese soil in November 1974, Ford arrived in a mood of repentance for his predecessor's jarring shocks of three years before.

Now prime minister, Kakuei Tanaka feared new quotas on Japanese exports, but Ford put him at ease by declaring his free-trade credentials. Tanaka did not want to repeat Sato's mistake of promising more than he could deliver, though with his close adherence to grassroots Japanese demands, he indicated a much tougher stance on trade. The Prime Minister called out the bloated US trade gap as Washington's internal problem, not Tokyo's.

He also confirmed that Japan would take a more unilateral course on Taiwan, perhaps agreeing with the PRC on a unification approach that the Americans opposed. Soon, Japan shifted toward a focus on the PRC, ending bans on credits as a means of expanding trade with the mainland. In September 1972—seven months after Nixon's trip to Beijing—Tanaka took his own visit to the Chinese capital where the PRC and Japan re-established diplomatic ties. This prompted protest from Washington, which feared a weakening of defense commitments to Taiwan. Above all, Tanaka's boldness showed that Japan was no longer a submissive follower of the United States in Asia.[25]

Japanese economists and diplomats urged their country to restore equilibrium in trade with the United States because of the risk of exacerbating protectionism just as Japan required more access for their exports. Congress had already tried to drop the volume of imports to the pre-Kennedy Round levels of the mid-1960s to the applause of unions. This was bad news for Japan, which shrewdly chose self-restraint by "orderly marketing" agreements for its exports. Tanaka and future prime ministers repeatedly gave genuine assurances of seeking to cut the US trade deficit by restraining Japanese goods flowing into the United States, though American consumers continued to buy them, thereby worsening the deficit.

Jimmy Carter took the cue. He fought off harsh mandatory congressional quotas on shoes in 1977 by settling instead on orderly marketing agreements that gave nations more leeway for their exports. The President endorsed free trade and, like his predecessors going back to Eisenhower, an export drive

---

[25]Ford, *A Time to Heal*, 210; "Premier Kakuei Tanaka . . . Tells it Like it Is," *Washington Post*, September 5, 1972, A20; George R. Packard, "The Pacific Rivals: Japanese Views of Japanese-American Relations," *New York Times*, October 29, 1972, BR2; Selig S. Harrison, "Japan Acts to Increase China Trade," *Washington Post*, July 27, 1972, A1; Selig S. Harrison, "Tanaka Hopes to Visit China Next Month," *Washington Post*, August 8, 1972, A17.

abroad. Facing 7 percent unemployment and rocketing prices, however, Carter knew that trade liberalization was politically problematic. Thus, he wrangled another export restraint agreement from Japan, this one on televisions. Tokyo responded with a warning that failure to stop protectionism had worsened the Great Depression; according to the Japanese, history seemed to be repeating itself in the inflationary hard times of the late-1970s.

Nevertheless, Americans labeled Japan an unfair competitor—a mantra of Detroit's car industry in particular—as Hondas and Toyotas poured into the United States. Assembly line workers made news by taking sledgehammers to them. When President George H. W. Bush visited Tokyo in 1992 with an US auto executive to demand that Japan buy US auto parts, the image of the former occupier coming hat in hand sparked bitterness back home. That he also became sick and vomited at a state dinner with the prime minister, perhaps subconsciously channeling the US trade deficit with Japan that had reached $49 billion, was an unfortunate optic as well.[26]

***

Japan not only beat the United States in trade but penetrated the American economy like never before. Ronald Reagan encouraged foreign investments in the United States as a means of buying up debt and keeping the budget afloat, which the President had spiraled into a deep deficit by massive defense spending and tax cuts. As a result, America became the world's largest debtor. And the world's largest creditor, Japan, held 20 percent of that debt in securities.

The more visible investments in marquee landmarks like Rockefeller Plaza in New York City, Universal Studios, CBS Records, Columbia Pictures, Westin Hotels, and Pebble Beach golf course in California, among many icons and targets, disturbed Americans. Japanese investors snapped up condominiums, housing developments, ranches, resorts, and other real estate. They delved into racehorses, ski areas, and the commercial rights to Yosemite National Park, a sale so galling that the Japanese company eventually sold them to a charity to improve its image. Japan dominated art auctions, sometimes even buying the auction houses themselves. What hallmark of Americana was next, the World Series? The Japanese came close by buying the trademark for the Indianapolis Motor Speedway to build an Indy oval near Tokyo and host the car race one day.

In essence Japan used its export revenues to go on an overseas shopping spree, especially after the dollar's crash by a third of its value after the Plaza

---

[26]Leonard Silk, "Japan Sheds Quantitative for Qualitative Goals," *New York Times*, June 7, 1972, 59; Zeiler, *Capitalist Peace*, 194–202; Michael A. Barnhart, "From Hershey Bars to Motor Cars: America's Economic Policy Toward Japan, 1945–1976," in *Partnership: The United States and Japan, 1951–2001*, eds. Akira Iriye and Robert A. Wampler (Tokyo: Kodansha International, 2001), 219.

Accord on exchange rates took effect in 1985. Five years later, Japan controlled four of the ten largest banks and 20 percent of retail banking in California alone, supplying a fifth of all credit in the state and financing half of its new housing starts. Hama Kikaku, a Tokyo real estate company, bought the property of St. Augustin Catholic Church on the main road facing Waikiki Beach in Hawaii by paying more than double the cost of any previous Hawaiian land purchases. Residents there and elsewhere decried their very identity seemingly carted away by a foreign intruder.

That sentiment soon permeated the view of Japan. Into the 1980s and early 1990s, a mentality of psychological warfare became the norm in the United States, undergirding the impulse of protectionism and threatening the tradition of trade liberalization. When the Japanese withdrew an enormous sum from the US bond market in 1987, an interest rate hike ensued that helped cause a Wall Street crash in October. Congress also insisted that Japan share the burden of its military defense either by paying the United States for its security or expanding its own defense capacity. Relatedly, Tokyo prompted much criticism for initially offering just $1 billion in aid for the American-led coalition in the Persian Gulf War in 1991, the same amount investors had paid for Pebble Beach golf course. Tokyo eventually raised its contribution to $9 billion, but its reputation as a reliable power—and friend—suffered.

Protests strengthened over Japan's interlocking system of trade and industry that unfairly deviated from America's cherished free-market principles and policies. MITI was not transparent and cared little for free trade unless it helped Japanese goods. As well, the Japanese were implacable bargainers at the negotiating table and also engaged in industrial espionage. Still, Americans seemed like crybabies. Until the United States played the same game, it would end up a loser regardless of the optimism of free traders. The dominance of "Japan Inc." had a chilling effect on the country's image.

Making Japan a scapegoat for their own failures in industrial policy, Americans fought back through the politics of trade and a culture war. Sure, the beloved Pokemon and manga captured the curiosity of young people. From the 1970s into the early 1990s, though, popular writers warned of a United States absorbed into Japan's "Co-Prosperity Sphere," an allusion to the Second World War. When the Cold War ended, Paul Tsongas, a candidate in the 1992 presidential election, quipped that "the bad news was that Germany and Japan won." Even the veteran journalist, Theodore White, wrote that MITI had "directed the guided missiles of the trade offensive" that converted the entire world into Japan's sphere of influence. Dozens of anti-Japanese diatribes accused Washington of being in Japanese corporate pockets and agents of Tokyo scouring the United States for profit and influence. Pundits screamed for Americans to wake up to the possibility of becoming a colony of Japan.

The unease over Japanese trade and investment reached into popular culture's most circulated media with scurrilous portrayals of Japan and American permissive feebleness. Take the best-selling book and movie: Michael Crichton's racist *Rising Sun* in 1992. The work showed Americans helpless in the face of Japan's sinister corporations, which controlled not only real estate but had captured the government through lobbyists and controlled the national security apparatus. Japan Inc. preyed on white women as well. A half-demented police officer yelled that the United States was at war "and some people are siding with the enemy!" In response, a pro-Japanese advisor noted that "All's fair in love and war, and the Japanese see business as war." Sensational and racialist (inscrutable predatory Orientals infiltrating the West) as it was, Crichton's point was not to call out Japan. Instead he aimed his darts at the United States for being complacent, arrogantly believing it could remain number one without adapting to new power structures. Americans had gone soft.[27]

Senator Joseph Lieberman of Connecticut noted in 1989 that when the Christmas tree lights were turned on at Rockefeller Center Americans would have to come to grips with the reality that this national celebration was occurring on Japanese property. On the fiftieth anniversary of the Japanese bombing in Hawaii that precipitated the Pacific War a radio announcement perfectly captured the irony. "We interrupt this program with a special bulletin," the grave voice stated on December 7, 1991, "the Japanese have just *bought* Pearl Harbor."[28] That summed up the crisis with Japan.

***

The United States could not stop the onslaught until the Japanese did themselves in with a real estate bubble that burst by 1993 and led to decades of misery. By the new millennium, anti-Chinese feelings had replaced Japan's rapacious image. But before this change in fortunes Japan asserted its permanent presence in the US economy.

For instance, after the collapse of the Chrysler Corporation in the late 1970s (and its eventual bankruptcy) and two oil crises made efficient Japanese cars very appealing, Tokyo signed a voluntary export restraint agreement on autos in 1981. The next year a Honda assembly plant opened in Ohio to meet new local content requirement laws. More companies followed in other states; by 2022, Japanese manufacturers in the United States accounted for some 2.8 million cars a year. This "transplant" practice bypassed formal protectionism like quotas

---

[27]Michael Schaller, "The United States, Japan, and China at Fifty," 59, also 57–8; Thomas W. Zeiler, "Business is War in U.S.-Japanese Economic Relations, 1977–2001," in *Partnership*, 242–243; Kunz, *Butter and Guns*, 313–6.
[28]Zeiler, "Business is War, 241–2.

and tariffs as a means of bowing to political pressure to produce in America. By the end of the 1980s Congress had legislated that trade officials identify nations (implicitly Japan) that discriminated against US products and retaliate by limiting their access to the American market. Protectionism had peaked again.

Protectionism had costs. The export restraint accord jacked prices on autos, profits that went straight into the hands of Japanese auto companies that plowed the money right back into its American plants or sent back home. As a result the transplant strategy won Japan nearly one-third of the US car market by the 1990s. Detroit developed a bunker mentality, always on the defensive by, for example, buying up cheap companies like Mazda and Suzuki to stake out market shares. By then the Japanese had moved on to advanced automation and high-end profitable cars like Lexus, Infiniti, and Acura.

American workers demanded an end to free-trade policies and complained of Japanese cartels that worked closely with government. Japan played on an unlevel playing field, they claimed. But even when leveled by trade restraint agreements the field still produced Japanese victories. America's uncoordinated market culture seemed unfit for competition. And US producers seemed like dinosaurs, unable or unwilling to adapt to new market conditions like high-priced oil and consumer demands for safety. The eventual end to the auto trade wars resulted only from acceptance of Japanese dominance.

There were some rare bright spots. The United States had some successes in stemming the tide of Japan's efficient quality goods. Take semiconductors, when a trade war ensued after Ronald Reagan imposed duties on Japanese exports. This time the US government stepped in with its own research and development partnership with the private sector—Japanese-style—through the Department of Defense funding of Sematech in 1986.

Yet on the whole America seemed like an aging prizefighter convinced of his own invincibility but failing to accept that a new heavyweight had passed him by. That lack of reality led to a doubling down on free-trade dogma among policymakers but a tripling-down of protectionist thinking among citizens and Congress. The fact was clear: in every industry Japan had targeted, it dominated until its own self-inflicted collapse in the 1990s.[29] Trade relations with Japan and other competitors provoked crises of confidence and performance in the United States. Even in the vibrant era of globalization this dark view percolated protectionism up through the ranks of workers to producers and politicians. Increasingly, Japan prompted them to call into question the postwar consensus on free trade.

***

---

[29]Zeiler, *Capitalist Peace*, 205; Zeiler, "Business is War," 227–39.

Like his predecessors (and most of his successors) President Nixon connected commerce to power, diplomacy, and America's role in world affairs. Although he did not favor economic nationalism he wanted Japanese markets open to US goods and services, much like decades later when Washington insisted the People's Republic of China grant wider access for exports.

The calculation involved a balancing act: fair-trade protectionism to protect jobs might win back labor to a freer trade stance which, in turn, might boost exports. Still, classical economists discredited this version of mercantilism, however moderate, as a violation of the law of comparative advantage in which nations produce and trade their most efficient goods and leave the rest to others. It also hurt consumers because the cost of imports rose. Besides, economists mocked the idea that America was an innocent victim of unfair trade practices of other nations, particularly Japan, since the US market was protected by more quota barriers and the highest tariffs than any of its trade partners. Republican Party economic ideology itself, moreover, was based on freedom and free markets. Thus, Nixon had veered close to hypocrisy by disregarding his party's postwar stance and engaging in his trade war with Japan.

It turned out that while the rather xenophobic approach of the second Nixon Shock and the third one of wielding the Trading with the Enemy Act represented demonstrative examples of economic nationalism, they were not the final word on the subject. Driven by a crisis atmosphere in the economy, protectionism grew stronger. After the Cold War—in the very era of globalization that supposedly made it obsolete—protectionism became an appealing weapon for liberals, conservatives, and certainly populists alike.

9

Aftershock Crises

The trade war with Japan foreshadowed an era of economic crises that proved much more significant than a war over textile exports. The textile wrangle also presaged debilitating years of predicaments in the foreign and domestic arenas, problems that stretched well beyond Nixon's presidency. It appeared that globalization created a paradox: more interdependence linked nations together—in crises as well as prosperity. Liberalization of money markets, for instance, led to more financial crunches.[1] One result was a loss of confidence in the postwar trade and monetary systems, with nationalism—expressed through protectionism—replacing internationalist optimism in many quarters.

This chapter serves as the connective tissue for the previous Nixon Shocks. All influenced the turn toward nationalism even if Nixon had intended to head off that very end. That shift ultimately involved a battle over liberal democracy itself at home and in the rest of the world.

***

At 5,712 pounds the luxurious Lincoln Continental Convertible was the heaviest American-produced automobile in 1960. This so-called "land yacht" came with a front seat about the size of a living-room couch. Its 315-horsepower engine and weight limited this behemoth to 9 miles per gallon in city driving and

---

[1] Niall Ferguson, "Introduction: Crisis, What Crisis? The 1970s and the Shock of the Global," in *The Shock of the Global: The 1970s in Perspective*, edited by Niall Ferguson, Charles S. Maier, Erez Manela, and Daniel J. Sargent, Cambridge: Harvard University Press, 2011, 18. For a moderate Democrat—Democratic Senator Chris Murphy of Connecticut—who turned on neoliberalism, see James Pogue, "The Most Interesting Democrat Not on the Ticket," *New York Times*, August 25, 2024, Sunday Opinion, 10–11.

14 mpg on highways. The Continental typified the nation's veneration of the automobile that built the suburbs and their shopping centers and magnificent interstate highway system, encouraging commutes into cities, promoting long-distance travel, and transforming American culture. And who cared that the Continental consumed loads of gasoline? Energy was cheap.

Five oil producer states—Iran, Iraq, Kuwait, Saudi Arabia, and Venezuela—founded the Organization of Petroleum Exporting Countries (OPEC) just a few weeks after families drove back from the Labor Day weekend holiday in their Lincolns in 1960. These nations chafed at mandated cuts in the price of oil by the powerful Seven Sister petroleum companies (five American, one Dutch, and one British) over the past decade. They sought an increase in prices by cutting production, but the Seven Sisters (also known as the Majors) continued the oil glut that reduced revenues for these Global South countries and kingdoms.

OPEC was impotent to compel changes in production (and thus prices) until Colonel Muammar Qaddafi led the Libyan revolution in 1969 that toppled the King. The next year, Qaddafi forced the Seven Sisters to raise the posted price of oil back to the levels of 1965. By 1971, Iran and Venezuela followed with laws allowing OPEC governments to raise prices. The next year, Iraq nationalized its major petroleum company holdings. Venezuela went further, taking full ownership of its oil fields. The Majors conceded by eventually turning over half of their control of oil reserves to OPEC.

American gas guzzlers and the Nixon administration had a problem that curdled into a crisis. Because environmental regulations prompted a decline in coal as an energy source, and lacking enough natural gas supply to fill the gap, America turned to cheap oil as its chief source of energy even though it had its own sizable reserves in Texas, Oklahoma, and other states. Petroleum supplied 47 percent of the market in 1972, but oil import quotas kept prices higher for Americans, protecting the domestic companies (called Independents). So did Nixon's price controls from the second Shock that began in November 1971 just when costs rose for winter so that refiners had incentives to produce more home-heating oil. With prices fixed artificially low, however, refiners reduced output and drove up costs. And because consumer demand still outpaced domestic supplies, pressure upward on prices grew even stronger.

Hope for price moderation and ample supplies lay with tapping into the mammoth oil fields in the Middle East for inexpensive oil. This solution had also made the nation complacent when it came to assured cheap sources of petroleum. Even when the Majors dumped oil on the American market, US Independents undersold them and their service stations flourished. By Spring 1973 the days of surplus petroleum and cheap gas were over, however. The Majors redirected their oil supplies to their brand-named filling stations, squeezing some 40,000 Independents to the extent that some 2,000 gas stations were shuttered.

Qaddafi and OPEC changed thinking by reducing production and excess capacity with it. As supplies abroad dwindled, prices were poised for a takeoff by the early 1970s. When Washington's friend, the Shah of Iran, demanded the sale of all Seven Sisters' properties and rights over oil in the country, the die was cast despite having another pro-Western major producer, Saudi Arabia, in America's corner when it came to cooperating with the big oil companies. This Kingdom understood its leverage as global oil reserves fell. "We are in a position to dictate prices," proclaimed Saudi oil minister, Sheik Zaki Yamani, "and we are going to be very rich."[2]

***

Washington resented such insolence, but the winter of 1972–3 witnessed an oil shortage in the United States and legislators started speaking of an "energy crisis." President Nixon doubted such overblown phrasing but brownouts of electric power grids and cancellations of natural gas contracts had already occurred. In short, there was not enough energy produced at home while world reserves were tight. When the third Arab-Israeli War erupted on the Jewish high holiday of Yom Kippur in October 1973 OPEC was in a perfect position to transform the world. Wrote a Nixon historian, the cartel precipitated "one of the most wrenching collective experiences of the American people in the post-World War II era."[3] The Yom Kippur War pitted Israel against Soviet-backed Egypt which swept to seeming victory before the Israelis reversed the tide, aided by the United States.

Yet Washington's foreign policy relied on Saudi Arabia and Iran, both Western-friendly oil-rich kingdoms, to defend US interests by buying American military hardware and serving as proxies of moderation in the region. In 1969, the Saudis also organized six small oil sheikdoms (including Dubai and Abu Dhabi) located in the eastern Arabian Peninsula into the United Arab Emirates for the same purpose. A week after the Nixon administration stepped into the Yom Kippur War to save Israel by airlifting arms and military supplies, however, Saudi Arabia announced an embargo on oil sent to the United States.

The rest of OPEC followed the Saudi lead. Because the organization also refused to negotiate prices with the Majors any longer, the oil nations unilaterally doubled the price per barrel by $2. The price hikes ended a long era when these Global South nations took orders from Western oil companies. Now OPEC would dictate the prices. An oil crisis was on.

***

---

[2]Matusow, *Nixon's Economy*, 258.
[3]Stein, *Pivotal*, 89; Matusow, *Nixon's Economy*, 241, also 241–54, 259.

The crisis really referred to the oil embargo, a related matter tied to forcing Israel to return to its 1967 borders and restore the rights of displaced Palestinians. The United States was best positioned to weather the embargo because of its limited use of Arab supplies; imports from Venezuela and Canada predominated in the American market. Nevertheless, production cutbacks ate further into US reserves, which forced oil companies to reduce allocations to gas stations across the country and to airlines as well. This raised the specter of the Second World War style rationing of gasoline.

Nixon faced a dilemma of favoring consumers or producers but either presented him with major headaches. The administration suggested voluntary curbs on automobile use such as carpools, reduced highway speeds to 55 miles per hour, and built new bus lanes to encourage commuting by mass transit. Embroiled in the Watergate scandal at this time the President was under great pressure to do more. Enraged Americans waited for hours in long lines at the pumps, some of which frequently ran out of gas.

In November 1973, Nixon urged voluntary oil conservation measures and asked Congress to legislate reduced hours for gas stations. He had already advocated construction of an Alaskan pipeline, deregulation of natural gas, a delay in clean air standards, a search for more offshore oil, and greater reliance on nuclear power. Fuel allocations were cut as well; New England power plants reduced voltage and filling stations shut on Sundays. Colleges canceled their mid-winter sessions and some schools closed early or altogether. Factories reduced hours to conserve energy and foot the bill of high fuel costs while airlines and auto companies announced layoffs. Truck drivers blocked highways to protest the price of diesel fuel. Independent producers accused Nixon of hurting them and appeasing the "Big Oil" Majors.

In December 1973, the Shah of Iran led OPEC to a new price hike that settled at $11.65 a barrel—a five-fold rise in the posted price. The Global South suddenly enjoyed a massive transfer of wealth for the first time in history. Of course, not all developing nations had oil deposits but they took cues from the OPEC cartel to form price-fixing associations of their own to determine production and export of other raw materials besides oil.

At the moment, there was little good cheer in the United States at Christmas. The Shah of Iran exalted that the industrial world's "terrific income and wealth based on cheap oil is finished. They will have to find new sources of energy, tighten their belts. If you want to live as well as now, you'll have to work for it."[4]

---

[4] Matusow, *Nixon's Economy*, 263. See also Stein, *Pivotal*, 90–100.

Into the late winter of 1974, outraged and anxious Americans continued to line up at the pumps while they watched Nixon's presidency unravel in the Watergate crisis. They ranked the oil crisis as their top concern, even above the political scandal. Activists Ralph Nader and Jesse Jackson told Americans to protest Big Oil by not paying their fuel bills. People grew suspicious, angry, devious, and even violent. In Miami, an enraged Cadillac driver tried to break into a gas line by nearly running over a service station attendant. In the Bronx, drivers rammed through oil drums to get at a gas station that was trying to close. Refused service in Gary, Indiana somebody shot and killed the station owner when refused gas. Drivers in huge Lincoln Continentals burned up 150 gallons an hour as they idled in mile-long lines. Panic and "gasoline fever" gripped America. Nixon's Silent Majority were not so silent now.[5] It was a bleak time.

***

Meanwhile, the administration looked at options to the oil shortage that no leaders had ever dealt with. Perhaps a gasoline tax would reduce consumption and save reserves. Maybe Nixon should do nothing and let market demand naturally clear out oil reserves. Rationing came up in Congress and the city of Portland, Oregon adopted it, allowing consumers to fill up on odd or even days according to the last digit of their license plate numbers.

Nixon turned instead to organizing consuming nations to combat OPEC but the Western powers lacked unity. The European Community, dependent on Arab oil, had already caved to OPEC's demands to pressure Israel to withdraw from lands taken in the Six-Day War. All Europeans except the Dutch were rewarded by an exemption from a petroleum production cutback. Under pressure from Arab oil ministers Tokyo followed by backing this demand even though Japan and Western Europe faced high oil prices and experienced recessions as a result. Furthermore, the oil sheiks realized that by permanently damaging the US economy they would kill the golden goose that made them rich. So they allowed the Seven Sisters to ship non-Arab OPEC oil to America, allowing nearly a half million more barrels a day to enter the country in February 1974.

Kissinger's "shuttle diplomacy" between Middle Eastern capitals got Israel to disengage from Egypt and Syria. As a result, by March 1974, Arab governments lifted the oil boycott. With the embargo over, by May, US oil imports rose more than one million barrels a day yet oil prices remained high, providing big profits for Big Oil but misery at the pumps for consumers. The administration and Congress spearheaded efforts for energy independence

---

[5]Matusow, *Nixon's Economy*, 267–8; Meg Jacobs, *Panic at the Pump: The Energy Crisis and the Transformation of American Politics in the 1970s* (New York: Hill and Wang, 2016), 65–85.

FIGURE 9.1. *During the first oil crisis and after the Yom Kippur War in November 1973, Nixon meets with Israeli Prime Minister Golda Meir, as Kissinger looks on. Courtesy: Richard M. Nixon Presidential Library and Museum (National Archives and Records Administration).*

from foreign oil which led to exploration of new oil fields at home, the development of new sources of energy, and a flood of small car imports from Japan that hurt Detroit automakers.[6]

***

Oil prices remained high into the Ford, Carter, and early Reagan years, depressing demand and contributing to what experts called the "Great Recession" of the 1970s and early 1980s. Persistent payments and trade deficits, surging imports, high unemployment, inflation, and a falling dollar were not recipes for prosperity. Indeed, capitalism seemed on the run as the industrialized West faced an existential economic crisis.

Jimmy Carter saw an opportunity for transformation. He injected principles into the oil crisis equation by declaring the "moral equivalent of war" in 1977 on energy use. Instead of siding with consumers and their love of cars, heating, and air-conditioning, he told them to be more frugal. The President even donned a cardigan to model how warm clothing in winter compensated for a reduction in home thermostats. Carter failed at persuasion; polls found Americans tuned out, resigned, or miffed by the preaching. Besides, domestic producers were drilling more oil fields. Furthermore, since the oil embargo,

---

[6]Matusow, *Nixon's Economy*, 270–4.

the United States had increased its share of OPEC oil imports from 22 percent to 37 percent. Thus, little adherence to conservation efforts and a greater dependence on OPEC oil made the country vulnerable to another oil crisis.

When the Shah of Iran was overthrown by the Ayatollah Ruhollah Khomeini in February 1979, that calamity came to pass. To be sure, the Shah had led the charge of the oil price explosion in 1978, but he was also the recipient of a quarter century of US aid as a long-time friend. Not so the fundamentalist Islamic Ayatollah, who looked on the United States as the Great Satan—the chief imperialist enemy of the Muslim world. His revolution and ensuing oil boycott against the West removed about two million barrels of OPEC oil a day from production. This led to fears of scarcity as prices nearly tripled to $34 a barrel by 1982.

The lines at gas stations were even longer than during the 1973 crisis. Congress acted for the first time to redistribute the massive profits that oil companies had enjoyed and also stimulated alternative energy sources. But the nation split. Seeking deregulation of energy markets, southerners trumpeted "freeze a Yankee" when northern liberals demanded that the government guarantee low prices for consumers. That funny slogan lost its humor when violence ensued over the oil crisis. Riots over shortages erupted in Pennsylvania when truckers protested at gas stations, and some demonstrations grew violent as drivers set fires to pumps. People also did not want to drive at 55 mph, and they demanded gasoline. Protesters carried signs reading "More Gas Now" and "No Gas, My Ass."[7]

Carter called for a massive synthetic fuel program and warned Americans of a "crisis of confidence," but voters reacted negatively. He seemed impotent to Iran, too, as the Ayatollah seized US Embassy employees in Tehran on November 4, 1979, and kept them hostage for fourteen months until Ronald Reagan was sworn in as President in January 1981. The year before the Iran-Iraq War had broken out, leading to another price hike and a recession. This finally abated by 1983 when oil prices began to drop, eventually settling at $19 a barrel in 1985 and then lower into the mid-1990s.

The oil crises ranked among the most traumatic events in the postwar era. Cheap oil sat at the heart of the American Century's prosperity, confidence, and identity for producers, workers, and consumers alike. Low gas prices fueled the transformation of society through suburbia and shaped culture. The United States held 6 percent of the world's population in 1973 but consumed one-third of its oil. At its peril, it was reliant on foreign sources of petroleum.

---

[7] Jacobs, *Panic at the Pump*, 161–307.

For many the oil crises—or more fittingly for this study, the oil shocks (as they are also called)—signaled the official end of the American Century and the beginning of a difficult, unsettled, and divisive era. What had been taken for granted after the Second World War—cheap and plentiful oil—had disappeared. One newspaper headline caught the atmosphere: "Things Will Get Worse Before They Get Worse."[8] That said, Americans balked at paying the price for energy conservation and came late to alternative sources. Nonetheless, because of the oil crises consumers became more efficient buyers and users. There was still a longing for the heyday of the Lincoln Continental, moreover, before OPEC made the West pay for its lifestyle.

***

Petrodollars gave OPEC members nearly three-quarters of all international monetary reserves by 1980 yet energy-poor less-developed countries faced impoverishment due to high oil prices. The oil shocks further hurt them by limiting their exports to the Global North that now endured from less capacity to buy raw materials and food because of the recession. Worse was to come for regions of the Global South.

Regardless of calls for a New International Economic Order in the 1970s and a reform of the market-oriented GATT in a more protectionist direction for poor nations, many countries relied on loans from the IMF and bankers in rich nations that soon ran them into massive debt. Latin America in particular suffered in the 1980s from the high interest rates charged by banks. Oil prices, lending, and recession prevented many poor countries from trading their way to surpluses that might pay off these debts. A crisis ensued that defied several rescue plans.[9] A bit like Japan Saudi Arabia and other OPEC nations invested in the United States, although unlike the Japanese they showed an eagerness to buy from America, especially in the category of high-tech weaponry. Politicians warned of the dangers of allowing foreign oil profits to purchase US assets and Treasury securities. The Arab oil boycotts gave these fears ominous undertones that played into xenophobic anti-Arab and anti-Muslim sentiment.

The debt crisis fizzled out in the mid-1990s as banks took their losses from defaulters. Before it ended the "Tequila Shock" of 1994 showed the danger of debt linked, in part, to the oil crises. Seeking to boost its exports Mexico converted its short-term debt of pesos into dollars, thus decreasing

---

[8]Patterson, *Grand Expectations*, 786, also 784–5. See also Matusow, *Nixon's Economy*, 252–4, 275, 301–2; Stein, *Pivotal*, 101–29, 148–53, 205–24.
[9]Robin Broad and Zahara Heckscher, "Before Seattle: The Historical Roots of the Current Movement Against Corporate-led Globalisation," *Third World Quarterly* 24, no. 4 (August 2003): 713–28; Giovanni Arrighi, "Global Capitalism and the Persistence of the North-South Divide," *Science & Society* 65, no. 4 (Winter /2002 2001): 469–78.

its foreign reserves and raising its debt. Investors got the default crisis they had predicted. The peso was devalued, causing a global currency crisis and resulting in a $50 billion IMF bailout of Mexico's economy arranged by the Clinton administration.[10] Oil and debt crises—and the Nixon Shocks—were only the beginning of decades of emergencies.

***

The world and the United States entered an era of inequality that was a product of the recessionary 1970s and the neoliberal war on labor power, worker rights, and regulation. At least, that is how critics of capitalism and crises viewed things. There seemed little difference between Democrats and Republicans when it came to economic policies—they were all pro-globalization neoliberals to some degree. Ronald Reagan and Republican successors might be less willing to spend on welfare and Bill Clinton and his Democratic followers less interested in cutting taxes. Nonetheless, the processes and results seemed the same to a growing number in free-market detractors in academia, the press, Congress, and the working and middle classes.

For them, manufacturing apparently played second to the focus on growth, mergers, stock trades and dividends—that is, profits through investments and tax cuts—that seemed like the objectives of financiers and government leaders more than fairly distributed incomes and productivity. Big box stores and internet exchanges and the tenuous nature of reliable well-paid work became more familiar than small business, community involvement, and decent jobs. As business journalist Robert J. Samuelson wrote, job insecurity moved beyond blue-collar to white-collar workers from the 1980s onward, creating a precarious prosperity from a capricious economy that held out a possibility of opportunity but often resulted in unequal distribution of wealth and disorder. Americans increasingly faced both of these problems after the Nixon dollar and trade shocks despite intermittent booms.[11]

One constant was recurring crises in the economy. The Mexican peso emergency preceded the Asian financial pandemic that came before the bursting bubble of venture capital investments in tech startups in the dot.com stock crash from 2000 to 2002.[12] This so-called "New Economy" of the neoliberal, free market "Washington Consensus" would supposedly lead to democracy and stability. While globalization reigned as king for elites, however, instability and collapse were always around the corner for masses of pawns.

---

[10]Kunz, *Butter and Guns*, 224–83; Herring, *The American Century*, 500–2, 506–7; Sargent, *A Superpower*, 131–61; Charles S. Maier, "Malaise," in *The Shock of the Global*, 25–48.
[11]Robert J. Samuelson, *The Great Inflation and Its Aftermath: The Past and Future of American Affluence* (New York: Random House, 2008), 175–202.
[12]For treatment of several of these crises, see Linda Yueh, *The Great Crashes: Lessons from Global Meltdowns and How to Prevent Them* (London: Penguin Business, 2023).

From the Nixon Shocks onward these were the anxious years. Pessimism abounded over the economy, environment, civil rights, and faith in authority. Many millions turned inward, withdrawing from the frustrations of the world and focusing on religion, personal health, and the outdoors. Gone were the "happy days" portrayed in the 1973 film *American Graffiti*, a nostalgic tour of the prosperous 1950s. More relevant was Archie Bunker of the hit situation-comedy *All in the Family*, who preferred the old American Century when women and people of color knew their place, men worked hard, and big bands played uncomplicated tunes. Archie believed his United States had gone to hell.

Blue-collar workers lost ground or worse, Nixon had conned them with nationalist economic rhetoric and a culture war against liberals. Cozying up to the working class became politically chic especially during election season. Nixon was not the last to do this, of course. His Republican successors, above all Donald Trump, fought a culture war designed to manipulate the resentments of the Archie Bunkers.

Some fought back, like actress Sally Field's brave union organizer in the movie *Norma Rae*. Sylvester Stallone in *Rocky* also overcame the odds or in the black version of such heroes who fought against injustice, so did *Shaft* and *Superfly*. Others just tried to forget the misery, like John Travolta who rebelled against his dead-end job selling paint in *Saturday Night Fever*. After having been "kicked around, since I was born" he and others retreated to the disco balls hovering over a dance floor that served as a refuge from reality.

Others understood the con. The film *Nashville* ridiculed the faux Southern cult Nixon had cultivated while rocker Bruce Springsteen's desperate character struggled alone in *Darkness on the Edge of Town*. In the words of the disco era's premier band, the Bee Gees, millions of average Americans were just "stayin' alive." They were under siege, losing as factories closed, gas prices skyrocketed, and unions dissolved under neoliberal corporate and governmental pressure.

From the mid-1970s onward many citizens had soured on America itself. Howard Beale, the seemingly deranged anchorman in the 1976 film, *Network*, expressed the emotions of the times. Look around, everyone was out of work or scared about losing a job, he pointed out. The dollar bought only a nickel's worth, banks were going belly up, and store owners kept guns under the counter. The military had been defeated while revolutions swept the world. The air was unfit to breathe and food inedible. Inflation and crime rampaged while elites and politicians just said everything was alright, concluded Beale, as if this were still the American Century.

It wasn't. Liberals unrealistically urged a return to the nearly extinct New Deal while conservatives pushed a patriotic illusion that the nation could have strong but smaller government, low taxes, and high deficits. Americans could have it all if they accepted greed as the rule and forgot about the rights of workers that had accrued over the past decades. Americans were confused, to be sure, but many were not buying the upbeat message regardless of the popularity of a Reagan or Clinton, a Bush or an Obama. Since the 1970s, said Howard Beale, they were "mad as hell" and getting madder.[13]

***

While globalization energized much of the world in the 1990s the Washington Consensus of austerity measures and neoliberalism as a solution to debt, nagging poverty, and inequality did not work for those who were not wealthy, college-educated, or high-tech and financial service providers. Opponents warned that the United States itself was just as much a target of the globalizers in banking and trade as the Global South. When the city of Seattle erupted against the World Trade Organization there were relatively few demonstrators against globalization on the populist right. They arrived with the Tea Party movement a decade later. The Seattle protesters hailed predominantly from the socialist, anarchist, and progressive left.

Their evidence, in the form of repeated crises, made a compelling case against globalization. During the Asian financial pandemic of 1997–8, Thailand's currency, the baht, suddenly lost half its value when plummeting stock market and real estate values sent investors into dollars and yen. This debacle spread throughout the region—to Malaysia, South Korea, Indonesia, Singapore, and the Philippines—which suffered similar enormous outflows of capital and plunging stock markets. Some 150 banks either closed, suspended operations, or were taken over by the International Monetary Fund during the Asian crisis as the contagion spread to Japan, Russia, and Brazil. The disaster prompted a dialogue about free-market ideology because Wall Street, Washington, and the IMF had encouraged emerging economies to deregulate their capital markets and open up to foreign banks. Such imprudent financial liberalization questioned the very idea that a borderless world shaped by free-trade capitalism would usher in prosperity for all.

---

[13]Kim McQuaid, *The Anxious Years: America in the Vietnam-Watergate Era* (New York: Basic Books, Inc., 1989), 319; Peter N. Carroll, *It Seemed Like Nothing Happened: America in the 1970s* (New Brunswick, NJ: Rutgers University Press, 1990), 22–70; Thomas Borstelmann, *The 1970s: A New Global History from Civil Rights to Economic Inequality* (Princeton, NJ: Princeton University Press, 2012), 53–72; Bruce J. Schulman, *The Seventies: The Great Shift in American Culture, Society, and Politics* (New York: Da Capo Press, 2001), 53–77, 159–89; Jefferson Cowie, *Stayin' Alive: The 1970s and the Last Days of the Working Class* (New York: The New Press, 2010), 176–209, 313–56; David T. Courtwright, *No Right Turn: Conservative Politics in Liberal America* (Cambridge, MA: Harvard University Press, 2010), 249–74; Dominic Sandbrook, *Mad as Hell: The Crisis of the 1970s and the Rise of the Populist Right* (New York: Alfred A. Knopf, 2011), ix–xi; Stein, *Pivotal*, 262–93; Charles Tilly, "Globalization Threatens Labor's Rights," *International Labor and Working-Class History* 47 (Spring 1995): 1–23.

Critics expressed their ire. Some agreed with the Prime Minister of Malaysia, Muhamad Mahathir, who blamed marauding capitalists for destabilizing the Global South. Others claimed that transnational production, mass consumption, and trillions of dollars in capital transfers had restructured capitalism itself for the benefit of the well-connected. Still others argued that there was still much to learn about the whipsaw nature of globalization that brought great profits and then sudden crisis. And yet a growing crescendo lashed out at the Washington Consensus that called for governments to cede sovereignty over health, safety, resources, and taxes to globe-trotting firms and institutions like the IMF and the WTO. The latter held secret meetings among unelected—and thus unaccountable—bureaucrats. Immune from the reach of national laws this administrative state directly threatened democratic governance and placed the livelihoods of the masses in jeopardy.

Protest stemmed from a reaction against neoliberalism and globalization themselves. Corporations and financial institutions had once provided benefits to society but now "market tyranny" drove them. The results were tragic and dangerous. Family and community withered, global crime ranging from terrorism to drug cartels exploded, the natural environment entered a period of alarming climate change and diminishing resources, and confidence in government, parties, and leaders evaporated as business lobbies seemingly purchased democratic power. The globalized supercharged growth that had promised utopia through technology and free markets failed to help the average person. When once government had stabilized markets and redistributed income in an egalitarian, regulated way in the American Century, now neoliberals ruled through a system of equality of opportunity rather than equality of outcomes.[14]

Economists and politicians might argue that protectionism was mere snake oil that played into the hands of demagogues but at least barriers to competitive imports promised concrete hope to the downtrodden. In 1996, when pundit Patrick Buchanan ran for president as a conservative populist in the mold of George Wallace before him and Donald Trump after, he showed

---

[14]David C. Korten, *When Corporations Rule the World* (West Hartford and San Francisco, CA: Kumarian Press, Inc. and Berrett-Koehler Publishers, Inc., 1996), 12, also 20–3, 141–8; Robert Went, *Globalization: Neoliberal Challenge, Radical Responses* (London: Pluto Press, 2000), 105–27; Joseph E. Stiglitz, *Globalization and Its Discontents* (New York: W.W. Norton & Company, 2002), 214–52; J. Bradford DeLong, *Slouching Towards Utopia: An Economic History of the Twentieth Century* (New York: Basic Books, 2022), 446; Pietra Rivoli, *The Travels of a T-Shirt in the Global Economy: An Economist Examines the Markets, Power, and Politics of World Trade* (Hoboken, NJ: Wiley, 2006), 139–56; James H. Mittelman, *The Globalization Syndrome: Transformation and Resistance* (Princeton, NJ: Princeton University Press, 2000), 165–222; C. Donald Johnson, *The Wealth of a Nation: A History of Trade Politics in America* (New York: Oxford University Press, 2018), 504–14.

that protectionism was an easy sell with economically anxious Americans. He lost but progressives took up his call against globalization's capacity to tear apart the social fabric. After all, markets were a social institution constructed by governments to let corporations run as freely as possible. Anti-globalizers saw markets as footloose institutions that required regulation to place societal harmony before profits.[15]

***

Progressives, or liberal populists, in the Democratic Party had risen in unison against free trade and their own president, Bill Clinton, and his support for globalization through North American Free Trade Agreement, the World Trade Organization, and engagement with China at the expense of human rights. His opponents saw unionized workers losing their jobs as factories fled the country. A member of organized labor once told the President that he would find no toys, gloves, or radios made by American workers who were being slaughtered by free trade. The WTO had come to represent the interests of the wealthy who benefited from globalization and not those who "felt left out and left behind," in Clinton's telling.[16]

Progressives stood up for the poor and oppressed around the world as well as for US workers slammed by imports and international financial transactions. That is why Clinton depended on Republicans to pass both NAFTA and the WTO, for Democrats, in his words, sent him a "big fuck you." He then showed up at the "Battle in Seattle" to admit there were real problems with globalization and to win back his average American constituents.[17]

All sorts of ideologies joined into a potent protesting bloc that took to the streets to object to the WTO at its ministerial meeting in Seattle in December 1999. Although mostly peaceful at first, huge demonstrations led to chaos. Marchers trapped delegates of the 135 WTO member nations in their hotels, including Secretary of State Madeleine Albright, and prevented discussion of an agenda for a new round of trade talks. Violence ensued as police tried to clear the streets with tear gas and rubber bullets then arrested over 600 people for spray-painting graffiti, smashing windows, and setting fires. Seattle inspired further demonstrations at other international meetings, including at the elite World Economic Forum in Davos, Switzerland in 2001. Even the Pope warned of globalization's perils.

In Seattle, a weird alliance across the political spectrum engaged environmentalists seeking to protect endangered species with stronger WTO standards and steelworkers and longshoreman who protested the flight of

---

[15]Dani Rodrik, *Has Globalization Gone Too Far?* (Washington, DC: Institute for International Economics, 1997), 69–71.
[16]Clinton, *My Life*, 878–9. See also Klein, *The Natural*, 80.
[17]Zeiler, *Capitalist Peace*, 238, 242, also 237, 240–1.

manufacturing jobs to nations with cheap labor. A sign read "Turtles and Teamsters" together, epitomizing the mix of protesters who also included human rights activists and spokespeople for poor nations' interests.

These critics did not necessarily desire a halt to the process of globalization because that was impossible as well as detrimental to economies worldwide. Instead, they wanted countries to enforce decent wage and labor standards, protect environmental rules, and promote human rights by engaging in fair trade that would also help vulnerable industries. They insisted on a halt to IMF austerity measures in poor nations as requirements for receiving loans to pay off their huge debts. The WTO must help reduce inequality across the world rather than penalize poor nations for focusing on local development. Maybe protectionism was a viable solution for the struggling masses. All also agreed that, in the words of Lori Wallach of the WTO watchdog organization Global Trade Watch, America "was the mother ship of neoliberalism." Washington privileged trade negotiators and corporations over "*human beings*" who detested the "beast" of globalized free-market dogma.[18]

The liberal Bill Clinton took issue with those like Wallach who, he chided, scapegoated trade for creating poverty. The President called protectionism an excuse for uncompetitive gripers and pointless discord. But he added that globalization needed a "human face" that gave communities dignity and hope. At Davos in 2000 Clinton criticized entrepreneurial acolytes of hyper-capitalism and their political supporters.[19] A decade later after the Great Recession of 2008–9, progressives took up his charge by revolting against the citadels of capitalism, wealth, and globalization. This time they were joined by rightwing activists as well.

***

The rise of the Occupy Wall Street movement of the populist progressive left occurred alongside the Tea Party movement of the populist right, though the latter would assume much more influence by transforming the Republican Party. Both were products of the Great Recession, the culture wars, and opposition to the interminable fruitless wars in Afghanistan and Iraq. No doubt they also arose from the decades of crises after the American Century as both ends of the political spectrum looked to the Nixon Shocks as a viable response.

Both also expressed the tribalism and nationalism that confronted a globalized consumerist ethic. Political scientist Benjamin Barber captured this battle over protecting or dissolving social and economic barriers in his book,

---

[18]DW Gibson, *One Week to Change the World: An Oral History of the 1999 WTO Protests* (New York: Simon & Schuster Paperbacks, 2024), 43.
[19]Eckes and Zeiler, *Globalization*, 249–56.

Jihad vs. McWorld, as did Thomas Friedman in *The Lexus and the Olive Tree*. For the jihadists and olive-tree cultivators history had certainly not ended, as Francis Fukuyama had so confidently claimed. Rather, neoliberalism bred pessimism, skepticism, and discontent with globalization and its constituent institutions like the IMF. These entities had not fulfilled promises; rather, they had betrayed them. That went for the United States as well, writes historian Fritz Bartel, by adopting a process of neoliberalism stretching back to the shocks of the 1970s that supplanted the government activism of the Cold War with a market doctrine unmindful of the average American's interests.[20]

It was during the financial crisis—the Great Recession starting in 2008—when decades of neoliberal globalization met its match. The United States took the blame for the meltdown due to its overheated and unstable housing market in which prices plummeted and credit markets collapsed due to unwise, greed-driven mortgage loans. Deregulation and devotion to the shaky theory of the Washington Consensus—that liberal economics assured an American-dominated system of political stability and the democratic rule of law—caused the disaster. Globalization ultimately offered a "false dawn" of progress. There was a disconnect between markets and democracy that only regulation could solve. Socialism and Marxism provided few answers and neoliberal conservatism made things worse. Above all, markets had to be embedded in society, and not the other way around.[21]

As the biggest financial disaster since the Great Depression emerged, protests mounted alongside the crisis. A staggering $50 trillion in wealth was erased in the year and a half of the Great Recession from October 2008 to April 2009. Banks and trading houses went under; Wall Street seemed on the verge of collapse. Those financiers and brokers represented the "one-percent" that Occupy Wall Street demonstrators accused of bilking the average American through inequality, greed, and the influence of money in politics. In those eighteen months, an average of 700,000 US workers lost their jobs each month in the worst sustained decline of employment since the 1930s. Earnings for those who kept their jobs dropped 48 percent to an annual average of just $23,000. Newcomers to the job market and older workers were hit hard, non-college and college-educated employees alike.

---

[20]Stiglitz, *Globalization*, 23–52; Benjamin R. Barber, *Jihad vs. McWorld: How Globalism and Tribalism Are Reshaping the World* (New York: Ballantine Books, 1996), 3–20; Fritz Bartel, *The Triumph of Broken Promises: The End of the Cold War and the Rise of Neoliberalism* (Cambridge, MAHarvard University Press, 2022), 18–9.

[21]John Gray, *False Dawn: The Delusions of Global Capitalism* (New York: The New Press, 1998), 17–21, 215–8. See also Jonathan Levy, *Ages of American Capitalism: A History of the United States* (New York: Random House, 2021), 719–49; DeLong, *Slouching*, 485–518.

FIGURE 9.2. *President George W. Bush speaks at a meeting of G7 leaders on October 11, 2008, as the Great Recession brings chaos to markets. Courtesy of the George W. Bush Presidential Library.*

GRAPH 9.1. *US Census—Foreign Trade Statistic Citation: "Balance of Trade," Higher Rock Education and Learning, Inc., https://www.higherrockeducation.org/glossary-of-terms/balance-of-trade.*

For many analysts the Great Recession represented the tip of the globalization iceberg. For three decades, tens of millions of white- and blue-collar jobs had been threatened by neoliberal free-market tax, outsourcing, and offshoring trends that sent manufacturing abroad. Even the dynamic information technology sector was vulnerable to offshoring, as were retail bankers, insurance companies, and pharmaceutical jobs. Indeed, the "big squeeze," as labor journalist Steven Greenhouse called it when describing the impact on US workers, had been in effect for everyone below executives for years. Downsizing, reengineering, and rightsizing had made job security a notion of the past. Meager or nonexistent healthcare, demands for faster production in a deregulated workplace, an assault on pensions, and widespread layoffs (known euphemistically as workforce reduction) in retail around the country added to the insecurity. Now the chickens had come home to roost. By Fall 2011, the leftist Occupy movement set up encampments in city parks across the country and extended a global reach as well.[22]

Alarm bells rang among liberals as well as progressives for a multi-pronged agenda to scale back the process of globalization and redistribute winners and losers. Even some dyed-in-the-wool free traders like liberal economists Alan Blinder and Paul Krugman confirmed that US manufacturing jobs were under attack from low-wage imports. They did, however, prefer expanding the social welfare safety net instead of promoting protectionism.

Further to their left, progressive solutions included monitoring or closing entirely the IMF and World Bank, replacing firms with non-profit organizations, imposing high taxes on business profits and sealing tax loopholes, breaking up monopolies, reforming business influence over the media, regulating the environment and consumer use of resources, and electing left-leaning politicians. In an influential book that had appeared as the Seattle protests began, Journalist Naomi Klein argued that corporate branding by Nike (sports), McDonald's (fast food), Microsoft (the information age), Starbucks (beverages), and others so dominated the economic culture that they had become more important than manufacturing and jobs. These marks even muscled into the school systems. Nations needed to reverse globalization by enhancing local control and rights over the economy. Anti-corporate activism, going mainstream, was a viable answer to corporate domination and the Washington Consensus.[23]

---

[22]Stein, *Pivotal*, 296; Washington Journal, "Occupy Wall Street Movement: Where Is It Headed," *C-SPAN*, https://www.c-span.org/video/?302103-2/open-phones (accessed April 30, 2024); Michael Greenstone and Adam Looney, "Unemployment and Earnings Losses: A Look at Long-Term Impacts of the Great Recession on American Workers," November 4, 2011, https://www.brookings.edu/articles/unemployment-and-earnings-losses-a-look-at-long-term-impacts-of-the-great-recession-on-american-workers/#:~:text=Losing%20A%20Job%20In%20the,employment%20since%20the%20Great%20Depression (accessed April 10, 2024); Herring, *The American Century*, 671; Steven Greenhouse, *The Big Squeeze: Tough Times for the American Worker* (New York: Alfred A. Knopf, 2008), 6–14, 204.

[23]Copeland, *The Wealth*, 557; Korten, *When Corporations*, 307–24; Timothy Noah, *The Great Divergence: America's Growing Inequality Crisis and What We Can Do About It* (New York: Bloomsbury Press, 2012), 179–95; Naomi Klein, *No Logo* (New York: Picador, 2002), xxiii, 27–61.

The political system convulsed in this crisis though not for the last time. Barack Obama rode the wave of uncertainty and angst to presidential victory; his election occurred a month after the start of the Great Recession. It was the Tea Party—shorthand for Taxed Enough Already—that shook the political rafters, however.

***

This conservative populist movement outlasted Occupy Wall Street, which ended up morphing into support for socialist Bernie Sanders' rebellion within the Democratic Party. Liberal centrists then effectively confronted Sanders. By contrast, the Tea Party seized roughly a third of the Republican Party. Rightwing populism stressed opposition to immigrants, minorities, and corporate power and favored authoritarian, anti-democratic leadership. Leftwing populists sought change and reform of the system; rightwing populists wanted the system overthrown entirely, including norms of accepted civil behavior.[24]

Centrism and compromise had no place in the Tea Party. These populists found their roots in Nixon's Southern Strategy and even in the libertarian, small-government ethic of Barry Goldwater before that, as well as in the conservative activism of neoliberalism since the Reagan years and the anti-globalization insurgencies of independents Ross Perot and Patrick Buchanan. Seeds of rebellion germinated with House Speaker Newt Gingrich's Republican capture of Congress in 1994 under the *Contract with America*, a plan to reduce the size of government, cut taxes, and restrict welfare.

The Tea Party fully bloomed on the political scene a month after President Obama's first inauguration in February 2009. Traditional conservatives despised taxes, too, but the Tea Party signaled a break from old-guard Republicans. Its nationalist, grassroots, and cultural appeal rendered it a potent force. The Tea Party demonized not only liberal and conservative agendas but the President himself. An example surfaced when an obscure congressman from South Carolina shouted "you lie" during Obama's State of the Union address in 2009. Others included a dozen or so real or threatened shutdowns of the government by Tea Party stalwarts—even against the wishes of members and House Speakers in their own Republican Party—over opposition to spending bills.

The Tea Party movement that reshaped the Republican Party itself demanded limited government but also absolute sovereignty for the United States. The agenda was not uniform among its followers but, in general, the Tea Party despised big government (including the Internal Revenue Service), recovery plans from the Great Recession, and Obama's Affordable Care Act of

---

[24]Barry Eichengreen, *The Populist Temptation: Economic Grievance and Political Reaction in the Modern Era* (New York: Oxford University Press, 2018), 15–16, 110–5, 135, 191.

universal and mandatory healthcare. It also defended freedoms, including gun rights, in constitutional amendments.

The movement was instrumental in the Republican sweep to power in both houses of Congress in 2010 and in the presidential electoral victories of Donald Trump in 2016 and 2024, supplying his base and that of significant Republican power in Congress thereafter. A foundation of chaos as well Tea Partiers even ruined or undercut their own Republican speakers of the House.[25]

Despite the globalized business interests inherent in conservatism, the Tea Party pushed the Republican Party toward populist-style protectionism and nationalism not seen since the Great Depression of the 1930s and the Nixon Shocks, though the latter turned out to be temporary expressions of chauvinism in 1971. The near-visceral reaction to immigrants showed the knee-jerk nationalism of the Tea Party. Donald Trump's lies that Obama was foreign-born (the "birther" issue) and thus not constitutionally qualified to be president appealed to this sentiment. These were xenophobic reactions that were inimical to internationalism and, in many cases, to rationale thought.

Post-Cold War populist challenges around the world created an existential crisis in the liberal order that concerned experts who worried about the threat to global cooperation, democratic governance, and stable economic relations. These fears intensified in the first two decades of the twenty-first century with authoritarianism in China, Russia, Hungary, and Brazil and with the rise of transatlantic illiberal populist parties as well. This was more than just an ideological debate; Brexit in the United Kingdom and Yellow Vest protests in France showed actions spoke as loudly as words.[26] International trade, moreover, took a front row seat next to immigration and taxation in the rightwing populist-nationalist theater.

***

The crisis of liberalism and internationalism epitomized and fueled by populist-protectionism converged in Donald Trump. He characterized trade not as a tool of foreign policy to promote shared prosperity, peace, and security but as a transactional endeavor in which the United States had long played the sucker. That is, just like American enemies like China, even allied nations acted like thieves who stole US copyrights, jobs, factories, livelihoods, and greatness

---

[25]John M. O'Hara, *A New American Tea Party: The Counterrevolution Against Bailouts, Handouts, Reckless Spending, and More Taxes* (Hoboken, NJ: Wiley, 2012), 21–50, 99–139, 175–233; Elizabeth Price Foley, *The Tea Party: Three Principles* (Cambridge: Cambridge University Press, 2012), 20–217; Obama, *A Promised Land*, 411.

[26]G. John Ikenberry, *A World Safe for Democracy: Liberal Internationalism and the Crises of the Global Order* (New Haven, CT: Yale University Press, 2020), 269–85, 300–7; Jussi M. Hanhimaki, *Pax Transatlantica: America and Europe in the Post-Cold War Era* (New York: Oxford University Press, 2021), 116–20.

through free-trade deals arranged by neoliberal policymakers. They allowed worse and worse trade deficits, themselves a sign of rip-off and decline.

The erosion would stop, Trump pledged, by the reassertion of protectionism. Higher tariffs, trade wars, and modification of or withdrawal from trade agreements like NAFTA and the Transpacific Trade Partnership were the weapons Trump promised to activate, and he did so. Nevertheless, the trade deficit and domestic struggles for workers remained and actually worsened. Still, Trump proclaimed to supporters in 2020 as he stood for reelection that he had overseen the restoration of America's greatness through protectionism. "We're in the greatest country anywhere in the world," he told an audience in Texas, "and we're taking care of you" through the trade war.[27] He echoed this sentiment in his successful campaign in 2024 and pledged to intensify protectionism once in office. He made good on that promise early on in his second administration, in 2025, by raising tariffs (and doing so unilaterally, in violation of WTO rules, rather than multilaterally) and even concocting a new approach to trade—reciprocity—which Trump interpreted as raising duties in line with other nations, even though the traditional meaning of reciprocity was to lower tariffs to the levels of others.[28]

Never over the past century or so had an administration spoken out so forcefully in favor of protectionism. This included Herbert Hoover during the Great Depression when he imposed the highest tariffs ever seen. Unlike Trump, however, Hoover believed in internationalism. Trump's successor, Joe Biden, also turned to a tough protectionist stance against China but like Hoover (and Nixon), at heart he eschewed nationalism and engaged with the world.

Trump fashioned himself as a populist, though he was an odd one being a supposed billionaire invested in the global economy rather than a victim of globalization. Nonetheless, his administration trumpeted the "America First" slogan first expressed by Nazi sympathizers before the Second World War and the pledge to "Make America Great Again" through protectionism. Nationalistic trade policies were designed to jolt allies abroad and supporters at home with the same intentions of domestic electoral advantage as Nixon displayed in his Shocks nearly a half century earlier.

This time around the Silent Majority and racist Southern Strategy were replaced by Tea Partiers, though they shared many of the same resentments toward educated elites, city-dwellers, minorities, feminists, atheists, and government at large. The anti-Trumpers were supposedly condescending and unpatriotic cosmopolitan globalizers and their traditionalist Republican

---

[27]Zoilor, *Capitalist Peace*, 277, also 270–8.
[28]Petros C. Mavroidis, "'Reciprocal' tariffs: what's in a word," *Bruegel*, February 27, 2025.

conservative and Democratic centrist enablers who ignored the average American. They also had let China run amok over trade norms and rules. Trump would famously save them by reversing course on engagement with Beijing and adopting a confrontational approach instead.

***

That was the logic of the protectionists, particularly the administration's energetic ideological point man in Trump's first term—a former international trade lawyer and now the US Special Trade Representative, Robert Lighthizer. He was the architect of the trade war with China, a warrior against the WTO and its free-trade bent, and proponent of pulling out of the TPP. Lighthizer was no destroyer for the sake of destroying, like other lieutenants such as Steve Bannon, Peter Navarro, and Trump himself. Yet he aggressively pursued a unilateral trade policy through negotiations that would, he designed, result in pragmatic and protectionist trade deals to correct the imbalance with the PRC and boost the fortunes of beleaguered US workers.

Lighthizer read trade history as a saga in which Washington had sold out labor by letting the country's industrial base erode. "I believe that American trade policy should revolve around helping working-class families" while all else—consumer prices, efficiency, and corporate profits—came second.[29] For Lighthizer, who grew up in the Rust Belt of Ohio and witnessed both its vibrant blue-collar life and devastating decline, manufacturing was the Holy Grail of trade as an ideal of American greatness. Furthermore, like Trump, Lighthizer believed that the trade deficit by itself explained that sad history.

In Lighthizer's analysis, America had lost its way in trade. From the Civil War to the advent of NAFTA and the WTO, history had been on the side of industry. Until the mid-1990s, even as tariffs gradually fell after the Second World War, trade liberalization was cautious and largely based on reciprocal concessions by other nations. There were also times when free-trading presidents applied protectionism, as in cotton textile and lumber restrictions under Kennedy and steel and auto restraints imposed by Ronald Reagan. The post-Cold War era of hyperglobalization was a disaster, however, particularly for the unskilled worker.

Oftentimes, US negotiators subsumed trade to security interests, generously allowing in massive imports to help allies prosper. These same partners also wielded protectionism against American goods and subsidized their exports in unfair trading practices. Relying on trade in services like

---

[29]Robert Lighthizer, *No Trade Is Free: Changing Course, Taking on China, and Helping America's Workers* (New York: Broadside Books, 2023), xiv. See also Gordon H. Hanson, "Washington's New Trade Consensus and What It Gets Wrong," *Foreign Affairs* 103, no. 1 (January/February 2024): 164–72.

banking or information was not the answer either, for manufacturing workers could not easily transition to such high-skilled work, nor did they want to.

American producers simply could not compete in this unfair trading landscape. In a world full of elitist thinking, "the benefits of globalization were very much in the forefront, while the concerns of those hurt by it were far away and easy to dismiss," complained Lighthizer. He determined to change that equation by hitching his star to "a great boss," Donald Trump who seemingly was the only leader with a plan (protectionism) to remedy the tragic situation of American industry and workers and give them hope.[30]

Historians, economists, and diplomats have picked apart Lighthizer's arguments, as they had long done with their wariness toward protectionist claims. They countered: the trade deficit actually improved in certain periods and was not the indicator of healthy trade patterns; prosperity depended on the service and technology sectors and not manufacturing; and raising tariffs to restrict imports actually hurt the very workers they are designed to help by boosting costs of production and punishing them as consumers through higher prices. Protectionism also led, inevitably, to foreign retaliation by tariff hikes that crossed over into poisoning political relations, international agreements, national security arrangements, and even peace.

Furthermore, this was déjà vu without a successful ending. That is, Donald Trump was no Richard Nixon. The abandonment of the dollar-gold peg and the Trading with the Enemy Act were tough measures but they had moved trade partners to meet US demands for currency revaluation and export restraints that set the table for later prosperity through globalization. The Lighthizer-Trump offensive merely compelled China to raise its own tariffs and worsened the US trade deficit while failing to boost employment at home.[31]

The approach, though, appealed to nationalist and populist sentiment in a swath of the United States. This protesting had been building for decades going back to the Nixon years. Crisis after crisis, coupled with free-trade globalization and worsened by a decline in traditional work, production, and business, scared and angered the working and middle classes. Their wallets and pocketbooks depleted by a cost of living that they could not sustain, they turned to protecting their way of life even if it meant backing untenable theories, extreme zealots, and a demagogue as a leader. Their feelings, perceptions, and experiences made them lash out for change.

They also had some facts to back them up. For instance, globalization had placed US employees into direct competition with lower-wage foreign

---

[30]Lighthizer, *No Trade*, 6, 12, also 31.
[31]Jack Rasmus, "Trump's Déjà vu China Trade War," *World Review of Political Economy* 0, no. 3 (Fall 2018): 346–63.

workers, which both depressed their earnings and lost some of their jobs. Due in part to imports and offshoring, more than 60,000 factories had closed from 2000 up to the pandemic in 2020. Since 1979, US manufacturing employment had dropped from 19.5 million to 12.9 million. Under these conditions, unions and workers were not prone to make demands or else they faced more job losses; some companies, like General Electric, made such threats.[32] For many, then, Trumpian protectionism—no matter how much of a siren song it was—provided an answer to their plight.

At bottom self-defense undergirded the protectionist impulse. The consequent growing inequality allowed an opportunistic showman like Trump to articulate the nationalist-populist sentiment of resentment, unfairness, and alienation. Nixon spoke to them as well when he played politics with trade and others had dipped their toes into protectionist waters. Nobody did so, however, more intensely and irrationally than Trump in both of his terms.

And the Trump stance had partially won the day. The Biden administration continued some protectionist policies by imposing economic restrictions on China and even curbing Japanese investments in steel plants, though without the nativism, denigration of allies, and fortress America mentality of Donald Trump and his associates. Biden also wheeled out a promising effort to bring jobs back home by various industrial policies designed to reverse the ruthlessly efficient supply chain and production model of globalization. Conservatives joined in the protectionist (and populist) crusade with the Heritage Foundation's Project 2025 during the second Biden/Harris-Trump election campaign. It considered Trump-style restrictions, even deportations on immigrants and tariffs on all on all goods regardless of where they came from.[33] Trump electoral victories meant that these ideas could become reality.

Protectionism signaled unhappiness and anxiety, whether in the Nixon years or a half century later in the Trump era. So did populism, which seemed ubiquitous in the United States and beyond its shores by the second decade of the twenty-first century. Repeated crises that destabilized lives and fractured society lay as root causes of the gloom and unease. Having faced such dilemmas in the past and perceiving a bleak future ahead, many people yearned for the American Century. Unfortunately, as even Richard Nixon had realized, it had already faded into history.

---

[32] Steven Greenhouse, *Beaten Down, Worked Up: the Past, Present, and Future of American Labor* (New York: Alfred A. Knopf, 2019), 11, 146.
[33] Roger Lowenstein, "It Hurts to See Biden Imitating Trump on Trade," *New York Times*, March 21, 2024, https://www.nytimes.com/2024/03/21/opinion/us-steel-merger-biden.html?searchResultPosition=1 (accessed April 18, 2024); Peter S. Goodman, *How the World Ran Out of Everything: Inside the Global Supply Chain* (New York: Mariner Books, 2024), 9, 296–313.

Conclusion

Consequences of the Nixon Shocks

By the early 1970s, the bell tolled for the American Century. Perhaps the United States did not suffer from a debilitating relative decline when compared to other nations, but the era of the Nixon Shocks onward was a troubled, oftentimes glum time. Already divided when Richard Nixon took office, he, in many ways, divided the country further. This book is an attempt to show his impact and enduring legacy in American history. To be sure, Nixon's imprint does not show up everywhere, but in areas like the economy, diplomacy, and politics, he oftentimes initiated policies (and outlooks) that resonate even today.

***

For instance, hard times, conflict, and anxiety greeted Nixon when he entered office, and he had to deal with them or he risked being a one-term president. That is, the psychological impact of the American Century's demise was telling and permanent. Jimmy Carter presciently nagged Americans to escape their "malaise." Ronald Reagan's optimism amounted to Hollywood bluster that covered up weaknesses by making Americans feel good, even as he set up the masses for a neoliberal cocktail of insecurity, struggle, and greed. It might sound good to the patriotic Archie Bunkers whom Nixon had targeted with his economic policies, but the Nixon remedy did little for them in real terms, even though educated service-sector employees fared better. Donald Trump picked up on the malaise, though his unsavory style of exaggerating the "American chaos" was blatantly self-serving and failed to bring meaningful results for the average American.

Americans were unhappy in 1971 and remained so a half century later. Nixon's first term had been revolutionary; opening the door to China and finally reforming the international monetary system were novel and bold initiatives that were also necessary. Educated, upper-middle-class, and wealthy Americans did fine (as they always do), but "average" working-class and lower-middle-class citizens increasingly struggled as the post-American Century decades wore on. Older Americans harked back to a better time, and younger people worried about their futures. They always do, as well. In the post-Cold War era, the American dream seemed more difficult to reach or, for many, entirely unattainable. Neither Nixon nor his successors, not even the cheery Reagan, could reverse the reality of the vanished American Century.

***

Although this book places the post-American Century largely in a foreign policy context, the abuse of power stemming from wars and foreign policy conflicts, confrontation with China, international tensions over finance, money, and trade, rivalry and fear toward Japan, anti-globalization, and protectionism symbolized the disintegration of political comity at home. The domestic arena connected closely, in other words, to the international scene. Deadlock, partisanship, and polarization occurred with growing frequency from the late 1960s and certainly since the Nixon years.

Disillusionment with politicians, disgust over moral issues, and resentment on the right and the left seemed the new norm. Moderates and so-called independents, who grew in number partly as a protest to traditional party politics, chafed at the discord. An impatience with divided government, while Washington seesawed between one party in the White House and the other controlling Congress, exhibited the dysfunction and rising popular discontent for over a half century.

Americans grew angrier. Talk of reconciliation, of coming together and uniting persisted, but the dividers occupied much of the forum since 1971. There were occasional bright spots—economic booms, the end of the Cold War, more diversity, technological feats, and even bipartisanship in Washington. Yet somewhat cynically, Americans believed that American Century unity among the public and within government had disappeared, perhaps forever.

***

Nixon abused the Constitution, and so did others after him. This behavior prompted anger and doubt from the electorate regarding the integrity of its leaders. He poisoned the political well, making Americans ever more cynical. To be sure, they were already confronted each other over the Vietnam War and civil rights, but starting with his attempted suppression of the *Pentagon Papers*, he infected the very faith in the democratic process. The scandal eroded public comity, especially in the moral, ethical, and constitutional spheres. Americans had less trust in leaders as elite professionals in service to communities and the nation—politicians, doctors, lawyers, the media, and academics—came under attack and faced rising skepticism about their intentions.

Society seemed to have unraveled from the postwar period, though it was never as consensual and forgiving as mythology holds. Nixon was responsible for the scorn, even the loss of whatever innocence remained. Trying to suppress the free press in June 1971, Nixon set in motion a process that destroyed his presidency. Trust in government never fully recovered. Distrust built up over the decades as various scandals and abuses of power occurred. Perhaps it hit a peak under a con artist like Donald Trump, who denounced government for supposedly persecuting him but used it to seek vengeance on his enemies, lied about the outcome (his loss) in the 2020 election, and undermined faith in democratic norms and processes on behalf of his own interests.

***

The economy painted broad strokes on this tableau of malaise. Hoping for honesty and reform, people can stomach corruption if their stomachs are full and their jobs secure. By 1971, however, Americans seriously worried for the first time since the Great Depression about inflation, wages, and inequality. After the first quarter century of the postwar period, blue-collar workers found their wallets shrinking. Poverty had always existed, and Lyndon Johnson's war against it had been a bold attempt at remedies, even if he had come up short. Yet in the 1960s, Americans believed they could grow out of their economic problems and keep their decent, stable postwar livelihoods intact.

In the decades to come, globalization held out a promise of enrichment through neoliberal prescriptions centered on the free market. That rush into international markets—led by the United States—transformed the global economy. Free trade and financial exchanges bolstered Free World security against communism and, after the Cold War, the unity of democratic capitalist nations in the face of illiberal and autocratic regimes through the revenue and cooperation wrought by open markets. That international order based on capitalist and democratic peace was created during the American Century and preserved thereafter. It was a foundation of post-Second World War US security and leadership and not to be sniffed at by any means, except by the narrow-minded and self-serving nationalistic propagandist, Donald Trump. And, on occasion, the post-Nixon Shocks economy also gave hope of new forms of prosperity for both elites and the masses.

For many Americans who had previously benefited from the American Century, however, that proved to be an increasingly erroneous assumption from the 1970s onward. Globalization's gains seemed to pass them by. Inflation and the oil crises, in particular, and free-market neoliberalism at home and abroad revealed stresses that hindered stable and affordable livelihoods for millions of Americans.

***

The resulting battles over the distribution of economic advantages played out in politics. Conflict led to periodic policy paralysis in Congress, with each party blocking the other's agenda in a form of political hostage-taking. Even decorum disintegrated, with catcalls directed at the president. There was even an invasion of the Capitol in 2021.

Ugly, bitter elections so polarized the electorate that small shifts in independents decided the electoral college count even as large majorities sided with one candidate (usually the Democrat, though in 2004 and 2024 the Republican got the edge) over the other. The fairness of the constitutionally mandated electoral college itself was called into question.

Unrelenting attacks on government and concentrated economic power led to the Tea Party and Occupy Wall Street movements and then even greater divisiveness. Fighting even over the merits of health safeguards, such as wearing masks, in a global pandemic revealed deep fissures. People of color protested in the Black Lives Matter movement, but so-called "deplorables," in candidate Hillary Clinton's terminology in reference to a white redneck class of people, showed others could protest right back. Elon Musk's efforts to eliminate or reduce federal government institutions and employment from the outset of Trump's second term spoke to the attack on the so-called "deep-(administrative) state"—the bureaucracy despised by populists for its overreach into their lives, its insularity from the democratic process, and its elitism.[1]

***

Richard Nixon's approach to politics and foreign policy, his agenda, and his personal imprint on the country itself very much foreshadowed this contentious history. Many of his accomplishments—bringing China into the global community, the reversion of Okinawa and treating Japan as an equal, competitive dollar devaluation and an end to the outmoded gold standard, and trade liberalization planting the seeds of globalization—were transformative. They changed the world and the United States, sometimes for the better and sometimes for the worse, depending on a nation's level of development and ability to compete in global markets and, at home, according to one's class, culture, and education.

Above all, Nixon recognized that America had entered a new era in which prosperity and stability would not come as easily and naturally as before. That proved to be true. Although he couched his messages in ways that benefited him politically, he told Americans the truth about the new circumstances of greater hardship at home and equality abroad. A hegemonic United States was no more in the post-American Century. As a result, faith in government and leaders as solvers of problems, political cooperation, and civility suffered

---

[1] Reichard, *Deadlock*, 333–4; Kevin M. Kruse and Julian E. Zelizer, *Fault Lines: A History of the United States Since 1974* (New York: W.W. Norton & Company, 2019), 288–358.

as the country's hold over the world economy itself suffered a relative decline. The empire seemed less able to strike back.

That Nixon undermined good deeds with corruption was both shameful and unfortunate, but there is a larger point. He was determined to issue a challenge to the country. Ever since the Nixon Shocks, Americans have questioned the efficacy of diplomacy, the capitalist system, and democracy. The Shocks represented an initial attempt at reform even though they seemed revolutionary at the time, and proved so.

In 1971, Richard Nixon pointed the way to solving big problems of adjustment in global affairs while he also showed the dangers of dwindling comity at home. For all his faults, he understood that cures for America's ills lay beyond the Nixon Shocks. In truth, over the succeeding decades since his Shocks, it was clear that the vibrancy of democracy and prosperity ultimately rested with Americans themselves.

Bibliography

Primary, Public, and Personal Sources

Baker, James A., Jr. *The Politics of Diplomacy: Revolution, War and Peace, 1989-1992*. New York: G.P. Putnam's Sons, 1995.

Brinkley, Douglas, ed. *The Reagan Diaries*. New York: HarperCollins Publishers, 2007.

Bush, George H.W. *"All the Best": My Life in Letters and Other Writings*. New York: Scribner, 2013.

Bush, George W. *Decision Points*. New York: Crown Publishers, 2010.

Byrnes, Malcom, and Peter Kornbluh. *The Iran-Contra Affair: The Making of a Scandal, 1983-1988*. Alexandria, VA: The National Security Archive, 1990.

Clinton, Bill. *My Life*. New York: Alfred A. Knopf, 2002.

Ellsberg, Daniel. *Secrets: A Memoir of Vietnam and the Pentagon Papers*. New York: Viking Penguin, 2002.

Ford, Gerald R. *A Time to Heal: The Autobiography of Gerald R. Ford*. New York: Harper & Row Publishers, 1979.

Gibson, D. W. *One Week to Change the World: An Oral History of the 1999 WTO Protests*. New York: Simon & Schuster Paperbacks, 2024.

Kissinger, Henry. *White House Years*. Boston, MA: Little, Brown, 1979.

Kornbluh, Peter, and Malcolm Byrne, eds. *The Iran-Contra Scandal: The Declassifed History*. New York: The New Press, 1993.

Luce, Henry R. "The American Century." *Life,* February 17, 1941, reprinted in *Diplomatic History* Vol. 23:2 (Spring 1999).

Mary Kay Company. "Quick Facts." February 2, 2017. https://www.marykay.com/en-us/about-mary-kay-company-and-founder/company-quick-facts (accessed March 12, 2024).

Nixon, Richard M. *RN: The Memoirs of Richard Nixon*. New York: Simon & Schuster, Inc., 1990.

Obama, Barack. *A Promised Land*. New York: Crown, 2020.

Office of the Director of National Defense. "Background to Assessing Russian Activities and Intentions in Recent U.S. Elections." January 6, 2017. chrome-extension://efaidnbmnnnibpcajpcglclefindmkaj/https://www.dni.gov/files/documents/ICA_2017_01.pdf.

Peterson, Peter G. *The United States in the Changing World Economy, Volume 1: A Foreign Economic Perspective*. Washington, DC: U.S. Government Printing Office, December 1971.

Ruby, Daniel. "TikTok User Statistics (2022): How many TikTok Users Are There?" *Demandsage,* October 16, 2022. https://backlinko.com/facebook-users (accessed May 5, 2024).

USTR. "European Union Trade and Investment Summary, 2022." https://ustr.gov/countries-regions/europe-middle-east/europe/european-union#:~:text=The%20U.S.%20goods%20trade%20deficit,(%2415.8%20billion)%20over%202021 (accessed March 15, 2024).
Walsh, Lawrence E. *Firewall: The Iran-Contra Conspiracy and Cover-up.* New York: W. W. Norton & Company, 1997.
Woolley, John, and Gerhard Peters. *The American Presidency Project.* University of California, Santa Barbara. https://www.presidency.ucsb.edu/.
World Trade Organization. "Countries 2024." https://worldpopulationreview.com/country-rankings/wto-countries (accessed March 15, 2024).

Media

ABC News
The Atlantic
BBC
BBC News
Business Insider
C-SPAN
FiveThirtyEight

Foreign Affairs

The Guardian
Los Angeles Times
NBC News
New York Times
Washington Post
https://www.britannica.com/topic/YouTube

Secondary Sources

Albrow, Martin. *The Global Age: State and Society Beyond Modernity.* Stanford, CA: Stanford University Press, 1997.
Ammon, Royce J. *Global Television and the Shaping of World Politics: CNN, Telediplomacy, and Foreign Policy.* Jefferson, NC: McFarland and Company, Inc., 2001.
Arrighi, Giovanni. "Global Capitalism and the Persistence of the North-South Divide." *Science & Society* 65, no. 4 (Winter/2002–2001): 469–78.
Bacevich, Andrew J. *American Empire: The Realities and Consequences of U.S. Diplomacy* Cambridge, MA: Harvard University Press, 2002.
Bacevich, Andrew J. *The Short American Century: A Postmortem.* Cambridge, MA: Harvard University Press, 2012.
Baker, Peter. *The Breach: Inside the Impeachment and Trial of William Jefferson Clinton.* New York: Scribner, 2000.

Barber, Benjamin R. *Jihad vs. McWorld: How Globalism and Tribalism Are Reshaping the World*. New York: Ballantine Books, 1996.
Barnhart, Michael A. "From Hershey Bars to Motor Cars: America's Economic Policy Toward Japan, 1945-1976." In *Partnership: The United States and Japan, 1951-2001*, (pp. 201–222), edited by Akira Iriye and Robert A. Wampler. Tokyo: Kodansha International, 2001.
Bartel, Fritz. *The Triumph of Broken Promises: The End of the Cold War and the Rise of Neoliberalism*. Cambridge, MA: Harvard University Press, 2022.
Bhagwati, Jagdish. *Protectionism*. Cambridge, MA: The MIT Press, 1989.
Black, Earl, and Merle Black. *The Rise of Southern Republicans*. Cambridge, MA: Harvard University Press, 2002.
Blackwill, Robert D., and Richard Fontaine. *Lost Decade: The U.S. Pivot to Asia and the Rise of Chinese Power*. New York: Oxford University Press, 2024.
Bluestein, Paul. *Schism: China, America, and the Fracturing of the Global Trading System*. Waterloo: Centre for International Governance Innovation, 2019.
Boot, Max. *Reagan: His Life and Legacy*. New York: Liveright Publishing Corporation, 2024.
Borstelmann, Thomas. *The 1970s: A New Global History from Civil Rights to Economic Inequality*. Princeton, NJ: Princeton University Press, 2012.
Brennan, Mary C. *Turning Right in the Sixties: The Conservative Capture of the GOP*. Chapel Hill, NC: University of North Carolina Press, 1995.
Broad, Robin, and Zahara Heckscher. "Before Seattle: The Historical Roots of the Current Movement Against Corporate-led Globalisation." *Third World Quarterly* 24, no. 4 (August 2003): 713–28.
Bunch, Will. *Tear Down this Myth: How the Reagan Legacy Has Distorted Our Politics and Haunts Our Future*. New York: Free Press, 2010.
Byrne, Malcolm. *Iran-Contra: Reagan's Scandal and the Unchecked Abuse of Presidential Power*. Lawrence, KS: University Press of Kansas, 2014.
Calleo, David P. "Since 1961: American Power in a New World Economy." In *Economics and World Power: An Assessment of American Diplomacy Since 1789*, (391–257), edited by William H. Becker and Samuel F. Wells, Jr. New York: Columbia University Press, 1984.
Cannon, Lou. *President Reagan: The Role of a Lifetime*. New York: Simon & Schuster, 1991.
Carroll, Peter N. *It Seemed Like Nothing Happened: America in the 1970s*. New Brunswick, NJ: Rutgers University Press, 1990.
Carter, Dan T. *The Politics of Rage: George Wallace, the Origins of the New Conservatism, and the Transformation of American Politics*. Baton Rouge, LA: LSU Press, 2000.
Chang, Gordon H. *Friends and Enemies: The United States, China, and the Soviet Union, 1948-1972*. Stanford, CA: Stanford University Press, 1990.
Christensen, Thomas J. *The China Challenge: Shaping the Choices of a Rising Power*. New York: W.W. Norton & Company, 2015.
Cohen, Warren I. *America's Response to China: A History of Sino-American Relations*, 6th ed. New York: Columbia University Press, 2019.
Collins, Robert M. "The Economic Crisis of 1968 and the Waning of the 'American Century.'" *The American Historical Review* 101, no. 2 (April 1996): 396–422.
Copeland, Dale C. *A World Safe for Commerce: American Foreign Policy From the Revolution to the Rise of China*. Princeton, NJ: Princeton University Press, 2024.

Courtwright, David T. *No Right Turn: Conservative Politics in Liberal America*. Cambridge, MA: Harvard University Press, 2010.
Cowie, Jefferson. *Stayin' Alive: The 1970s and the Last Days of the Working Class*. New York: The New Press, 2010.
DeBenedetti, Charles, and Charles Chatfield. *An American Ordeal: The Antiwar Movement of the Vietnam Era*. Syracuse, NY: Syracuse University Press, 1990.
DeLong, J. Bradford. *Slouching Towards Utopia: An Economic History of the Twentieth Century*. New York: Basic Books, 2022.
Del Pero, Mario. *The Eccentric Realist: Henry Kissinger and the Shaping of American Foreign Policy*. Ithaca, NY: Cornell University Press, 2009.
Destler, I. M., Haruhiro Fukui, and Hideo Sato. *The Textile Wrangle: Conflict in Japanese-American Relations, 1969-1971*. Ithaca, NY: Cornell University Press, 1979.
Dikotter, Frank. *China After Mao: The Rise of a Superpower*. London: Bloomsbury Publishing, 2022.
Draper, Robert. *To Start a War: How the Bush Administration Took America into Iraq*. New York: Penguin Books, 2012.
Eckes, Alfred E., Jr., and Thomas W. Zeiler. *Globalization and the American Century*. Cambridge: Cambridge University Press, 2003.
Economy, Elizabeth. "Is Engagement Still the Best US Policy For China?" In *The China Questions 2: Critical Insights Into US-China Relations*, edited by Maria Adele Carrai, Jennifer Rudolph, and Michael Szonyi, 31–7. Cambridge, MA: Harvard University Press, 2022.
Economy, Elizabeth. *The Third Revolution: Xi Jinping and the New Chinese State*. New York: Oxford University Press, 2018.
Egerton, John. *The Americanization of Dixie: The Southernization of America*. New York: Harper's Magazine Press, 1974.
Eichengreen, Barry. *The Populist Temptation: Economic Grievance and Political Reaction in the Modern Era*. New York: Oxford University Press, 2018.
Eisenberg, Carolyn. *Fire And Rain: Nixon, Kissinger, and the Wars in Southeast Asia*. New York: Oxford University Press, 2023.
Eisenberg, Carolyn. "Remembering Nixon's War." In *A Companion to the Vietnam War*, edited by Marilyn B. Young and Robert Buzzanco, 262–4. Malden, MA: Blackwell Publishing, 2008.
Engel, Jeffrey A. *When the World Seemed New: George H.W. Bush and the End of the Cold War*. Boston, MA: Houghton Mifflin Harcourt, 2017.
Farber, David. *The Age of Great Dreams: America in the 1960s*. New York: Hill and Wang, 1994.
Ferguson, Niall. *The Ascent of Money: A Financial History of the World*. New York: Penguin Press, 2008.
Foley, Elizabeth Price. *The Tea Party: Three Principles*. Cambridge: Cambridge University Press, 2012.
Friedberg, Aaron L. "Stopping the Next China Shock: A Collective Strategy for Countering Beijing's Mercantilism." *Foreign Affairs* 103, no. 5 (September/October 2024): 177–89.
Friedman, Thomas L. *The Lexus and the Olive Tree: Understanding Globalization*. New York: Farrar, Straus and Giroux, 1999.
Friedman, Thomas L. *The World is Flat: A Brief History of the Twenty-First Century*. New York: Picador, 2007.

Fry, Joseph A. *The American South and the Vietnam War: Belligerence, Protest, and Agony in Dixie*. Lexington, KY: University Press of Kentucky, 2015.
Fukuyama, Francis. *The End of History and the Last Man*. New York: The Free Press, 1992.
Galbraith, John Kenneth. *The Affluent Society*. New York: Houghton and Mifflin Co., 1958.
Garten, Jeffrey E. *Three Days at Camp David: How A Secret Meeting in 1971 Transformed the Global Economy*. New York: Harper, 2021.
Gilpin, Robert. *The Challenge of Global Capitalism: The World Economy in the Twenty-First Century*. Princeton, NJ: Princeton University Press, 2000.
Goldberg, Edward. *Why Globalization Works for America: How Nationalist Trade Policies are Destroying Our Country*. Sterling, VA: Potomac Books, 2020.
Goodman, Peter S. *How the World Ran Out of Everything: Inside the Global Supply Chain*. New York: Mariner Books, 2024.
Gowa, Joanne. *Closing the Gold Window: Domestic Politics and the End of Bretton Woods*. Ithaca, NY: Cornell University Press, 1983.
Gray, John. *False Dawn: The Delusions of Global Capitalism*. New York: The New Press, 1998.
Greenhouse, Steven. *Beaten Down, Worked Up: the Past, Present, and Future of American Labor*. New York: Alfred A. Knopf, 2019.
Greenhouse, Steven. *The Big Squeeze: Tough Times for the American Worker*. New York: Alfred A. Knopf, 2008.
Greenstone, Michael, and Adam Looney. "Unemployment and Earnings Losses: A Look at Long-Term Impacts of the Great Recession on American Workers." November 4, 2011. https://www.brookings.edu/articles/unemployment-and-earnings-losses-a-look-at-long-term-impacts-of-the-great-recession-on-american-workers/#:~:text=Losing%20A%20Job%20In%20the,employment%20since%20the%20Great%20Depression (accessed April 10, 2024).
Greider, William. *One World, Ready or Not: The Manic Logic of Global Capitalism*. New York: Simon & Schuster, 1997.
Gungwu, Wang. "How Does the Past Serve the Present in Today's China." In *The China Questions 2: Critical Insights Into US-China Relations*, edited by Maria Adele Carrai, Jennifer Rudolph, and Michael Szonyi, 415–22. Cambridge, MA: Harvard University Press, 2022.
Hanhimaki, Jussi M. *Pax Transatlantica: America and Europe in the Post-Cold War Era*. New York: Oxford University Press, 2021.
Hanhimaki, Jussi M. *The Rise and Fall of Détente: American Foreign Policy and the Transformation of the Cold War*. Washington, DC: Potomac Books, 2013.
Harris, John F. *The Survivor: Bill Clinton in the White House*. New York: Random House, 2005.
Herring, George C. *America's Longest War: The United States and Vietnam, 1950-1975*, 4th ed. New York: McGraw-Hill, 2002.
Herring, George C. *The American Century and Beyond: U.S. Foreign Relations, 1893*. New York: Oxford University Press, 2017.
Ikenberry, G. John. *A World Safe for Democracy: Liberal Internationalism and the Crises of the Global Order*. New Haven, CT: Yale University Press, 2020.
Isikoff, Michael, and David Corn. *Hubris: The Inside Story of Spin, Scandal, and the Selling of the Iraq War*. New York: Crown Publishers, 2006.

Jackson, Kenneth T. *Crabgrass Frontier: The Suburbanization of the United States*. New York: Oxford University Press, 1987.

Jacobs, Meg. *Panic at the Pump: The Energy Crisis and the Transformation of American Politics in the 1970s*. New York: Hill and Wang, 2016.

James, Harold. *International Monetary Cooperation Since Bretton Woods*. Washington, DC: International Monetary Fund, 1996.

James, Harold. *Seven Crashes: The Economic Crises that Shaped Globalization*. New Haven, ct: Yale University Press, 2023.

Jian, Chen. *Zhou Enlai: A Life*. Cambridge, ma: Harvard University Press, 2024.

Johnson, C. Donald. *The Wealth of a Nation: A History of Trade Politics in America*. New York: Oxford University Press, 2018.

Khan, Sulmaan Wasif. *Haunted By Chaos: China's Grand Strategy from Mao Zedong to Xi Jinping*. Cambridge, MA: Harvard University Press, 2018.

Khan, Sulmaan Wasif. *The Struggle for Taiwan: A History of America, China, and the Island Caught Between*. New York: Basic Books, 2024.

Kirkendall, Andrew J. *Hemispheric Alliances: Liberal Democrats and Cold War Latin America*. Chapel Hill, NC: University of North Carolina Press, 2022.

Klein, Joe. *The Natural: The Misunderstood Presidency of Bill Clinton*. New York: Doubleday, 2002.

Korten, David C. *When Corporations Rule the World*. West Hartford and San Francisco, CA: Kumarian Press, Inc. and Berrett-Koehler Publishers, Inc., 1996.

Korzeniewicz, Miguel. "Commodity Chains and Marketing Strategies: Nike and the Global Athletic Footwear Industry." In *The Globalization Reader*, edited by Frank J. Lechner and John Boli, 173–83. Malden, MA: Blackwell Publishers, 2001.

Kruse, Kevin M., and Julian E. Zelizer. *Fault Lines: A History of the United States Since 1974*. New York: W.W. Norton & Company, 2019.

Kunz, Diane B. *Butter and Guns: America's Cold War Economic Diplomacy*. New York: The Free Press, 1997.

Kutler, Stanley I. *The Wars of Watergate: The Last Crisis of Richard Nixon*. New York: Alfred A. Knopf, 1990.

LaFeber, Walter. *Michael Jordan and the New Global Capitalism*. New York: W.W. Norton & Company, 2002.

LaFeber, Walter. *The Clash*. New York: W.W. Norton & Company, 1997.

Lampton, David. *Living U.S.-China Relations: From Cold War to Cold War*. Lanham, MD: Rowman & Littlefield Publishers, 2024.

Landes, David S. *The Wealth and Poverty of Nations: Why Some Are So Richa and Some So Poor*. New York: W.W. Norton & Company, 1999.

Lang, Tim and Colin Hines. *The New Protectionism: Protecting the Future Against Free Trade*. New York: The New Press, 1993.

Lassiter, Matthew D. *The Silent Majority: Suburban Politics in the Sunbelt South*. Princeton, NJ: Princeton University Press, 2006.

Leffler, Melvyn P. "An Illuminating Hand-Off." In *Hand-Off: The Foreign Policy George W. Bush Passed to Barack Obama*, edited by Stephen J. Hadley, Peter D. Feaver, William C. Imboden, and Meghan L. O'Sullivan, 635–57. Washington, DC: Brookings Institution Press, 2023.

Leffler, Melvyn P. *Confronting Saddam Hussein: George W. Bush and the Invasion of Iraq*. New York: Oxford University Press, 2023.

LeoGrande, William M. *Our Own Backyard: The United States in Central America, 1977-1992*. Chapel Hill, NC: University of North Carolina Press, 1998.

Levinson, Marc. *The Box: How the Shipping Container Made the World Smaller and the World Economy Bigger*. Princeton, NJ: Princeton University Press, 2006.

Levy, Jonathan. *The Ages of American Capitalism: A History of the United States*. New York: Random House, 2021.

Lighthizer, Robert. *No Trade Is Free: Changing Course, Taking on China, and Helping America's Workers*. New York: Broadside Books, 2023.

MacMillan, Margaret. *Nixon and Mao: The Week That Changed the World*. New York: Random House, 2007.

Maier, Charles S. "'Malaise': The Crisis of Capitalism in the 1970s." In *The Shock of the Global: The 1970s in Perspective*, edited by Niall Ferguson, Charles S. Maier, Erez Manela, and Daniel J. Sargent, 25–48. Cambridge, MA: Harvard University Press, 2010.

Mansbach, Richard W. "Globalization: Love It or Loathe It?" In *Introducing Globalization: Analysis and Readings*, edited by Richard W. Mansbach and Edward Rhodes, 301–6. Los Angeles, CA: Sage, 2013a.

Mansbach, Richard W. "The Many Meanings of Globalization." In *Introducing Globalization: Analysis and Readings*, edited by Richard W. Mansbach and Edward Rhodes, 1–11. Los Angeles, CA: Sage, 2013b.

Markovitz, Andrei S., and Lars Rensmann. *Gaming the World: How Sports are Reshaping Globa Politics and Culture*. Princeton, NJ: Princeton University Press, 2010.

Marsh, David. *The Euro: The Politics of the New Global Currency*. New Haven, CT: Yale University Press, 2009.

Mastro, Oriana Skylar. "Is China a Challenge to US National Security?" In *The China Questions 2: Critical Insights Into US-China Relations*, edited by Maria Adele Carrai, Jennifer Rudolph, and Michael Szonyi, 177–84. Cambridge, MA: Harvard University Press, 2022.

Matusow, Allen J. *Nixon's Economy: Booms, Busts, Dollars, and Votes*. Lawrence, KS: University of Kansas Press, 1998.

Matusow, Allen J. *The Unraveling of America: A History of Liberalism in the 1960s*. New York: Harper & Row, Publishers, 1984.

Mavroidis, Petros C. "'Reciprocal' Tariffs: What's in a Word." *Bruegel*, February 27, 2025, 1–8.

Mavroidis, Petros C., and Andre Sapir. *China and the WTO: Why Multilateralism Still Matters*. Princeton, NJ: Princeton University Press, 2021.

McQuaid, Kim. *The Anxious Years: America in the Vietnam-Watergate Era*. New York: Basic Books, Inc., 1989.

Millwood, Pete. *Improbable Diplomats: How Ping-Pong Players, Musicians, and Scientists Remade U.S.-China Relations*. Cambridge: Cambridge University Press, 2022.

Millwood, Pete. "(Mis)perceptions of Domestic Politics in the U.S.-China Rapprochement, 1969-1978." *Diplomatic History* 43, no. 5 (November 2019): 890–913.

Minami, Kazushi. "Perpetual Foreigners: Chinese Americans and the U.S. Opening to China." *Diplomatic History* 47, no. 3 (June 2023): 446–71.

Mittleman, James H. *The Globalization Syndrome: Transformation and Resistance*. Princeton, NJ: Princeton University Press, 2000.

Mohl, Raymond A. *Searching for the Sunbelt; Historical Perspectives on a Region*. Knoxville, TN: University of Tennessee, 1990.

Nye, Joseph S., Jr. "Is the American Century Over?" *Political Science Quarterly* 130, no. 3 (Fall 2015): 393–400.

O'Hara, John M. *A New American Tea Party: The Counterrevolution Against Bailouts, Handouts, Reckless Spending, and More Taxes*. Hoboken, NJ: Wiley, 2012.

Olson, Keith W. *Watergate: The Presidential Scandal That Shook America*. Lawrence, KS: University Press of Kansas, 2016.

Olveiro, Vernie. "The United States, Multinational Enterprises, and the Politics of Globalization." In *The Shock of the Global The 1970s in Perspective*, edited by Niall Ferguson, Charles S. Maier, Erez Manela, and Daniel. Sargent, 143–57. Cambridge, MA: Harvard University Press, 2010.

O'Neill, Shannon K. *The Globalization Myth: Why Regions Matter*. New Haven, CT: Yale University Press, 2022.

O'Neill, William L. *American High: The Years of Confidence, 1945-1960*. New York: Free Press, 1986.

Patterson, James T. *Grand Expectations: The United States, 1945-1974*. New York: Oxford University Press, 1997.

Perlstein, Rick. *Nixonland: The Rise of a President and the Fracturing of America*. New York: Scribner, 2008.

Pomfret, John. "US-China Relations: How Did We Get Here, Where Can We Go?" In *The China Questions 2: Critical Insights Into US-China Relations*, edited by Maria Adele Carrai, Jennifer Rudolph, and Michael Szonyi, 21–30. Cambridge, MA: Harvard University Press, 2022.

Pottinger, Matt, and Mike Gallagher. " No Substitute for Victory: America's Competition With China Must be Won, Not Managed." *Foreign Affairs* 103, no. 3 (May/June 2024): 25–39.

Rasmus, Jack. "Trump's Déjà vu China Trade War." *World Review of Political Economy* 9, no. 3 (Fall 2018): 346–63.

Reeves, Richard. *President Reagan: The Triumph of Imagination*. New York: Simon & Schuster, 2005.

Reichard, Gary W. *Deadlock and Disillusionment: American Politics Since 1968*. Malden, MA: Wiley-Blackwell, 2016.

Reston, James, Jr. *The Lone Star: The Life of John Connally*. New York: Harper & Row Publishers, 1989.

Ricks, Thomas E. *The American Military Adventure in Iraq*. New York: Penguin Books, 2006.

Rigger, Shelley. "How Does Taiwan Affect US-PRC Relations?" In *The China Questions 2: Critical Insights Into US-China Relations*, edited by Maria Adele Carrai, Jennifer Rudolph, and Michael Szonyi, 204–10. Cambridge, MA: Harvard University Press, 2022.

Rivoli, Pietra. *The Travels of a T-Shirt in the Global Economy: An Economist Examines the Markets, Power, and Politics of World Trade*. Hoboken, NJ: Wiley, 2006.

Rodrik, Dani. *Has Globalization Gone Too Far?*. Washington, DC: Institute for International Economics, 1997.

Rudenstine, David. *The Day the Presses Stopped: A History of the Pentagon Papers Case*. Berkeley, CA: University of California Press, 1996.
Sage, George H. *Globalizing Sport: How Organizations, Corporations, Media, and Politics are Changing Sports*. Boulder, CO: Paradigm Publishers, 2010.
Samuelson, Robert J. *The Great Inflation and Its Aftermath: The Past and Future of American Affluence*. New York: Random House, 2008.
Sandbrook, Dominic. *Mad as Hell: The Crisis of the 1970s and the Rise of the Populist Right*. New York: Alfred A. Knopf, 2011.
Sandbrook, Dominic. "Salesmanship and Substance: The Influence of Domestic Policy and Watergate." In *Nixon in the World: American Foreign Relations, 1969-1977*, edited by Fredrik Logevall and Andrew Preston, 85–106. Oxford: Oxford University Press, 2008.
Sargent, Daniel J. *A Superpower Transformed: The Remaking of American Foreign Relations in the 1970s*. New York: Oxford University Press, 2015.
Schaller, Michael. *Reckoning with Reagan: America and Its President in the 1980s*. New York: Oxford University Press, 1992.
Schaller, Michael. "The United States, Japan, and China at Fifty." In *Partnership: The United States and Japan, 1951-2001*, (pp. 33–61), edited by Akira Iriye and Robert A. Wampler. Tokyo: Kodansha International, 2001.
Schippers, David P. *Sellout: The Inside Story of President Clinton's Impeachment*. Washington, DC: Regnery Publishing, Inc., 2000.
Schulman, Bruce J. *The Seventies: The Great Shift in American Culture, Society, and Politics*. New York: Da Capo Press, 2001.
Schulzinger, Robert D. *A Time for War: The United States and Vietnam, 1941–1975*. New York: Oxford University Press, 1997.
Smil, Vaclav. *Two Prime Movers of Globalization: The History and Impact of Diesel Engines and Gas Turbines*. Cambridge, MA: The MIT Press, 2010.
Solomon, Robert. *The International Monetary System, 1945–1981*. New York: Harper & Row Publishers, 1982.
Spigel, Lynn. *Make Room for TV: Television and the Family Ideal in Postwar America*. Chicago, IL: The University of Chicago Press, 1982.
Stein, Judith. *Pivotal Decade: How the United States Traded Factories for Finance in the Seventies*. New Haven, CT: Yale University Press, 2010.
Stiglitz, Joseph E. *Globalization and Its Discontents*. New York: W.W. Norton & Company, 2002.
Talley, Christian. *Forgotten Vanguard: Informal Diplomacy and the Rise of United States-China Trade, 1972-1980*. Notre Dame, IN: University of Notre Dame Press, 2018.
Taylor, Alan M. "The Global 1970s and the Echo of the Great Depression." In *The Shock of the Global: The 1970s in Perspective*, edited by Niall Ferguson, Charles S. Maier, Erez Manela, and Daniel J. Sargent, 97–112. Cambridge, MA: Harvard University Press, 2010.
Tilly, Charles. "Globalization Threatens Labor's Rights." *International Labor and Working-Class History* 47 (Spring 1995): 1–23.
Tomlinson, John. *Globalization and Culture*. Chicago, IL: The University of Chicago Press, 1999.
Tucker, Nancy Bernkopf. *Strait Talk: United States-Taiwan Relations and the Crisis with China*. Cambridge, MA: Harvard University Press, 2009.

Walker, Breck. "'Friends but Not Allies' – Cyrus Vance and the Normalization of Relations with China." *Diplomatic History* 33, no. 4 (September 2009): 579–94.

Watson, James L., ed. *Golden Arches East: McDonald's in East Asia*. Stanford, CA: Stanford University Press, 1997.

Weber, Arnold R. *In Pursuit of Price Stability: The Wage-Price Freeze of 1971*. Washington, DC: The Brookings Institution, 1973.

Went, Robert. *Globalization: Neoliberal Challenge, Radical Responses*. London: Pluto Press, 2000.

Westad, Odd Arne. "Sleepwalking Toward War: Will America and China Heed the Warnings of Twentieth-Century Catastrophe?" *Foreign Affairs* 103, no. 4 (July/August 2024): 78–89.

Xia, Yafeng. *Negotiating with the Enemy: U.S.-China Talks During the Cold War, 1949–1972*. Bloomington, IN: Indiana University Press, 2006.

Yergin, Daniel, and Joseph Stanislaw. *The Commanding Heights: The Battle Between Government and the Marketplace That Is Remaking the Modern World*. New York: Touchstone, 1999.

Yueh, Linda. *The Great Crashes: Lessons from Global Meltdowns and How to Prevent Them*. London: Penguin Business, 2023.

Zeiler, Thomas W. "Business is War in U.S.-Japanese Economic Relations, 1977–2001." In *Partnership: The United States and Japan, 1951–2001*, (pp. 223–248), edited by Akira Iriye and Robert A. Wampler. Tokyo: Kodansha International, 2001.

Zeiler, Thomas W. *Capitalist Peace: A History of American Free-Trade Internationalism*. New York: Oxford University Press, 2022.

Index

9/11 attack   45–9, 51, 56, 95, 152

Abrams, Elliott   42
Albright, Madeleine   91, 191
Ali, Muhammad   140
Al-Qaeda, *see* Bush, George W;
   Osama bin Laden
American Century   1, 2, 5, 7–13, 15,
   27, 30–2, 41, 47, 64, 65, 102,
   111, 113, 116, 122, 124, 154,
   156, 157, 159, 185, 187, 188,
   190, 192, 201, 203–6
American Graffiti   188
American Textile Manufacturers
   Institute   157
Asian financial crisis (1997)   142, 187,
   189, 200
Asian-Pacific Economic Cooperation
   (APEC)   148
Association of Southeast Asian
   Nations (ASEA)   148, 150

Bagdikian, Ben   18
Baker, James   87, 88
balance-of-payments   114–16, 120,
   161, 163, 169, 170, 184
Barber, Benjamin   192
Barr, Bill   54–5, 58–9
Bee Gees   188
Biden, Hunter   57
Biden, Joe   52, 57
   on China   100, 101, 103, 105, 198,
      201
   mishandles classified
      documents   56, 59
Black Lives Matter movement   105,
   206
Blair, Tony   50
Boland Amendment   33, 39

Bork, Robert   25
Bretton Woods monetary
   system   111–19, 122–4,
   128–31, 135, 142, 163
Brexit   147, 197
Brookings Institution   21, 22
Bryan, William Jennings   120
Buchanan, Patrick   88, 190, 196
Bunker, Archie   157, 188, 203
Burns, Arthur   119, 120, 122
Bush, George H. W.   43
   Iran-Contra involvement of   40–2
   negotiates NAFTA   149–50
   presidential approach to China
      of   83–8
   as US liaison in China   69, 75
   Vice President   30
   visits Japan   173–4
Bush, George W.   45, 194
   9/11 response   46, 47
   abuse of power by   48–9,
      51–2
   on China   95–7
   supports globalization   153

Cambodia   13–14, 18, 22, 66, 78, 87,
   88, 167
Carter, Ash   99
Carter, Jimmy   30, 31, 33, 83, 139,
   173, 203
   on China   77–8, 80, 90
   and oil crisis   184–5
Casey, William   31–5, 38, 41
Castro, Fidel   32, 33
Central European Free Trade
   Area   147
Central Intelligence Agency (CIA)   21,
   25, 31, 33, 35, 42
Cheney, Dick   47–50

INDEX

China, People's Republic of 11, 12, *see also* pandas; Taiwan; Tiananmen Square massacre
   American critics of 65, 66, 69, 85–7, 96, 98, 107, 109, 204
   Belt and Road Initiative of 100, 103
   economic growth of 94, 97, 104, 145
   espionage of 98, 100
   hardline anticommunism in 64, 77, 88, 92–3
   human rights violations in 87–90, 97, 103, 106
   military expansion of 95, 96, 98, 100–1
   and Most-Favored-Nation (MFN) treatment 86–9
   normalization with US 78, 79, 81
   reform in 65, 79–80, 84, 94–5
   Shock 63–70
   Summer Olympics in 95, 96
   trade relations 78, 80, 82–3, 89–91, 93–4, 96, 102, 106, 173, 177
   US engagement of 66, 75, 87, 90, 93–5, 98, 105, 106, 109
   US trade war with 102–5, 198, 200, 201
   WTO membership of 89–91
civil rights 6, 8–10, 30, 47, 157, 188, 204
classified documents 20, 52, 58–9
Clinton, Bill 13, 27, 56
   abuse of power by 44–6
   backs NAFTA 149
   China approach of 88–93
   on globalization 144–5, 187, 191, 192
Clinton, Hillary 44, 49, 53, 54, 97, 98, 206
CNN 85, 144
Cohen, Michael 54
Cold War 6–8, 11, 23, 29–32, 40, 42, 43, 63, 64, 66, 75, 79, 82–3, 87, 94, 101, 106, 114, 116, 123, 132–4, 138, 139, 143, 144, 146, 148, 163, 175, 178, 193, 197, 199, 204, 205

Colson, Charles 117
Comey, James 53
Connally, John 118–22, 127–31, 161, 162, 172
consumerism 8, 192
Contras, *see* Reagan, Ronald
Coors, Joseph 34
COVID-19 (coronavirus) pandemic 58, 102, 103, 132, 139, 206
Cox, Archibald 24, 25, 27
Crichton, Michael 176
culture 8, 10, 182, 183, 185, 187–8

Dalai Lama 87, 89, 98
Davos meetings 136, 191, 192
Democrats 9, 10, 22, 24, 37–9, 44, 56, 57, 78, 89, 91, 125, 149, 156, 187, 199, 206
Deng Xiaoping 77, 78, 81, 83–7
détente 63–4, 75
Disney parks 137, 138, 148
Dole, Bob 41

Ehrlichman, John 22
Eisaku Sato 68, 69, 76, 158–60, 163–72
Eisenhower, Dwight D. 7, 10, 11, 41, 117, 159, 173
Ellsberg, Daniel 17–22, 61
Enlai, Zhou 63, 66–8, 70–3, 77, 159
Ervin, Sam 24
Europe, Western 12, 50, 69, 87, 89, 113, 114, 122, 128, 132, 134, 135, 155–6, 162
   European Community 129, 130, 183
European Union 147–9
exchange rates 2, 112, 113, 125, 128–31, 135, 139, 142, 175
executive privilege 17, 20, 24, 25, 27, 39, 53

Fang Lizhi 84–6
Federal Bureau of Investigation (FBI) 4, 18, 21, 25, 44, 53, 58
Field, Sally 188
Flanigan, Peter 168
Flynn, Michael 53

Ford, Gerald   26, 77, 173, 184
Foreign Intelligence Surveillance Act (FISA)   47
Four (Asian) Tigers   148
Friedman, Milton   139
Friedman, Thomas   193
Fujita, Den   137
Fukuyama, Francis   144, 193
Fulbright, J. William   17

Gates, Bill   143
General Agreement on Tariffs and Trade (GATT)   8, 88, 130, 131, 135, 146, 149, 151, 156, 158, 164, 165, 186
Gingrich, Newt   44, 196
Giuliani, Rudy   56
Global South   11, 31, 32, 93, 100, 103, 134–6, 142, 143, 151, 180–2, 186, 188
Global Trade Watch   192
Globalization   142–3, *see also* Seattle protests
   Bill Clinton and   144–5, 150
   corporate   137–9
   critics of   135, 146, 152, 153, 189–93, 198, 200
   defined   133–5, 141
   supporters of   138, 140, 150, 152, 153
gold   1, 10, 111–25, 128–32, 134, 169, 200
Goldwater, Barry   30, 34, 69, 196
Gorbachev, Mikhail   31, 37, 43, 82, 84, 143
Gore, Al   45
Gravel, Mike   18, 19
Great Depression   10, 52, 111, 112, 135, 174, 193, 197, 198, 205
Great Recession   52, 97, 139, 192–6
Guofeng, Hua   77

Hadley, Stephen   51
Haig, Alexander   33, 81
Haldeman, H. R.   20, 25, 70, 122, 127
Hall, Fawn   37
Harvey, Paul   127
Hirohito, Emperor   137, 170

Homeland Security, Department of   47
Hong Kong   87, 89, 102, 105, 107, 148
Hoover, Herbert   163, 198
Hoover, J. Edgar   21
Hu Jintao   95, 100
Humphrey, Hubert   156
Hunt, E. Howard   21, 22, 24
Hussein, Saddam   35, 45, 48–51, 87
Huston Plan   14

impeachments   25
   of Clinton   44–6, 91
   of Trump   52, 55–8
independents (petroleum companies)   180, 181
Ing-wen, Tsa   101
insurrection of January 6, 2021   52, 56, 58
International Monetary Fund (IMF)   113, 115, 119, 128–30, 133, 152, 186, 189–92, 195
internationalism   103, 144, 158, 171, 197, 198
Iran-Contra scandal   35–43

Jackson, Jesse   183
Jackson-Vanik Amendment   80
Japan   112, 132, 183, 204, *see also* MITI; Okinawa
   and automobile trade   176–7
   and China   68–9, 74, 76, 87, 98, 100
   and globalization   137, 140
   investments in US by   174–6
   as a scapegoat   160–3, 175–7
   and Second Nixon Shock   118, 122, 123, 128–30
   trade surplus with US of   160, 161, 172–4
   US textile trade war with   155–71
Jiang Jeshi   66, 71, 73, 78, 96
Jiang Qing   66
Jiang Zemin   90, 95, 107
Johnson, Lyndon B.   7, 9, 11, 14, 17, 23, 114, 156, 205
Jordan, Michael   140, 141

Kakuei Tanaka   76, 170, 172–3
Kendall, Donald   167

Kennedy, David   168–70
Kennedy, John F.   7, 9, 114, 199
Kerry, John   49
Khomeini, Ayatollah   35, 185
Kim Il-un   137
King, Martin Luther, Jr.   9
Kinzinger, Adam   59
Kislyak, Sergey   53
Kissinger, Henry   11, 19–22, 25, 63, 68, 70–7, 86, 119, 130, 159, 164
Klein, Naomi   195
Krogh, Egil   21

labor   8, 15, 69, 99, 135, 140, 156–8, 176, 187–9, 191–5, 197, 199–200
Lee, Martin   89
Lee Teng-hui   91
Lenin, Vladimir   64, 119
Lewinsky, Monica   44–6, 91, 92
Li Peng   88
Liddy, G. Gordon   21, 22, 24
Lieberman, Joseph   176
Lighthizer, Robert   102, 104, 199–200
Luce, Henry   5, 15, 65

McConnell, Mitch   58
McCracken, Paul   119
McDonald's   8, 137, 138, 144, 195
McFarlane, Robert   35–7, 42
McGovern, George   17, 23
McNamara, Robert   17
Mahathir, Muhamad   190
Manafort, Paul   54
Mao Zedong   63, 65, 66, 70–2, 100, 107
Mary Kay Cosmetics   137, 138
Meany, George   69
Meir, Golda   184
MERCOSUR   148
Mexico ("Tequila Shock") crisis   186
Meyer, Armin   76
Mills, Wilbur   158, 160, 167–9
Milosevic, Slobodan   45
Ministry of International Trade and Industry (MITI)   62, 164, 166, 167, 169, 170, 175
Mitchell, George   85
Miyazawa, Kiichi   167
MoveOn.org   49

Mueller, Robert   53–7
Mulroney, Brian   149
multinational (transnational) corporations   135, 136, 138, 147, 152
Mulvaney, Mick   57
Musk, Elon   206

Nader, Ralph   183
Nashville   188
National Basketball Association (NBA)   105, 140, 141
National Security Council (NSC)   14, 21, 31, 34, 35, 37, 38, 52
nationalist-populism   155, 178, 179, 189, 192, 195–8, 200, 201, 205
Navarro, Peter   102, 189
neoconservatives   30, 47–8, 88
neoliberalism   3, 30, 128, 131, 134, 139–41, 150, 152, 154, 179, 187–90, 192, 193, 196, 198, 203
Network   188
New International Economic Order (NIEO)   186
Nike shoe company   140, 195
Nixon, Richard M.   10–11, 56, 203, 206–7
   abuse of power by   17–21, 23–7, 60, 204–5
   births dollar globalization   130
   boldness of   123
   Camp David economic decisions of   115, 119–21, 123
   and dollar devaluation   1, 2, 7, 12, 111, 113–25, 128–32
   during the oil embargo   181–3
   election calculations of   22, 23, 127, 157–8, 168, 171
   enemies list   14, 23
   financial policies of   111, 115–26, 158
   "Grand Design" of   63–5, 69, 75
   invokes Trading with the Enemy Act   155
   and Japan   159
   at the "Kitchen Debates"   7
   resignation of   25–6
   Southern Strategy of   157–8, 198
   talks with Mao   71–2

and Vietnam War 12–13, 22
views of China 65–7, 83, 86
wage and price controls of 111, 117, 118, 120, 127, 139, 180
and Watergate scandal 21–5, 33, 77, 182
North American Free Trade Agreement (NAFTA) 47, 149, 150, 191, 197, 199
North Atlantic Treaty Organization (NATO) 2, 103, 116, 122, 130
North Korea 32, 75, 87, 89, 90, 92, 96–8, 101, 137
North, Oliver 34, 37, 39, 41

Obama, Barack 51, 196
  on China 97–101
  supports globalism 153
O'Brien, Lawrence 24, 125
Occupy Wall Street movement 192, 193, 195, 206
oil crises 127, 134, 176, 181, 182, 184–6, 205
Okinawa reversion 76, 159, 160, 163, 164, 166–8, 170, 206
Operation Iraqi Freedom 50
Orban, Viktor 102
Organization of Petroleum Exporting Countries (OPEC) 136, 180–6
Ortega, Daniel 33, 43
Osama bin Laden 45–7

pandas 73, 144
Pelosi, Nancy 86, 87, 89
Pentagon Papers 17–21, 25, 27, 60, 204
Perot, Ross 44, 196
Peterson, Peter 132, 162, 168–71
ping-pong diplomacy 67, 72
Plaza Accord 131
plumbers 21–2, 24
Poindexter, John 36, 37, 41
Pol Pot and Khmer Rouge 78, 88
Pompidou, Georges 128
Powell, Colin 47–52
Project Democracy 35–7
protectionism 82, 89, 93, 97, 102, 112, 127, 130, 135, 155–7, 167, 171, 173, 175–9, 190, 192, 195, 197–201, 204
Putin, Vladimir 53, 101, 105, 144

Qaddafi, Muammar 180, 181
Qian Qichen 87

Reagan, Nancy 30
Reagan, Ronald 27, 77, 146, 157, 184, 199, 203
  abuse of power by 34, 37, 39–42
  anticommunism of 29–33, 39
  and China 66, 68–70, 80–3
  decision-making by 30, 31, 37–8, 40
  deregulation under 139
  as a free trader 82, 140, 150, 187
  and Japan 177
  and Nicaraguan Contras 32–4, 43
Republicans 25, 41, 44, 45, 50, 56, 57, 78, 150, 156, 168, 178, 187, 191, 196–8, 206
Reston, James 74
Ribicoff, Abraham 156
Rice, Condoleezza 49, 52
Rogers, William 73, 120, 123, 172
Romney, Mitt 58
Roosevelt, Franklin D. 7, 9, 41, 113, 119, 156
Rumsfeld, Donald 47–8, 120
Russia (Trump) probe 53–6

Safire, William 119, 123
Salinas, Carlos 149
Saturday Night Fever 188
Saudi Arabia 136, 180, 181, 186
Schroeder, Patricia 29
Scowcroft, Brent 86
Seattle protests 191–2
Second World War 5–7, 11–12, 74, 93, 113, 120, 125, 127, 130, 155, 158, 159, 175, 182, 186, 199, 205
Sematech 177
Seven Sister (Majors) petroleum companies 180–3
Shah of Iran 181, 182, 185
Shanghai Communique 73–4, 81
Sheehan, Neil 17

Shultz, George 31, 34, 35, 82, 119, 127, 131
Silent Majority 10, 182, 198
Smith, Jack 58, 59
Smithsonian Agreement 131
Sondland, Alexander 56
Soviet Union 5, 11, 12, 20, 30, 41, 43, 63–4, 66, 68, 69, 72, 75, 79–81, 93, 106, 107, 143–5, 171
Springsteen, Bruce 188
Stallone, Sylvester 188
Stans, Maurice 162–4, 167–8, 171
Starr, Kenneth 44
Stone, Roger 54
Strategic Arms Limitation Talks (SALT) 68, 78
Summers, Larry 91

Taiwan 66–9, 71, 72, 74–83, 88, 91–2, 94–7, 100, 105, 109, 159
Taliban 48, 95
tariffs 80, 88, 98, 102, 103, 105, 111, 112, 120–2, 124, 129, 130, 135, 149–51, 158, 176, 178, 197–201
Tea Party movement 189, 192, 195–7, 206
textiles, see Japan; Nixon, Richard M.
Thurmond, Strom 157, 158, 160, 163, 167–9
Tiananmen Square massacre 84–6, 91, 92, 144
Tibet 87, 89, 90, 95, 97, 107
TikTok 143
Tower, John 39–40
Trading with the Enemy Act 3, 155, 170, 178, 200
transnationalism 142, 145, 153, 190
Trans-Pacific Partnership (TPP) 99, 198
Travelgate 44
Travolta, John 188
Trudeau, Pierre 128
Trump, Donald 41, 203
    abuses of power by 55, 59–61, 205
    America First stance 60, 101, 154, 155, 171, 190
    crimes of 42, 45, 53, 57
    trade views of 101–3, 197–201

Trump, Donald, Jr. 54
Tsongas, Paul 175
Turner, Ted 144

Uighurs 95, 107
Ukraine 32, 53, 56–8, 101, 103, 105
United Nations 50, 69, 87, 91
USA PATRIOT Act 47

Vance, Cyrus 77, 80
Vietnam War 9, 11–15, 18, 22, 25, 27, 64, 66, 75, 156, 158
Vindman, Alexander 56, 57
VISA 137, 138, 142
Volcker, Paul 119

Wallace, George 10, 23, 69, 157, 158, 190
Wallach, Lori 192
Walsh, Lawrence 39–43
War Powers Act 25
Washington Consensus 152, 187, 189, 193, 195
Watergate scandal 14, 21–5, 37, 45
weapons of mass destruction (WMDs) 8, 51, 160
Weinberger, Caspar 31, 34, 35, 38, 41, 42, 119
Whitewater investigation 44
Wikileaks 54
Woods, Tiger 141
World Bank 108, 113, 124, 130, 152, 195
World Trade Organization (WTO) 91–2, 95, 96, 102, 107, 151–3, 190–2, 198, 199

Xi Jinping 99–101, 103, 107, 108

Yamani, Ahmed Zaki 136, 181
Yellow Vest protests (France) 197
Young, David 21

Zelensky, Volodymyr 56, 57
Zhang Yimou 97
Zoellick, Robert 106